Free Trade Agreements and Globalisation

Arne Melchior

Free Trade Agreements and Globalisation

In the Shadow of Brexit and Trump

Arne Melchior
Norwegian Institute of International Affairs
Oslo, Norway

ISBN 978-3-319-92833-3 ISBN 978-3-319-92834-0 (eBook)
https://doi.org/10.1007/978-3-319-92834-0

Library of Congress Control Number: 2018946237

Cover illustration: Sandema / Alamy Stock Photo

Printed on acid-free paper

This Palgrave Macmillan imprint is published by the registered company Springer Nature Switzerland AG
The registered company address is: Gewerbestrasse 11, 6330 Cham, Switzerland

Acknowledgements

Main parts of this book were written as contributions to the research project "Europe in transition—small states in an age of global shifts (EUNOR)", funded by the Research Council of Norway (project no. 238017) during 2014–2017. The model presented in Chap. 6 and Appendix B was partly developed as part of the research project "Trade Integration, Geopolitics and the Economy of Russia (TIGER)", funded by the Research Council of Norway during 2013–2016 (project no. 228244). I would like to gratefully acknowledge the financial support provided by the Research Council of Norway. I thank Natalia Turdyeva and other TIGER projects' participants for useful feedback when the preliminary material was presented at a project workshop at Centre for Economic and Financial Research (CEFIR), Moscow (21 April 2016). I also thank Natalia Turdyeva and Roman Vakulchuk for guidance in accessing regional data for Russia and Kazakhstan, respectively, and Sergei Golovan for useful advice on aspects of MATLAB programming. Parts of the material included in the book were also presented at seminars during 2017 at the University of Oslo and at the Norwegian Institute of International Affairs, Oslo, Norway, and at the conference on "Trade and Integration in a Time of Anti-Globalisation" in Malmö, Sweden, on 25–27 October 2017. I thank the participants at these seminars and conferences for their valuable comments. Finally, I thank the anonymous referees of Palgrave Macmillan for their useful comments on the plan for the book as well as a preliminary version of it. I also thank Laura Pacey and Clara Heathcock at Palgrave Macmillan for their excellent follow-up as well as patience when the book deadline had to be postponed for unforeseen reasons. As usual, the responsibility for remaining errors, if any, stays with the author.

Contents

Abbreviations

ACP	Africa, Caribbean and Pacific countries
AD	Anti-dumping
AfCFTA	African Continental Free Trade Area
AGOA	African Growth and Opportunity Act (US trade preferences)
ANZCERTA	Australia-New Zealand Closer Economic Relations Trade Agreement
BEA	Bureau of Economic Analysis (US agency)
BITs	Bilateral Investment Treaties
CBI	Caribbean Basin Initiative (US trade preferences)
CD	Countervailing Duties (WTO measure against subsidies)
CES	Constant Elasticity of Substitution
CGE	Computable General Equilibrium
COMTRADE	United Nations Commodity Trade Statistics Database
CTS	Consolidated Tariff Schedules (of the WTO)
DESTA	Design of Trade Agreements database
DSM	Dispute Settlement Mechanism
EAEU	Eurasian Economic Union
EBA	Everything But Arms (EU trade preferences for LDCs)
EEA	European Economic Area
EFTA	European Free Trade Association
EPA	Economic Partnership Agreements (EU trade agreements with ACP)
FAO	Food and Agriculture Organization

FATF	Financial Action Task Force
FMINCON	Constrained Non-linear Minimization Algorithm in MATLAB
FSB	Financial Stability Board
FTA	Free Trade Agreement
GATS	General Agreement on Trade in Services
GATT	General Agreement on Tariffs and Trade
GDP	Gross Domestic Product
GSP	Generalised System of Preferences
GVC	Global Value Chain
HM	Her Majesty
IAIS	International Association of Insurance Supervisors
ICP	International Comparison Program (mapping international price differences)
ICT	Information and Communication Technology
IIT	Intra-industry Trade
ILO	International Labour Organization
IMF	International Monetary Fund
IOSCO	International Organization of Securities Commissions
IPR	Intellectual Property Rights
ISDS	Investor-State Dispute Settlement
ITU	International Telecommunication Union
LDCs	Least Developed Countries
MAI	Multilateral Agreement on Investment
MFN	Most Favoured Nation
MRA	Mutual Recognition Agreement
NAFTA	North American Free Trade Agreement
NQTM	New Quantitative Trade Models
NTM	Non-tariff Measures
OECD	Organisation for Economic Co-operation and Development
PPP	Purchasing Power Parity
PSAs	Partial Scope Agreements (between developing countries, notified under WTO's enabling clause)
REACH	Registration, Evaluation, Authorisation of Chemicals (EU chemical regulation)
RO	Rules of Origin
RTA	Regional Trade Agreement
SACU	South African Customs Union

SBO	Substantial Business Operations (origin criterion for services)
SDT	Special and Differential Treatment
SPS	Sanitary and Phytosanitary Measures
SQP	Sequential Quadratic Programming sub-algorithm in MATLAB
STRI	Services Trade Restrictiveness Index (OECD)
TBT	Technical Barriers to Trade
TFEU	Treaty of the Functioning of the European Union
TISA	Trade in Services Agreement
TPP	Trans-Pacific Partnership
TRAINS	Trade Analysis Information System (UNCTAD)
TRIMS	Trade-Related Investment Measures (WTO agreement)
TRIPS	Agreement on Trade-Related Intellectual Property Rights (WTO)
TSCA	Toxic Substances Control Act (US law on chemical regulation)
TTIP	Transatlantic Trade and Investment Partnership
UAE	United Arab Emirates
UNCTAD	United Nations Conference for Trade and Development
UNECE	United Nations Economic Commission for Europe
USTR	United States Trade Representative
VAT	Value Added Tax
WB	World Bank (not usual but used in appendix)
WCO	World Customs Organization
WDI	World Development Indicators (World Bank database)
WITS	World Integrated Trade Solution
WTO	World Trade Organization

List of Figures

List of Tables

1

Introduction and Overview

1.1 The Race for Free Trade Agreements

In this book, we use FTAs (Free Trade Agreements) as a broad term, covering all types of agreements between subsets of countries with an aim to liberalise trade in goods or services.[1] FTAs have developed since the 1950s, starting with trade in goods and within geographical regions. For a long time, there was a perceived conflict of interest between the GATT (General Agreement on Tariffs and Trade, part of the WTO—World Trade Organization—from 1995) and the FTAs. The GATT had a strong focus on non-discrimination, expressed in the MFN (Most Favoured Nation) criterion—trade partners should be treated equally. Article XXIV (=24) of the GATT allowed FTAs as an exception from the MFN principle, and hence FTAs have been legal according to GATTs rules since 1947. At the same time, major actors such as the USA and later the EU had the perception that if all trade was covered by FTAs, it would undermine the world trade system. For this reason, an FTA between the USA and the EU was not on the agenda for decades. FTAs were mainly within world regions and not across—we had the EU and NAFTA (North American Free Trade Area) and agreements in all world regions, but not FTAs across the Atlantic and Pacific. There was peaceful coexistence

A. Melchior, *Free Trade Agreements and Globalisation*,
https://doi.org/10.1007/978-3-319-92834-0_1

between the FTAs and the GATT/WTO, except some moments when the USA feared that European integration would undermine the global trade system.

All this changed from the turn of the century, when the spread of FTAs accelerated and several countries revised their trade strategies. There were several reasons underlying this change. The potential virtues of FTAs had been demonstrated during the 1990s, with the establishment of NAFTA (1993) and the EU internal market (1992), plus the EU enlargement and the European Economic Area Agreement in 1994. Another reason was globalisation and the rise of Asia, expanding trade with Asia and creating a need for inter-regional FTAs. China became a WTO member in 2001, and there was globalisation in harmony. A third reason was the slowdown of the WTO: From great success when the WTO was established in 1993/1995, to growing North-South frictions and dwindling support for new reforms. The mixture of lukewarm developing countries and anti-globalisation protests, with the "Battle of Seattle" in 1999 as a turning point, cooled down WTO reforms and the organisation never recovered fully in spite of wholehearted attempts. With a need for governance and demand for FTAs that the WTO could not satisfy, FTAs became an alternative. A fourth reason for the new approach to FTAs was the pioneering change of policies by some small countries such as Chile, Singapore and European Free Trade Association (EFTA) countries, aiming at inter-regional FTAs across the globe. The FTA race had started, and big nations gradually changed their minds and became more proactive. From the economics of FTAs, outsiders may lose from the trade discrimination inherent in FTAs—so there can be "domino effects" (Baldwin 1993; Baldwin and Jaimovicz 2016; discussed in Chap. 9).

For all these reasons, there was an exponential spread of FTAs across the globe from the turn of the century (Chap. 3). The last turn of this spiral was President Obama's initiative for "plurilateral" FTAs across the Pacific (TPP, Trans-Pacific Partnership) and the Atlantic (TTIP, Transatlantic Trade and Investment Partnership). A large number of other FTAs were also in the making (Chap. 3). The global FTA network was not only extended but so was the agenda of the agreements, with an ever-growing appetite for complexity and regulatory issues beyond tariffs for trade in goods—the archetypical FTA backbone. When the EU went to Washington for TTIP negotiations during 2013–2016, their delegations typically counted about 90 persons—an army of experts covering different areas.[2] International agreement on regulation is however not an easy task; parallel to the escalating travel expenditures often came difficulties in achieving the requested regulatory cooperation: At the end of Obama's presidency, TTIP was still quite far from the "gold standard" promised at the outset.

1.2 The Crash of 2016

Year 2016 dealt two heavy blows to the FTA agenda: First came Brexit, the British referendum interrupting a 60-year cycle of ever deepening and widening economic integration in Europe. Second, Donald Trump was elected President of the USA, with a nationalist and protectionist trade agenda, leaving the TPP on his first day in the White House. The election of Trump ended a 70-year history with the USA at the front seat of the liberal world trade order. There were signs of retraction even some years ago, but Trump jumped across the fence, into a new terrain of trade policy bilateralism with a nationalist scent and "America first" replacing multilateralism.

The two shocks have by no means cancelled the FTA agenda; on the contrary the "Brexiteers" of the UK promise to be the "champions of free trade" (HM Government 2017, p. 51), aiming at FTAs across the globe, including with emerging economies. At the time of writing, Trump's trade policy is yet in the making, but the aim is to go for bilateral rather than multilateral trade agreements, and renegotiation of trade agreements with a sharp focus on the US trade balance.

In spite of the promise of a continued FTA agenda, the "shock of 2016" challenges global trade policy in fundamental ways. First, there is an earthquake for existing institutions. The UK Government has promised to start trade policy more or less from scratch, with full autonomy and having to build up a new set of agreements across the globe that took other countries decades to develop.[3] For the EU, Brexit is a serious challenge, raising fundamental questions about the entire EU project. In the absence of UK, the EU will become different—not least in the trade area where the UK has been the eloquent spokesman for the "liberal North" (see Elsig 2010; Young and Peterson 2014). Trump deceived USA's trade partners and allies by withdrawing from TPP, which was signed in 2016 after arduous negotiations and with a result strongly influenced by US priorities (and largely even in line with the priorities of the Trump team). He has also signalled that if WTO's decisions are in conflict with US priorities and laws, these may not be followed (USTR 2017, 2018). At the US national level, the change of policy was also an institutional earthquake, with heads rolling and internal struggles.

While less explicit from the outset, Brexit and Trump also challenge the ever-widening regulatory agenda of the FTAs. The UK and the USA share a wish to retain national autonomy and avoid ceding authority to international bodies. For the UK, it is the EU supranational governance that is rejected (not the multilateral trade institutions), but for Trump even the more modest powers of the WTO are questioned (ibid.). In this field, the road from rhetoric to practice is unclear for both. Trump will have to understand that the "USA first" slogan has little appeal beyond US borders. The issue of national autonomy is certainly not new—it is a standard element in national debates on trade policy. But only on a few occasions has the "populist" rejection of regional or global governance overruled the mainstream.

Paradoxically, Trump's cancellation of TPP and possibly TTIP could also strengthen the global trade system since these "megalaterals" aimed at creating a regulatory system that might compete with the WTO. According to Subramanian (2017), "deep is out" and "super-globalization" with global rule-setting will be toned down. According to this, the demise of the megalaterals could revitalise the WTO and leave the rule-making to national or regional institutions. The truth of this prediction remains to be seen.

Trump has also challenged trade policy by linking issues. For theory and discussion on issue linkages, see e.g. Harstad (2015) or Horstmann et al. (2001). In his morning twitters or messages to car companies ("make in USA or pay big border tax"), investment, trade and taxation are linked. In Trump's trade policies, especially as portrayed by Navarro and Autry (2011) with China as the chief culprit, the US trade deficit is a key problem along with "unfair" trade practices (currency manipulation, counterfeiting, lax regulations and subsidies). While some of these issues have been part of trade agreements in the past, the Trump administration has broadened the agenda by linking trade to macroeconomic issues and investment. With the tariffs on steel and aluminium announced by the USA in March 2018, the USA linked trade to security, using American law but also referring to the WTO security exception in GATT's Article XXI. Trump's main trade policy advisor Navarro is considering the risk of military conflict with China on top of a trade war (Navarro 2015). Rather than proposing new international regimes for currency misalignment or lax standards, the USA under Trump wants to solve problems by means of bilateral bargaining power. "Fair trade" has got a new meaning—formerly a left-leaning concept of safeguarding the interests of the poor and vulnerable—with Trump eagerly taking this role as a victim of cheating and manipulation by the trade partners of the USA. (Who said decline of the West?) At the WTO, the USA is obstructing the appointment of new members of the Appellate Body for dispute settlement—to the extent that the dispute settlement system may be inoperative unless the conflict is resolved. This conflict started under Obama, and so the problem is deeper than Trump.

In some countries, populist movements have also challenged the liberal agenda more fundamentally, arguing that trade liberalisation is detrimental to segments of the population and that protection is needed to save domestic jobs. This is certainly the message of Trump, supported by left wing democrats such as Bernie Sanders. On this issue, the signs of Brexit and Trump are however opposite: The "Brexiteers" are free traders who do not question the virtues of free trade. But there is something to it in Britain as well; an element of the Brexit campaign was the rejection of "expert assessments" predicting large economic losses from leaving the EU. With comparatively high UK growth after the referendum in spite of all the gloomy expert predictions, the critics are cheering and claiming the experts were all wrong.

The year this book is published, 2018, is therefore a year of confusion and havoc in global trade policy. The 11 remaining parties in TPP proceed without the USA, but the feast is not the same with the main guest missing. Under President Trump, protectionism is on the rise, dominating the headlines and forcing the trade negotiators of other countries to respond rather than think of new FTAs. The trade policy "shock of 2016" has, at least to some extent, put the FTA race on halt. The future of global trade institutions is in jeopardy when a major player such as the USA has made its support so conditional. Will Brexit and Trump 2016 become footnotes in the history of global trade policy or a turning point towards reversal of the liberal trade order? While the answer to these questions is yet unknown, it is timely in this situation to undertake a reassessment of FTAs in global trade policy. This book is a contribution to this endeavour. Such reassessment may be necessary; it may also be useful since global trade policies are far from perfect, and Brexit and Trump provide an opportunity for change even if we do not like it.

1.3 The Key Pillars of the Book

With globalisation, we need global analysis. This book therefore has a global perspective; it is about globalisation and trade and not about the details of Trump or Brexit, although it is highly relevant for both. The chapters examine global trade policy, FTAs across the globe and world trade. In the analysis, we divide the world into seven major regions and examine the trade interactions within and between them: Trade (Chap. 2); trade agreements (Chaps. 3, 4 and 5); and trade policy options (Chaps. 7 and 8). In the analysis of trade policy options and effects in Chaps. 7 and 8, we use a numerical world trade model with 110 countries and regions (Chap. 6, Appendix B), and many of the results are aggregated for the same world regions. In addition to this world region perspective throughout the book, interested readers can find results for their own country and most countries in the world (Appendix C).

A second key feature and motivation of the book is to combine empirical analysis and economic theory, with a broad and holistic approach that is possible in a book; including economic, institutional and trade policy aspects. The first part of the book (Chaps. 2, 3, 4 and 5) contains empirical analysis of trade and trade agreements; the second part (Chaps. 6, 7 and 8) uses a numerical model of the world economy to shed light on trade policy effects and options—we call it "theory with numbers"; and the final part (Chap. 9) discusses how regulatory cooperation in FTAs should be handled in economic research. Finally, Chap. 9 also discusses some implications for current trade policy, and reviews some questions that remain unanswered.

Another contribution of the book is to bring commodities back onto the trade policy stage. While commodities were a hot issue in global trade in the 1970s and partly the 1980s (see e.g. Newbury and Stiglitz 1981; Jones and Kenen 1984), it was somewhat forgotten later in the trade circles. Chapter 2 shows that more than half the world's countries rely on commodity exports, and the same applies to four out of the seven major world regions. The general equilibrium model used in Chaps. 6, 7 and 8, and presented in Appendix B therefore includes commodities. With this tool, we shed light on the trade policy effects and interests for commodity exporting nations, including terms-of-trade effects that play a key role for these nations. While GVCs (global value chains) have plausibly become a hot topic in the trade literature recently (see e.g. Timmer et al. 2014), the most archetypical and fundamental GVC is the one between manufacturing and commodities, and in this book it is part of the analysis and not left in the shades.

This book addresses the major changes in the world economy during recent years, particularly the rise of Asia in general and China in particular. The rise of Asia is addressed in the analysis of trade (Chap. 2) and FTAs (Chap. 3). In Chap. 7, we shed light on the rise of China and its impact on the world economy: Using the numerical model, we shrink China to its 1990 size and see what happens so we study "growth in reverse". In Chaps. 7 and 8, the impact of trade integration with Asia is a core issue.

Research on trade policy often assumes that trade liberalisation is balanced and symmetrical. The empirical study of trade policy shows that this is often not the case: Some countries have higher tariffs than others; some have more liberal services trade and investment policies; and some have efficient customs offices while their exporters face corruption and red tape abroad. Trade policy is to a considerable extent non-reciprocal. For non-tariff issues in FTAs, trade reforms are often non-discriminatory and so there is a free-rider effect. In this book, we take the issue of non-reciprocity seriously and address it in the analysis of tariffs (Chap. 4); non-tariff issues in FTAs (Chap. 5); and the analysis of trade policy options also examines non-reciprocal trade reforms (Chaps. 7 and 8).

The issue of reciprocity or not is linked to North-South issues in trade policy; for example, the GSP (Generalised System of Preferences) is systematic non-reciprocity in order to promote development. In the book, we ask some questions about these policies: 80% bound tariffs for some developing countries do not promote development and this "water in the tariffs" transforms the WTO into a parody with less credibility. Similarly, there is now "water in the GATS" (General Agreement on Trade in Services), with practices on the ground much more liberal than GATS commitments in many cases and a similar undermining effect on the world trade system. This is one of the North-South issues discussed in this book (Chaps. 4 and 5). Using the world trade model in Chaps. 6, 7 and 8, we show that poor countries have an interest in FTAs and can gain even more if they are able to reduce their higher tariffs and non-tariff barriers.

With the numerical model analysis, this book aims to introduce a novel approach. Rather than abstract theoretical predictions about all countries gaining from trade and the like, the aim is to make specific predictions that are realistic in some dimensions, for real and existing countries. The aim is not to produce "the correct number", for example, on the impact of Brexit or Trump's trade policies; it is to obtain qualitative knowledge about proportions, options, comparisons and mechanisms. To obtain such knowledge, we sometimes run unrealistic scenarios; for example, we redistribute the world's stock of human and physical capital fairly across countries. This will never happen, but it sheds light on the importance of capital for country performance and welfare. The model is not fully realistic: It has no money, no public sector, no cross-border investment, no unemployment and so on. We do not expect it to match the real world perfectly, and we do not calibrate model parameters to create a perfect match. We accept that it is quasi-realistic or "theory with numbers". It captures some important mechanisms and interactions between factor endowments, trade and markets across the globe. Compared to standard CGE (Computable General Equilibrium) models such as GTAP, it is a small-scale macro-model with three sectors only, and so data requirements are more limited. It is a more "lean" model which sheds light on particular aspects of FTAs without promising to be all-encompassing and providing the full truth, but providing qualitative insight on some issues.

In terms of research methodology, the most important contribution in the book is therefore the numerical model presented in Chap. 6 and Appendix B, and used further in Chaps. 7 and 8. This is a mathematical model with an exact solution, solved numerically using MATLAB (Matrix Laboratory) software. It is a macro-model with three sectors (services, manufacturing and commodities), where production structure, wages, prices and trade are endogenous and determined in the model, based on a limited number of (mostly) observable variables: Factor stocks (labour, capital and natural resources), technology parameters and elasticities (taken from existing research) and trade costs (based on existing research and other data). With the structure imposed by the model, every scenario creates a complete "synthetic universe". By changing factor stocks or trade costs, we can examine the impact of various policy scenarios. Trade patterns and the number of manufacturing firms are determined endogenously in the model, and so we can study how China's growth or trade integration affect jobs as well as welfare. The model realistically allows some commodity exporting countries to become fully specialised, with no manufacturing production, and is solved technically for this. In the base scenario using data for 2014, 12 out of 110 countries and regions are completely specialised. The model is more macro and "lean CGE" with fewer sectors that standard CGE models such as GTAP[4]. The way commodities are included and the endogenous determination of industrial structure (the number of manufacturing firms) also makes the model different from the "Ricardian" model of Eaton and Kortum (2002) and some recent "new quantitative trade models" building on this (e.g. Felbermayr et al. 2018).

Empirical research on international trade strongly confirms that trade is affected by distance, and the impact of trade policy is therefore affected by geographical location. The model used in this book is a "geographical economics" world trade model building on Melchior (2010, 2011). According to this, EU integration affects Germany and the UK differently, and the growth impact of EU enlargement towards Central Europe had a strong East-West gradient (Melchior 2011). The model used here captures this and all trade policy effects have a geographical "footprint". The numerical model shows that location has a strong influence on the outcome for individual countries or regions: Your own characteristics matter, but also whether your neighbour is, for example, Alaska or China.

We also take economic geography seriously by decomposing large nations into subregions: Seven countries (Brazil, Canada, China, India, Kazakhstan, Russia and the USA) are split into regions, to capture geography in a better way. Russia spans half the globe and so whether you are east or west matters a lot. China and India each have 30 regions with average populations at the size of France, and so they deserve more detail than Iceland or Luxemburg. This is obvious but mostly neglected in trade research, and in this book we take it into account.

In Chap. 6, we quantify the importance of trade for welfare: On average, the countries and regions of the world would lose 27% of their real income if all trade is eliminated. Small countries, and countries with very little or very much natural resources, will lose more—Iceland would lose 61%. As a trade researcher, one would like to think that trade is immensely important, and the results confirm this. On the other hand, we also show that even if trade is important, factor endowments and technology rank above: Human and physical capital endowments are the most important driver of cross-country income differences. Natural resource endowments also matter, but on average less than trade. In modern trade policies addressing investment and migration, it is therefore important to take factor market effects into account. In the case of Brexit, factor market effects could easily outnumber the pure trade effects. We illustrate this but make no attempt of a realistic quantification—that is left to the more specialised studies.

Finally, we address some future research challenges. The world trade model we use is ridden by the "tariff equivalent syndrome"—assuming that FTAs are about discriminatory reductions in trade barriers, just like tariffs. The analysis of non-tariff issues in FTAs in Chap. 5 shows that trade is often not discriminatory in this way; for example, in the case of unilateral liberalisation for services or investment. In Chap. 9, we discuss the "tariff equivalent syndrome" through the lens of so-called trade policy spillovers, whereby trade cost reductions within an FTA also benefits third countries. While some forms of trade policy spillovers can be handled by standard trade models, others require new approaches.

1.4 Chapter Overview

Chapter 2 analyses world trade during 1995–2015, using a new data set constructed for the purpose. Dividing the world into seven major regions, we find that all regions have approximately the same proportion of manufacturing in their imports, but for exports they diverge: Asia, Western Europe and North America are the factories of the world, with a high share of manufactures in their exports. Among these, Asia is on the rise, and the two others, especially North America, are in relative decline. The remaining four regions, and more than half the world's nations, rely on commodity exports. Commodity trade is more "globalised" than manufacturing trade, which is more intra-regional. About three-fourth of world trade is within or between the three manufacturing regions, and much of this is two-way trade in manufacturing. About one-fifth of world trade is between the manufacturing and commodity regions, mostly consisting of exchange of manufacturing for commodities. Influenced by rising commodity prices, the share of two-way manufacturing trade in world trade declined considerably during 1998–2012.

Chapter 3 examines the fast spread of FTAs during recent decades, with about 300 agreements in force and notified to the WTO in 2017. Recent agreements often include services, and FTAs across rather than within world regions are on the rise. Counting agreements does not tell too much since the members of the WTO could in principle make more than 13,000 FTAs between them! So how much is 300? In order to find out more, the chapter examines the coverage of FTAs between the 40 largest countries in the world, plus the EU. On average for the 41, FTAs covered only 10 out of 40 trade relations in 2017. Small countries such as Chile, Singapore and EFTA countries top the list, the EU is on the rise, but the USA is below average. Within Asia, the FTA coverage has increased particularly fast since the turn of the century. More than half of world trade in goods is between countries that had an FTA in 2017. For the majority of world regions, trade within the region is fully or largely covered by FTAs, but the share is much lower and more variable for trade with other world regions. Hence a large share of the world's trade relations is still ruled by the WTO.

Contrary to the allegation that tariffs are low and do not matter anymore, Chap. 4 shows that tariffs still matter. Many countries have high tariffs, and countries with low tariff averages often have "sensitive" sectors with high tariffs. For many countries, the bound tariffs (= upper tariff ceilings) at the WTO are much higher than the applied rates, and this so-called "water in the tariffs" reduces the credibility of the WTO and its negotiations. Tariffs are still a key element in FTAs, and FTAs lead to substantial tariff cuts. Tariff preferences are discriminatory, and the hierarchy of tariff discrimination by the EU and the USA are shown as illustrations. Paradoxically, the "Most Favoured Nations" are sometimes the "Least Favoured" ones, since the majority of trade partners have some kind of trade preference. As a digression in the analysis, the chapter also reflects on why countries have up to 15,000 tariff lines: Imagine that the value added tax (VAT) varied across 15,000 products! The chapter argues that the excessive detail is a historical anomaly, and tariff classifications should be grossly simplified.

Chapter 5 reviews non-tariff issues in FTAs. This is a complex area with endless detail, and we attempt to simplify and obtain a general and coherent picture. A key issue is whether FTAs lead to discrimination across trade partners in non-tariff areas, in the same way as they do for tariffs. The conclusion is that in non-tariff areas, FTAs are often not discriminatory as for tariffs. This is because countries have liberalised unilaterally; for example, OECD countries have liberalised investment and services on a voluntary basis but as part of a 50-year process at the OECD, with binding codes and aims. In some areas, discrimination is also technically impossible; for example, standards are the same for all. Another key issue is whether FTAs lead to deeper liberalisation than the WTO in non-tariff areas. In several areas, we find that he majority of FTAs do not go much beyond the WTO. However, some agreements do, and these are sometimes more discriminatory. Deep FTAs are mainly intra-regional and the analysis suggests that deep integration across continents is a high-hanging fruit. In some non-tariff areas, for example, services and investment, unilateral liberalisation has created an issue of non-reciprocity that complicates international trade negotiations.

Chapter 6 and the accompanying Appendix B introduces the world trade model used in the book. The model is simulated numerically with MATLAB software, using data from 2014. There is intra-industry trade in manufacturing along with commodity trade. The model replicates country income levels realistically and sheds light on the difference between rich and poor countries in trade. It includes commodities and sheds light on terms-of-trade effects and the trade policy interests of commodity exporters. As an experiment that also serves to demonstrate the model properties, we quantify the value of trade and compare it to the quantitative impact of factor endowment differences on national income levels. The world stock of human and physical capital is reallocated proportionally to the labour force of countries, and so some countries lose and others gain. The capital-labour ratio is a key driver of productivity, and changes in this ratio have strong impact on income levels. A similar experiment is undertaken for natural resources, and so Russia loses most of its natural resource wealth while others gain. As the third experiment, illustrating the importance of trade, we prohibit trade and derive the model outcome in autarky. On average, countries and regions lose 27% of their real income if trade is no longer possible. Comparing the three experiments, we find that human and physical capital endowments are the most important driver of cross-country income differences, but trade is the second largest welfare determinant. Applied to Brexit, it means that factor market implications may be important along with trade effects—we illustrate this but make no attempt to quantify it realistically.

Chapter 7 focuses on US trade policies and the rise of China. Using the model presented in Chap. 6 and Appendix B, we simulate China's growth and show that it generates a welfare gain for the whole world. The gain is larger for countries close to China, and for commodity exporters that gain is from improved terms of trade. There is a reduction in manufacturing production in other countries, and for the USA and Western Europe, these "pains" are large compared to the gains. Simulating trade policy options for the USA, the analysis suggests that trade integration, also with Asia, improves welfare as well as US manufacturing. But trade liberalisation has to be reciprocal; otherwise it hurts manufacturing. Hence President Trump is right about reciprocity, but wrong about trade agreements: FTAs are part of the solution and not the problem. Chapter 7 also shows that with data for the recent decades, the US trade deficit looks about the same with or without China. The China deficit has become larger mainly because China's economic growth. The USA has a trade deficit with many countries; so if unfair trade practices are the cause, almost the whole world has to be cheaters—which seems unlikely. According to the analysis, the USA loses economically from lagging behind in the FTA race, and so it may be the lack of trade agreements that is the problem. FTAs normally promote reciprocity with respect to the height of tariffs and other barriers, and so they also help addressing the problem of non-reciprocity in world trade policy.

Chapter 8 examines the balance between global versus local integration, for all seven world regions but with an extra focus on Western Europe. For Western Europe, trade integration with other world regions could provide larger gains than intra-European integration, if a similar depth of integration could be achieved—however, this is not so easy. We find again that trade liberalisation must be reciprocal if a loss of manufacturing is to be avoided. Integration between Europe and Asia could even relocate manufacturing to Europe. With a growing share of Asia in the world economy, Chaps. 7 and 8 alike demonstrate that trade integration with Asia has become a key issue. With respect to trade integration within each world region, Asia and surprisingly Africa have most to gain from this, whereas Eastern Europe is at the other end of this scale—Russia should therefore "go global" and engage in FTAs beyond its neighbourhood.

In Chap. 8, we also show that small countries and countries with high trade barriers gain more from global trade integration than others. Poor countries benefit along with others, and so they should not hesitate to engage in FTAs, also beyond their own regions. For developing countries, a problem is that many countries are small and so their partners may not have a strong interest in spending the resources needed to negotiate FTAs. This size asymmetry in trade policy—small trade partners are less interesting and important—is an argument that a multilateral trade system is of particular importance to the smaller countries. This book also shows that commodity exporters often gain from FTAs and such agreements may promote diversification of industry, in addition to the welfare gains from trade and potential terms-of-trade gains. It is therefore no surprise and no paradox that several commodity exporters have pursued FTAs proactively; for example, the Gulf Cooperation Council.

Chapter 9 discusses some implications and challenges. Beyond the area of tariffs, FTAs are often not discriminatory and we discuss so-called "trade policy spillovers", whereby trade reforms within an FTA "leak out" to third countries. This may occur if liberalisation is non-discriminatory; if harmonisation within FTAs reduces fixed trade costs for third countries; if the FTAs boost imports from third countries involved in global value chains (GVCs); or there are trade policy "domino effects" where third countries initiate new FTAs in order to avoid trade discrimination. We argue that trade policy spillovers are a real and existing phenomenon but more evidence is needed about their nature and magnitude. Some spillovers can be analysed in standard trade models but other types require other tools.

Chapter 9 also addresses challenges to worldwide regulatory cooperation in the field of trade. How can we avoid the fact that world regions are "drifting apart" in the regulatory field, leading to segmentation of world markets into different regulatory clubs? We examine the hierarchy of regulatory cooperation, with special focus on European integration as an illustrative case. The extension of the EU internal market to EFTA countries illustrates that deep regulatory cooperation requires an extent of legal homogeneity that is impossible on a global scale. Global regulatory cooperation is therefore the "art of the possible", depending on coalitions and finding the right moment. The WTO found the right moment in 1995, and the WTO is a success in terms of global governance. But WTO's last negotiation round (the Doha development Agenda) mainly failed. This creates a need for more plurilateral initiatives or international negotiations with systematic representativity. After Brexit, the UK will face a dilemma between accepting the legal homogeneity of the internal market, and negotiating FTAs with the USA or other countries having different practices and standards.

We end the book by addressing the "fatigue of numbers"—people are no longer convinced by the estimated gains from trade, and they "cannot fall in love with the internal market" (Delors 1989). We argue that research should aim to present qualitative knowledge and reason rather than "the right number" about trade agreements, and this book aims to contribute to this endeavour.

Appendix D also includes some additional teaching material, in the form of a simple model of regional economic integration. This is suitable for teaching at the master of science level, while the model in Appendix B could be used at the PhD level.

Notes

1. FTAs can be customs unions (with a common external tariff); free trade agreements in WTO's technical sense—with liberalisation between partners but no common trade policy viz. third countries; FTAs for trade in services; or FTAs between developing countries notified under WTOs "Enabling Clause" from 1979; see Chap. 4 for more on this.
2. Source: Melchior (Ed.). (2016). A typical EFTA delegation to FTA negotiations counts 30–40 persons, with delegations from counterparts counting up to about 100 (ibid.).
3. In the book, we leave out the institutional details of Brexit but address broader trade and trade policy issues that are relevant for Brexit (most of the book, but especially Chaps. 6, 8 and 9).
4. GTAP = Global Trade Analysis Project, trade model maintained at Purdue University, see https://www.gtap.agecon.purdue.edu/. The current version of the GTAP model has data for 57 sectors.

References

Baldwin, R. (1993). *A Domino Theory of Regionalism. CEPR (Centre for Economic Policy Research)* (Discussion Paper 857. Working Paper 4465). Cambridge, MA: NBER (National Bureau of Economic Research).

Baldwin, R., & Jaimovicz, D. (2016). Are Free Trade Agreements contagious? *Journal of International Economics, 88*(1), 1–16.

Delors, J. (1989). Address given by Jacques Delors to the European Parliament (17 January 1989). Bulletin of the European Communities, Supplement 1/89. Luxembourg: Office for Official Publications of the European Communities.

Eaton, J., & Kortum, S. (2002). Technology, Geography, and Trade. *Econometrica, 70*(5), 1741–1779.

Elsig, M. (2010). European Union Trade Policy after Enlargement: Larger Crowds, Shifting Priorities and Informal Decision-making. *Journal of European Public Policy, 17*(6), 783–800. https://doi.org/10.1080/13501763.2010.486975.

Felbermayr, G., Gröschl, J., & Heiland, I. (2018). *Undoing Europe in a New Quantitative Trade Model.* Munich: Ifo Institute, Leibniz Institute for Economic Research at the University of Munich, Ifo Working Paper No. 250.

Harstad, B. (2015). Issue Linkages and Negotiations – Basic Theory, Chapter 4. In A. Melchior & U. Sverdrup (Eds.), *Conflicts of Interest in Norwegian Trade Policy* (pp. 86–104). Oslo: Universitetsforlaget. In Norwegian.

HM Government. (2017). *The United Kingdom's Exit from and New Partnership with the European Union.* @ Crown copyright, Cm 9417, Presented to the Parliament by the Prime Minister, February 2017.

Horstmann, I. J., Markusen, J. R., & Robles, J. (2001). *Multi-Issue Bargaining and Linked Agendas: Ricardo Revisited or No Pain No Gain* (NBER Working Papers 8347). Cambridge, MA: National Bureau of Economic Research.

Jones, R. W., & Kenen, P. B. (Eds.). (1984). *Handbook of International Economics. Vol. 1. International Trade.* Amsterdam: North-Holland.

Melchior, A. (2010). Globalisation and the Provinces of China: The Role of Domestic Versus International Trade Integration. *Journal of Chinese Economic and Business Studies, 8*(3), 227–252.

Melchior, A. (2011). East-West Integration: A Geographical Economics Approach. In Dabrowski, M. & Maliszewska, M. (Eds.). *EU Eastern Neighborhood. Economic Potential and Future Development* (Chapter 2, pp. 23–44). Heidelberg: Springer.

Navarro, P. (2015). *Crouching Tiger. What China's Militarism Means for the World.* Amherst: Prometheus Books.

Navarro, P. & Autry, G. (2011). *Death by China. Confronting the Dragon – A Global Call to Action.* New Jersey: Pearson Education. Note: The Cover Page Also Says First Printing (2015) so Publication Year is Not Fully Clear.

Newbury, D. M. G., & Stiglitz, J. E. (1981). *The Theory of Commodity Price Stabilization. A Study in the Economics of Risk.* Oxford: Oxford University Press.

Subramanian, A. (2017). The WTO Reborn? *Arab News*, 3 March 2017. http://www.arabnews.com/node/1062406.

Timmer, M. P., Erumban, A. A., Los, B., Stehrer, R., & de Vries, G. J. (2014). Slicing Up Global Value Chains. *Journal of Economic Perspectives, 28*(2), 99–118.

USTR. (2017). *2017 Trade Policy Agenda and 2016 Annual Report of the President of the United States on the Trade Agreements Program.* Washington, DC: Office of the United States Trade Representative.

USTR. (2018). *2018 Trade Policy Agenda and 2017 Annual Report of the President of the United States on the Trade Agreements Program.* Washington, DC: Office of the United States Trade Representative.

Young, A. R., & Peterson, J. (2014). *Parochial Global Europe. 21st Century Trade Politics.* Oxford: Oxford University Press.

2

A Portrait of World Trade

In order to understand trade agreements, it is essential to know key properties of world trade. There is a two-way relationship: Trade drives FTAs, and FTAs drive trade. There is trade in goods and services; in components and parts; and in manufactures and commodities. There is "inter-industry" trade whereby goods or services from different sectors are exchanged and "intra-industry" trade with two-way trade within the same sectors. The "new trade theory" of the 1980s (see e.g. Krugman 1980) was particularly motivated by the growing share of intra-industry trade (Grubel and Lloyd 1975). Descriptive evidence is therefore also important by framing research on causal mechanisms and telling us "what to look for".

Global trade developments are regularly analysed by international institutions such as the IMF (International Monetary Fund) and the WTO (World Trade Organization, see e.g. WTO 2017), and also by major banks. These reports typically cover recent years only, and there is a need for research covering longer time periods—also addressing the

A. Melchior, *Free Trade Agreements and Globalisation*,
https://doi.org/10.1007/978-3-319-92834-0_2

data challenges involved in constructing consistent data for extended periods. This chapter contributes to this endeavour.

This chapter compactly portrays some key characteristics of world trade in goods. We divide the world into seven major regions and examine trade within and between them. The same regional subdivision is applied in subsequent chapters on the spread of FTAs (Chap. 3) and on the economic impact of FTAs (Chaps. 7 and 8). In this way, this book attempts to provide a coherent analysis of descriptive, institutional and analytical aspects of FTAs.

Key messages from the analysis of this chapter are as follows:

- The growth of Asia has led to a dramatic re-composition of world trade with a growing share for Asia and intra-Asian trade.
- The world has evolved into two clubs, the manufacturers and the commodity exporters. North America, Western Europe and Asia are the manufacturing exporters of the world and by far the largest traders, while the other four regions (Latin America, Eastern Europe, Africa and the Middle East) are commodity exporting regions with a modest share of world trade.
- Three-fourth of the world trade is between and within the manufacturing world regions; and a large share of this is two-way trade in manufacturing. About one-fifth of the world trade is between manufacturing and commodity regions, mainly exchange of manufacturing for commodities. The manufacturing regions have more intra-regional trade, while commodity trade is more globalised.
- The shares of manufacturing and commodities in world trade have changed considerably over time, with commodity price fluctuations as a key driver. Until recently, commodity price increases led to a falling share for manufacturing in world trade and a considerable reduction in the share of two-way trade in manufacturing (intra-industry trade).

The analysis raises a number of questions about FTAs and their role. Do manufacturing and commodity exporters have a similar interest in FTAs? Will poor countries obtain similar gains from FTAs as the rich ones? How large are the gains from trade integration within the regions, compared to inter-regional with distant countries? In later chapters, we revert to such questions.

2.1 Data and Regional Aggregation

In the following, we analyse world trade in goods during 1995–2015, using a newly created data set for the purpose, constructed from trade data from the United Nations' Commodity Trade Statistics Database (COMTRADE); retrieved using the search engine World Integrated Trade Solution (WITS).[1] A data issue is that the number of reporting countries varies over time between 136 and 178, with the maximum in 2007. This is shown in Fig. 2.1 (left axis).

For the analysis of changes over time, we need to have a consistent time series. For this purpose, we fill in most of the data gaps by using *mirror data*: For the missing countries, bilateral trade flows are still reported by most of their trading partners, including major countries that are generally among the reporters. We therefore use such mirror data to extend the data; for example, if country X is missing among the data reporters, we use USA's imports from country X to quantify country X's exports to the USA and so on. In this way, the overall trade value covered by the data set is increased by up to 6% for the years with the lowest number of reporters. This is shown in Fig. 2.1 (right axis). Our expanded data set thereby covers virtually all of world trade in goods, and it has consistent country coverage over time.[2]

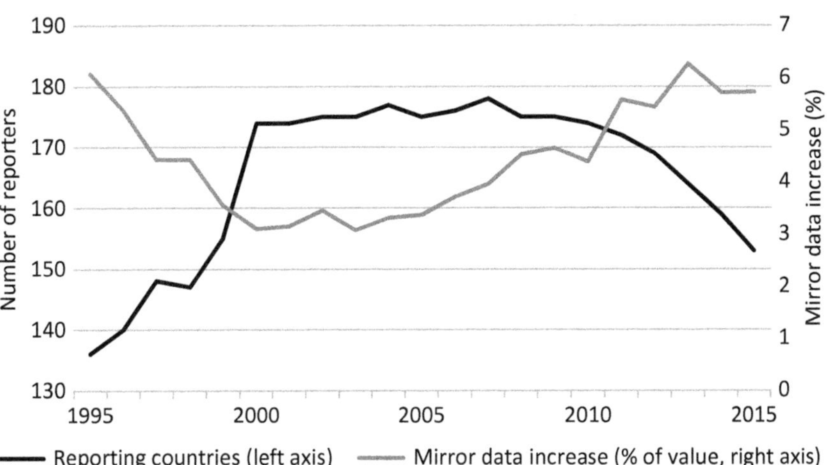

Fig. 2.1 Data increase due to mirror data. (Source: Own calculations based on data from WITS/COMTRADE)

In the analysis throughout this book, we often divide the world into the following seven major world regions (with the number of countries in brackets, counting from trade data):

- North America (6): Includes Mexico, Bermuda and Greenland.
- Latin America (48): The rest of the Americas and the Caribbean.
- Western Europe (38): All of EU and European Free Trade Association (EFTA) plus some very small states.[3]
- Eastern Europe (12): The former Soviet Area.
- Africa (58): All of Africa except Egypt.
- Middle East (23): An expanded region including the non-EU Balkan countries, Turkey, Egypt, Afghanistan and Pakistan in addition to the "standard" Middle East countries.
- Asia/Pacific (55): Includes South Asia and Pacific countries including Australia and New Zealand.

In the expanded trade data set that we use, there are 240 countries. As we shall see, some world regions have a tiny share of world trade, in spite of their inclusion of a large number of countries. In the figures throughout the book and in some tables, we use slightly abbreviated region names in order to save space.

The price to pay for limiting the number of regions is some heterogeneity within regions; for example, Turkey may not like to be in the expanded Middle East and so on. The intention here is to provide a stylised macro-picture of world trade and for this endeavour we limit the number of regions and thereby the extent of detail. In the analysis of trade, an issue is whether intra-regional trade should be included or not; for example, sometimes intra-EU trade is excluded in the analysis of world trade (see e.g. WTO 2011, p. 67). In the following analysis, intra-EU trade is included.

2.2 Manufacturing Versus Commodity Regions

Stylised fact 1: *All world regions have a similar import propensity for manufactured goods, but on the exporting side, they diverge into commodity versus manufacturing exporters.*

Figures 2.2 (for exports) and 2.3 (imports) show this divergence across world regions.

Figure 2.3 shows that for all world regions, manufactured goods have a relatively similar share of total imports of goods; starting above 70% for most regions in 1995 and falling somewhat over time for most regions. The falling share was mainly due to the commodity price increases; this is discussed in Sect. 2.4.

For exports, Fig. 2.2 reveals a dramatic difference between the "factories of the world" (Asia, Western Europe and North America) and the remaining four regions. In this book, we use the terms commodity regions and manufacturing regions; although, it should be recalled that the pattern may change over time, and also that there is heterogeneity within these major regions—Turkey and Saudi Arabia are different. Covering the period 1970–2010, Melchior (2012) shows that over this longer time span, Central Europe grew into the manufacturing league. Hence in the future, the classification may change.

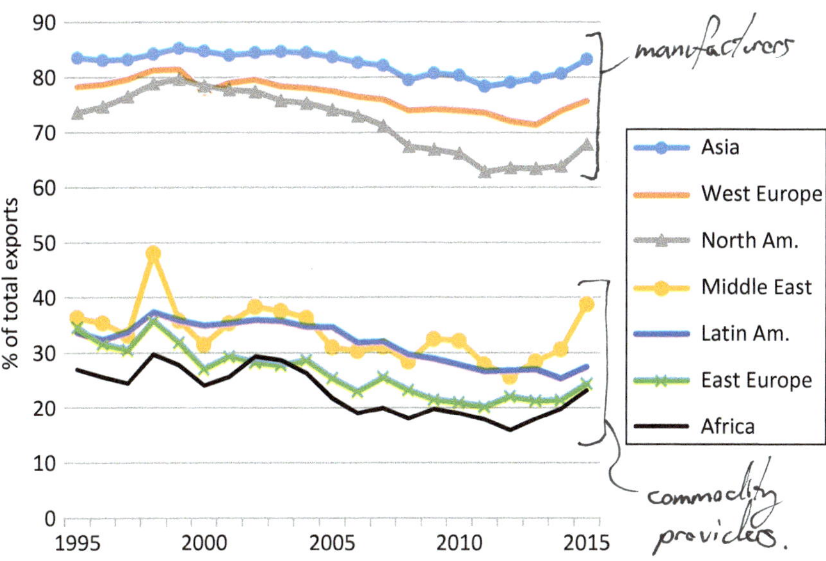

Fig. 2.2 Share of manufacturing in the exports of major world regions. Percentage of total exports, average based on reported export and import data. (Source: Own calculations based on data from WITS/COMTRADE)

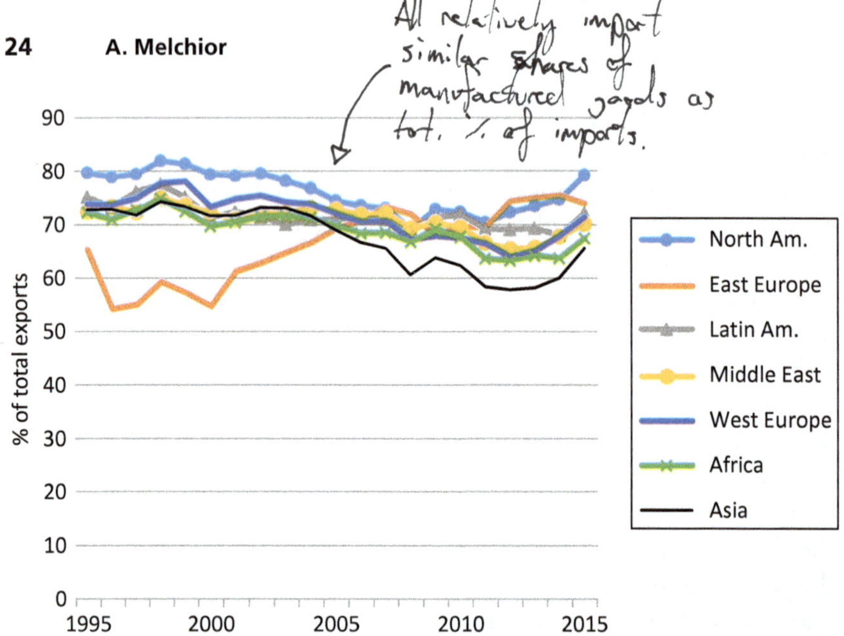

Fig. 2.3 Share of manufacturing in the imports of major world regions. Percentage of total imports, average based on reported export and import data. (Source: Own calculations based on data from WITS/COMTRADE)

From Sect. 2.1, we may observe that more than half the world's countries (131) are in the commodity regions of the world. Commodity exports are of vital importance to half the world. One of the main aims of this book is, therefore, to include commodities properly in the analysis of FTAs and trade policy. The world economy model we present in Chap. 6 and Appendix B, and which is used in the trade policy analysis of Chaps. 6, 7 and 8, includes commodities and sheds light on the trade policy interests and the impact of trade policy for these countries.

2.3 The Giants of Trade

The manufacturing regions are also the giants of world trade. Figure 2.4 shows shares of world trade for the seven regions during 1995–2015.

The three industrial regions are clearly the giants of world trade. Among the three, there was a sharp reallocation of shares over time: While Asia rose from 27% to 34% of world trade during this period, Western Europe declined from 44% to 35% and the North American share fell from 19%

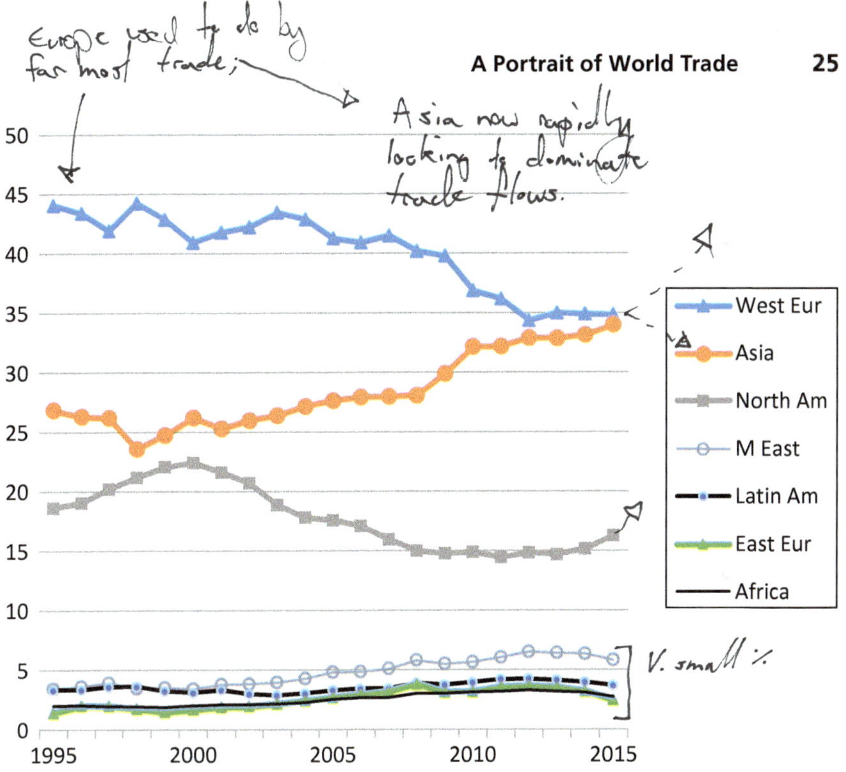

Fig. 2.4 Shares of world trade in goods (%) for major world regions, 1995–2015. (Source: Own calculations based on data from WITS/COMTRADE)

to 16%. The share of these three world regions taken together declined from 90% in 1995 to 85% in 2015. Hence the four commodity regions had on average faster trade growth during the period; however, their combined share of world trade remains modest. Their trade growth was fuelled by commodity price increases, and with the commodity price boom ending in 2011, their trade share started falling thereafter.

For the analysis of FTAs, it is of interest to see not only "who is trading", but "who is trading with whom". Appendix Table A.1 presents shares of world trade and the growth of trade flows for the full 7x7 matrix of trade between the seven world regions. To gauge the bigger picture and provide a "grand view" that is easy to recall, we aggregate our world regions further into the "Industrial 3" (Western Europe, North America and Asia) and the "Commodity-4" (Africa, Eastern Europe, Latin America and Middle East). Table 2.1 shows the shares of world trade for trade within and between these mega-regions and the share of manufacturing in the respective trade flows.

Table 2.1 Trade patterns between industrial and commodity regions (%)

			% of world trade		% manufacturing in trade	
			Importing region			
			Industrial-3	Commodity-4	Industrial-3	Commodity-4
Exporting region	Industrial-3	1995	81.5	8.5	79.2	79.2
		2005	76.6	8.3	79.0	82.5
		2015	74.4	11.3	77.5	79.6
	Commodity-4	1995	7.9	2.1	29.9	46.0
		2005	11.7	3.4	24.8	43.9
		2015	10.5	3.9	24.8	45.1

Source: Own calculations based on data from WITS/COMTRADE

In 2015, 74% of world trade was within and between the Industrial-3 regions; 22% was trade between Industrial-3 and Commodity-4 regions; and only 4% was within and between the Commodity-4 region. Trade within and between the Industrial-3 region was mainly manufacturing; whereas trade between Industrial-3 and Commodity-4 regions was mainly exchange of manufacturing for commodities. For trade within and between the Commodity-4 regions, the manufacturing share was intermediate.

Figure 2.5 shows the shares of world trade for the respective flows. Here we have also split up trade within the mega-regions into intra-regional trade (e.g. within Western Europe, North America, etc.) and inter-regional trade (e.g. between Western Europe and North America, etc.). Figure 2.6 shows the annual nominal growth rates for these trade flows. For trades involving both Industrial-3 (IND-3) and Commodity-4 (COMM-4), the exporting region is mentioned first.

While trades within and between the Industrial-3 region are the largest trade flows, these had the lowest growth rates. The fastest growing trades were those within and between the Commodity-4 regions, with trade between Industrial-3 and Commodity-4 regions at an intermediate level. Again, the footprint of commodity prices is seen from the reversal of trends from 2012.

Stylised fact(s) 2 is therefore as follows: *Half of world trade is intra-regional trade within the Industrial-3 region. Another one-fourth of the world trade is trade between the Industrial-3 region, and a bit more than one-fifth of the world trade is between Industrial-3 and Commodity-4 regions. While the latter trades are mainly exchange of manufacturing for commodities, manufacturing dominates trade within and between industrial*

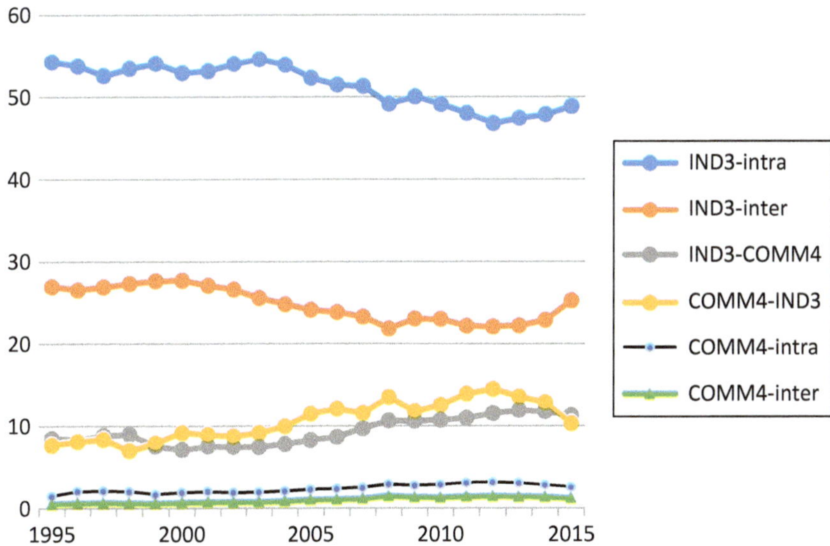

Fig. 2.5 Shares of world trade (%) for major trade flow types, 1995–2015. (Source: Own calculations based on data from WITS/COMTRADE)

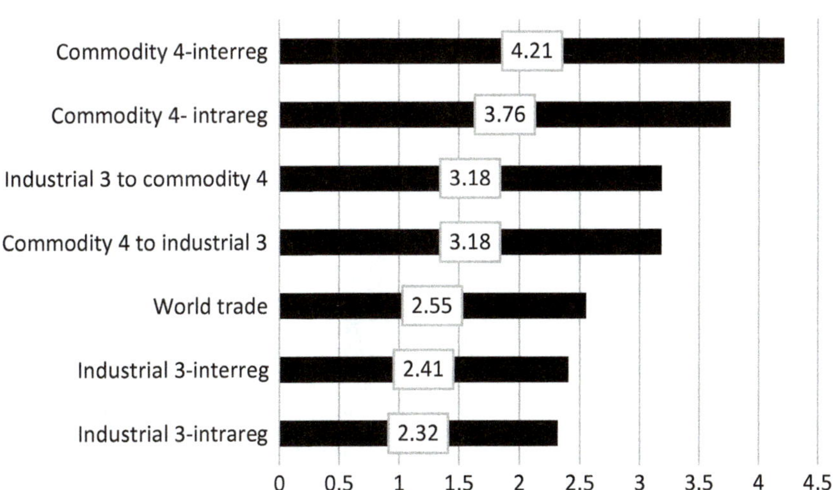

Fig. 2.6 Annual growth rates (nominal) for major world trade flows, 1995–2015. (Source: Own calculations based on data from WITS/COMTRADE)

regions. Trade within and between the Commodity-4 region has a share of merely 4% of world trade, but this is the fastest growing component of world trade, followed by trade between industrial and commodity regions.

2.4 Intra-regional and Intra-industry Trade

For the development and spread of FTAs, an issue is to what extent trade is intra-regional—within Western Europe, North America and so on—or inter-regional, across oceans and between world regions. This is shown in Fig. 2.7.

Stylised fact 3 is immediately visible: *For the manufacturing regions, the share of intra-regional trade (as opposed to trade with other world regions) is larger.*

Geography and the number of countries in each world regions affect the share of intra-regional trade in total trade; this is part of the explanation that, for example, North America has a lower share of intra-regional trade than Asia or Europe (where intra-EU trade is included). The major pattern is still clear; the manufacturing regions have a larger share of intra-regional trade. Commodity trade is more "globalised" and inter-regional.

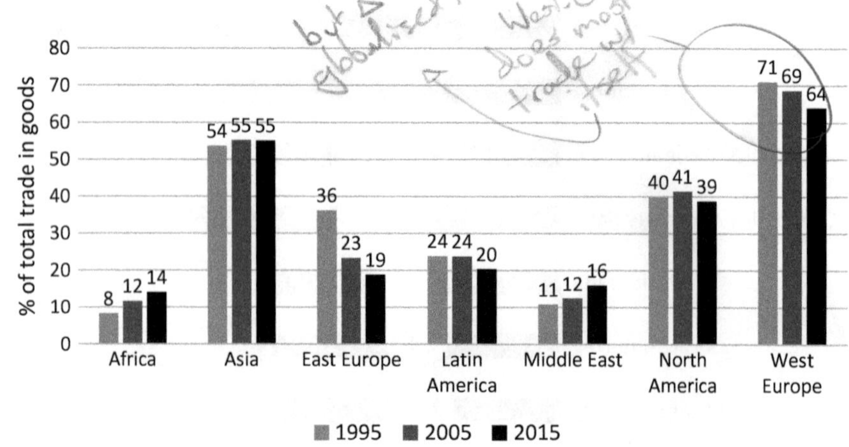

Fig. 2.7 The share of intra-regional trade in total goods trade for major world regions. (Note: For data reasons, the left bar for East Europe shows 1996. Source: Own calculations based on data from WITS/COMTRADE, using import data)

With faster growth for trade within the commodity regions, this p may change over time.

For the industrial regions, the trends over time differ: Fig. 2.7 suggests that globalisation was stronger for Western Europe, with a stronger fall in the share of intra-regional trade. This decline is interesting and perhaps surprising, given that EU enlargement (and the preceding Europe agreements) contributed to stronger intra-European integration during the period. Commodity price increases contributed to a lower intra-regional share for Western Europe, and the trade and value chain effects of further European integration were not enough to reverse this trend. A more detailed analysis is needed to disentangle the relative impact of commodity prices, globalisation, value chains and integration effects.

As noted in the introduction; the extent of two-way trade in similar goods motivated the new trade theory; which is an important foundation for modern economic theory of regional integration. Intra-industry trade may be measured at different aggregation levels; for example, Brülhart (2009) calculated intra-industry trade at the three-digit and five-digit of the SITC trade classification, with 177 and 1161 product categories, respectively.[4] With so many product categories, the measurement of intra-industry trade (IIT) for all of world trade becomes a larger data exercise. Conceptually, it is also not clear that more detail is "more accurate"; if we aim to identify the "industrial capacity" of nations and its role for trade, it may not be important whether they make bicycles or radios. As a shortcut here which allows a characterisation of IIT more broadly with less data requirements and still captures the aggregate industrial capacity, we simply use two-way trade in manufacturing as a measure. We have compared this more aggregated measure of IIT with Brülhart's calculations for 200 countries in 2006, giving a correlation coefficient for levels of IIT across countries at 0.81 with Brülhart's three-digit measure, and 0.74 with the five-digit measure. The high correlation suggests that two-way manufacturing trade is a useful proxy measure. While the level of IIT is higher, the more aggregated is the measure. Brülhart's results verify that comparisons across countries are highly correlated between different aggregation levels.[5] For comparison across countries and over time, an aggregated measure may therefore serve the purpose.

ard IIT index of Grubel and Lloyd (1975): If, for xports manufacturing worth 100 from country B, opposite direction, the trade overlap or two-way is 50*2=100. Expressed as a share of total trade gregate), this is the Grubel-Lloyd measure of intra- ue. For example, we first calculate the amount of two-way in manufacturing bilaterally for each country pair, and then aggregate for the world regions. For brevity, we call our measure IIT.

Table 2.2 shows the share of two-way trade in manufactured goods in world trade flows 2015.

As we might expect, the share of IIT is particularly high in the intra-regional trade of the industrial regions. It is also high in Western Europe's trade with North America and Asia, but surprisingly low between Asia and North America. While the shares of Western Europe as well as North America in world trade have dropped, the manufacturing export decline was stronger for the USA. In our seven by seven matrix of trade flows between the seven world regions (see Appendix Table A.1), North American exports to Asia had the second lowest growth of all the 49 trade flows during 1995–2015 (only beaten by North American imports from Africa!).

For the commodity regions, the IIT's share in intra-regional trade is lower than for the industrial regions. The share is even lower for the off-diagonal trade flows of the commodity regions; here trade is mainly exchange of commodities for manufacturing. Figure 2.8 shows that for all

Table 2.2 The share of two-way trade in manufacturing in world trade flows, 2015 (%)

		Importing region							
		Africa	Asia	East Europe	Latin Am	Middle East	North Am	West Europe	World
Exporting region	Africa	12	8	5	8	7	21	21	14
	Asia		40	15	6	11	23	47	34
	East Europe			31	3	18	26	18	19
	Latin Am				26	8	28	17	18
	Middle East					25	19	39	23
	North Am						57	56	46
	West Europe							61	52
	World								39

Source: Own calculations based on data from WITS/COMTRADE

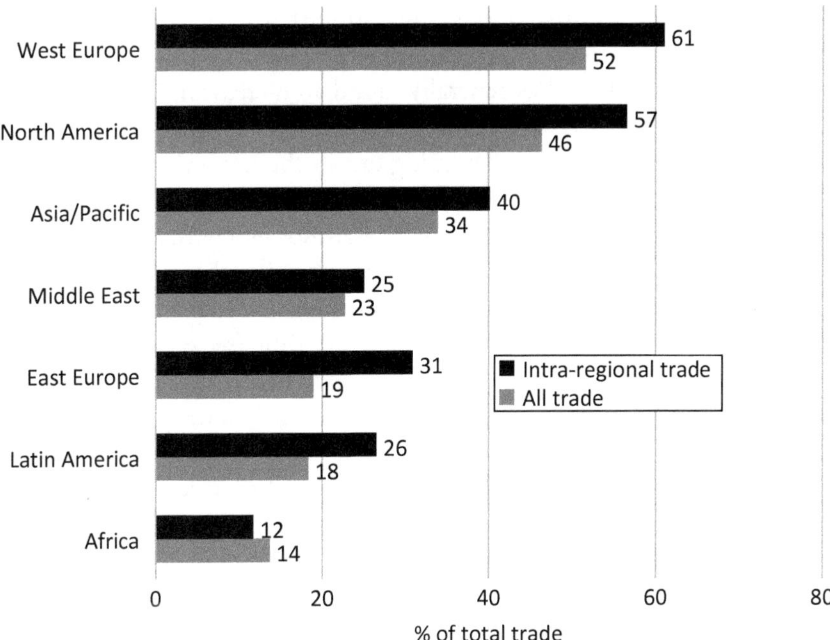

Fig. 2.8 Two-way bilateral manufacturing trade in % of total trade for major world regions in 2015. (Source: Own calculations based on data from WITS/COMTRADE)

world regions except Africa, the share of two-way manufacturing trade is higher for intra-regional trade than in trade with other regions.

Stylised fact 3 is therefore as follows: *Two-way manufacturing trade is higher within and between the manufacturing regions and higher for intra-regional than for inter-regional trade.*

The results here are in line with those of Brülhart (2009), who finds that IIT is positively correlated with income levels and inversely related to distance—implying that it will be larger within regions than between them. These results are in line with the earlier literature on IIT, dating from, for example, Balassa (1966). The early literature also found that IIT was higher for countries at similar income levels, but this was not supported by Brülhart (ibid.), who found a strong increase in IIT for middle-income countries. At the same time, IIT was in fact higher for intermediate than for final goods; suggesting that a considerable part of IIT is linked to international production networks.[6]

Earlier analysis of IIT has generally found an increase in IIT over time; for example, Brülhart (2009) found a sizeable increase in IIT during the period 1962–2006; however flattening out in the late 1990s and declining slightly at the five-digit level after the turn of the century. Given that IIT is measured from value figures, the author notes that commodity price increases provide a possible explanation for the reversed trend. Considering the evidence in support of the Prebisch-Singer hypothesis on the relative decline in commodity prices other time (see e.g. Harvey et al. 2010), the argument also applies for periods with a rising share of IIT.

For the period covered by the analysis here, it is indeed the case that the share of two-way manufacturing trade in total trade changes over time. It is also strongly affected by commodity price fluctuations. Figure 2.9 shows the share of two-way manufacturing trade in world trade (%, left axis) and an IMF commodity price index (right axis).[7]

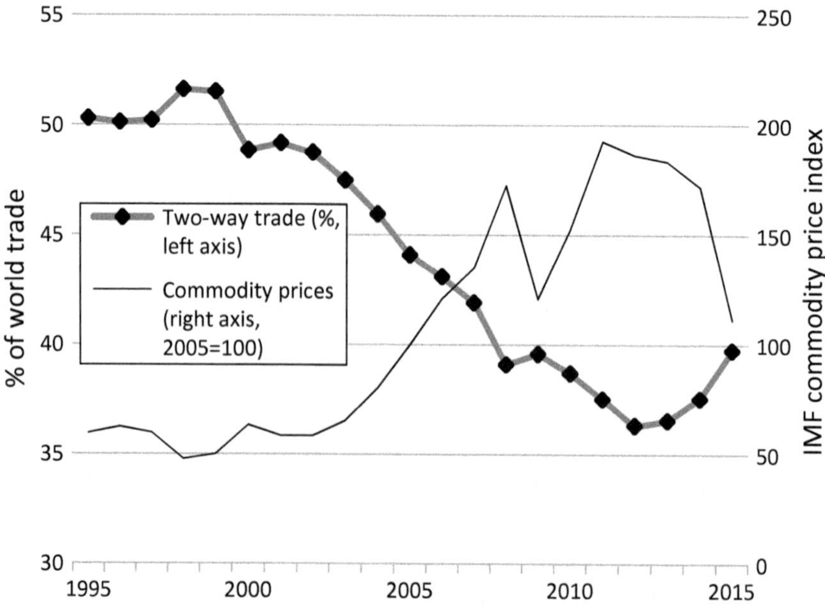

Fig. 2.9 Two-way manufacturing trade as % of world trade, 1995–2015. (Source: Own calculations based on data from WITS/COMTRADE and IMF)

The "scissors" symmetry illustrates the influence of commodity prices. Because of higher commodity prices during most of the period, the share of manufacturing in world trade dropped, including the share of IIT. From 2012, the development was reversed.

Stylised fact 4 is therefore that *the share of IIT in world trade fell from 1998 to 2012, mainly due to commodity price changes.*

The share of IIT could also fall for other reasons; a more detailed analysis is beyond the scope here. The analysis indicates an "omitted variable bias" in some earlier analysis of IIT, in the sense that commodity prices are a key driver that has not always been taken fully into account.

2.5 Implications for Trade Policy

This chapter has several messages that are important for trade policy.

First, the growth of Asia, with a corresponding increase in its share of world trade, implies that trade policy related to Asia becomes more important. In later chapters, we will undertake numerical simulation of trade policy options, and we will see this "body mass factor" of Asia in the results. This is indeed a key issue in the Brexit debate in the UK: An example is the billionaire James Dyson, who has argued that the business opportunities are in Asia.[8] In later chapters, we will examine and quantify this argument.

Second, it is important for trade policy that a majority of bilateral trade flows across the globe are predominantly exchange of commodities for manufacturing. It is therefore essential to answer the question: Are FTAs good for Saudi Arabia and other countries that rely on commodity exports? In the later analysis, we will see that the answer is often "Yes indeed."

Third, the commodity regions comprise more than half the world's countries, but the trade within and between these countries adds up to a modest 4% of world trade, with a lower share of manufacturing in trade. Do FTAs make sense also for these trade flows? In absolute numbers, the impact of such FTAS will be smaller. On the other hand, these are the fastest growing world trade flows, and so perhaps there is more to gain in relative terms? In Chap. 8, we show that there is indeed hope also for the commodity regions: Africa can benefit significantly from intra-regional FTAs even if the volume of trade is currently small.

A standard prediction from modern trade research is that trade liberalisation that leads to inter-industry specialisation (across sectors) entails higher adjustment costs compared to trade liberalisation leading to more intra-industry trade. According to this, the low share of IIT in US trade with Asia is a possible explanation of the anti-trade sentiments in the 2016 US election, fuelled by Trump but also Sanders. In Chap. 6, we analyse further this "threat" from Asia and China, and what it means for US trade policy.

Commodity countries are often more or less specialised in commodity exports, and in such cases, there is no room for more inter-industry adjustment and so the adjustment cost argument above does not apply. In this case, the impact of trade policy on prices and the terms of trade is more essential. In this book, we will therefore use a world trade model that takes the issue of complete specialisation and terms-of-trade effects properly into account.

In terms of methodology, this chapter relies on scientific tools such as the use of mirror data for constructing the data set. Our simplified IIT index is also a contribution, simplifying analysis and reducing the data burden for examining the role of two-way trade. The analysis is mainly descriptive, using tables and graphs in order to derive the stylised facts. We do not test econometrically particular hypotheses about what is driving the changes or explaining the patterns; we are content here by showing the key characteristics and the book format allows this. Our belief is that descriptive and historical analysis should have an important role in economics; beyond short introductions to narrow articles. Major breakthroughs in research on international trade, such as the new trade theory, have been motivated by descriptive empirics, such as the observed growth of intra-industry trade (Grubel and Lloyd 1975). Trade researchers should know about trade and this chapter aims to contribute by revealing some of the key stylised facts about world trade. While some issues, such as the main properties of intra-industry trade, are well-known from the literature, some aspects have changed over time (e.g. the share of IIT) and an up-to-date analysis is therefore warranted.

The analysis is about trade in goods, so the omission of services trade is a limitation. For analysis of services trade, see, for example, Loungani et al. (2017). As shown by these authors, services currently constitutes about one-fourth of world trade but has been growing faster than goods trade, partly due to the ICT (information and communication technology) revolution. In the global value chains, there is interaction between goods and services in a number of ways. In Chap. 3, we will see that more and more FTAs cover services, with a sharp acceleration after the turn of the century. Global value chains are also important for goods trade. While we address the "mother of all value chains"—the role of commodity trade—we do not examine trade in manufactured components, and this is a limitation. This may be studied further using recently developed databases for the purpose; see, for example, Timmer et al. (2014).

Notes

1. Data were downloaded on 18 August 2017, using the WITS software/search engine.
2. A technical issue is that import data are reported "cif" (with cost, insurance and freight included) whereas exports are reported "fob" (free-on-board and without these costs). The import value should therefore be somewhat higher than the export value of the same bilateral trade flow. When constructing mirror data, we use the rule of thumb often applied by the IMF (International Monetary Fund) in their balance of payments data; the import value is 10% larger than the export value.
3. In the charts and tables, we often use abbreviations such as West Europe, East Europe, North Am, etc., in order to save space.
4. Brülhart used the SITC1 vintage of this classification. The latest version (SITC4) has 263 and 2970 categories at the three- and five-digit levels, respectively.
5. Brülhart finds that global IIT in 2006 was 27% at the five-digit level and 44% at the three-digit level. With our measure, we obtain global IIT at 43%.The reason why this is lower than Brülhart's three-digit result is likely that we do not include two-way trade for non-manufacturing products.

6. For the EU-27 and Japan, Domit and Shakir (2010, p. 185) show that the share of intermediate components in goods imports increased during the period 1999–2009, reaching a share above 50% for Japan and above 60% for the EU.
7. IMF Primary Commodity Prices, all commodities and energy, 2005=100. Available at http://www.imf.org/external/np/res/commod/index.aspx.
8. See, for example, "Brexit: UK should make a 'clean break' from the EU, says James Dyson"; The Independent, 14 September 2017.

References

Balassa, B. (1966). Tariff Reductions and Trade in Manufactures among Industrial Countries. *American Economic Review, 56*, 466–473.

Brülhart, M. (2009). An Account of Global Intra-industry Trade, 1962–2006. *The World Economy, 32*(10), 401–459.

Domit, S., & Shakir, T. (2010). Interpreting the World Trade Collapse. *Bank of England Quarterly Bulletin, 50*, 183–189.

Grubel, H., & Lloyd, P. J. (1975). *Intra-industry Trade*. London: Macmillan.

Harvey, D. I., Kellard, N. M., Madsen, J. B., & Wohar, M. E. (2010). The Prebisch-Singer Hypothesis: Four Centuries of Evidence. *Review of Economics and Statistics, 92*(2), 367–377.

Krugman, P. (1980). Scale Economies, Product Differentiation, and the Pattern of Trade. *American Economic Review, 70*(5), 950–959.

Loungani, P., Mishra, S., Papageorgiou, C., & Wang, K. (2017). *World Trade in Services: Evidence from A New Dataset* (IMF Research Department Working Paper WP/17/77). Washington, DC: International Monetary Fund.

Melchior, A. (2012). *World Trade 1970–2010: Globalization, Reallocation and Regionalization* (Working Paper No. 805). Oslo: Norwegian Institute of International Affairs. https://brage.bibsys.no/xmlui/handle/11250/277242.

Timmer, M. P., Erumban, A. A., Los, B., Stehrer, R., & de Vries, G. J. (2014). Slicing Up Global Value Chains. *Journal of Economic Perspectives, 28*(2), 99–118.

WTO. (2011). *World Trade Report 2011. The WTO and Preferential Trade Agreements: From Co-existence to Coherence*. Geneva: World Trade Organization.

WTO. (2017). *World Trade Statistical Review 2017*. Geneva: World Trade Organization.

3

The Global Landscape of FTAs

It is well-known that the worldwide number of Free Trade Agreements (FTAs) has exploded. The recent surge in the number of FTAs is documented by World Trade Organization (WTO) (2011, Part II): From around 1990, the number of FTAs exploded, increasing from about 70 in 1990 to about 300 in 2010. The DESTA (Design of Trade Agreements) database of Dür et al. (2014) also includes FTAs not notified to the WTO, and the authors identify 393 agreements in force in 2009. According to Acharya (2016), 265 FTAs were in force and notified to the WTO by October 2015, and about 100 more FTAs were in force but not notified to the WTO. Lynch (2010) provides a more qualitative analysis and overview of the evolution of FTAs. This chapter starts by updating the FTA accounting, using WTO data as of August 2017. The "FTA race" continued after 2010, and there was particularly high growth for the number of FTAs covering services. The majority of current FTAs are youngsters: As of August 2017, 72% of the FTAs in force and notified to the WTO were of vintage 2001 or later.

Counting the number of agreements usefully illustrates the "FTA race" and its recent acceleration. The number of agreements is however a very imprecise measure if we want to shed light on the importance of FTAs.

A. Melchior, *Free Trade Agreements and Globalisation*,
https://doi.org/10.1007/978-3-319-92834-0_3

Standard math tells us that if we have N countries, they may enter into N*(N−1)/2 agreements between them. So three countries can have 3*2/2=3 agreements, ten countries can have 10*9/2=45 agreements and so on. According to this, the WTO had 164 members in 2017 and they could hypothetically enter into a stunning 13,366 bilateral FTAs!! So is 300 or 400 really all that much?

Many FTAs also have more than two partners, and counting, for example, the EU as one FTA is misleading. The 28 members of the EU could have 378 bilateral agreements between them (using the same formula), but they have simplified the matter for us by having one "plurilateral" agreement. With EU's eastward enlargement in 2004, the number of FTAs in force decreased since former FTAs between EU and the new members were discontinued and replaced by EU membership. Hence deeper integration was reflected in a reduction in the number of FTAs. In this case, counting the number of FTAs obviously provides a misleading picture of integration.

In this chapter, we therefore try another way of counting the FTAs: We pick out the 40 largest non-EU countries in terms of Gross Domestic Product (GDP) or population and construct the matrix of FTAs between them, in addition including the EU as one observation/unit. Using a number of information sources, we collect information on FTAs in force, FTA negotiations, failed FTAs and more. In this way, we map not only who has an FTA, but also who does not. We do not count FTAs, but trade links covered by FTAs. Later, we sum up the trade value covered by FTAs, dividing the world into regions as in Chap. 2.

Between our 41 key players in the global race for FTAs, we find that 10 out of 40 trade relations were on average covered by an FTA in August 2017. Hence the majority of trade relations had no FTAs, and the WTO still rules for a large majority of the trade links. Since FTAs are more frequent among richer and more economically important countries, the prevalence of FTAs is likely much lower worldwide than in our 40+EU sample. Within our sample, FTAs are particularly prevalent within and between the industrial regions. Within Asia, the coverage of FTAs has expanded particularly fast during the last 15 years. Hence, in value, more than half of the world trade in goods is between countries that had FTAs.

In the sample of 41, we find that small countries such as Chile, Singapore and European Free Trade Association (EFTA) countries have been particularly proactive in the FTA race. Among the big powers, the EU, China and India are in the upper half of the FTA counting, whereas the USA, Brazil and Russia are in the lower half. In later chapters, we examine the potential economic loss from this lack of activism from, for example, the USA.

3.1 An Explosion in the Number of FTAs

As of August 2017 there were about 300 FTAs in force, according to the WTO online data base. If two trade partners have one goods FTA and another services FTA, we count this as one. Table 3.1 provides an overview.

The table illustrates the rapid expansion of FTAs after the turn of the century: More than two-thirds of the agreements entered into force 2001 and later. About one half of the FTAs covered trade in goods only, and the other half goods and services. Trade in services is a new element in many agreements: Before 2001, only 11 agreements covered services; by 2017, this number was 147. Although not visible from the table, the following analysis will show that from the turn of the century, more agreements were between countries in different world regions.

As an alternative counting of FTAs, we select the 35 largest countries in the world; in terms of GDP (2015) or population (2016). With the EU counting as one, we obtain a sample of 41, with 40 individual countries plus EU-28, covering 94% of world GDP (92% for GDP in purchasing power parities), 92% of world trade and 85% of the world's total

Table 3.1 The vintage of free trade agreements in force August 2017

	Number of agreements			% of agreements		
Year of entry into force	Goods	Goods and services	All	Goods	Goods and services	All
Up to 1990	19	4	23	13	3	8
1991–2000	53	7	60	35	5	20
2001–2010	51	81	132	34	55	44
2011–	27	55	82	18	37	28
All years	150	147	297	100	100	100

Source: WTO online database for trade agreements (rtais.wto.org); data downloaded August 2017

population.[1] The sample is not representative due to the selection criteria, but includes all the countries that are most active with respect to FTAs (Acharya 2016, p. 8). On the other hand, we are not counting the FTAs these countries have with countries outside the sample, and the results should be interpreted with this in mind. For example, Russia has many FTAs with former Soviet republics but only Russia and Ukraine are in the sample; the USA has agreements in Central America that are not covered; and the EU with countries in Africa and so on.

Within this chosen sample, each country and the EU have 40 trade links that could be covered by FTAs. Between the 41, there are 820 trade links that could potentially be covered by FTAs. Using several sources, we map FTAs in this universe, as well as negotiations on FTAs and the year of their entry into force. Appendix Table A.2 shows the number of trade links covered by FTAs by country, as well as negotiations and failed negotiations. Table 3.2 provides a summary.

The picture presented here is a snapshot at a particular point in time (August 2017). For example, the Trans-Pacific Partnership (TPP) is classified as "Failed" whereas later, the 11 partners except the USA agreed on a modified agreement. The "final count" is impossible to be arrived at since it changes all the time; the aim is to examine some major patterns. The list will soon become obsolete, but the patterns may be more durable.

In 2017, there were 198+14=212 trade links covered by FTAs in force or completed between the 41; that is, a bit more than one quarter (26%) of the potential of 820. Compared to the potential of 40, each country

Table 3.2 FTAs between 41 countries/regions as of August 2017

	Number	% of relationships
FTAs in force	198	24.1
FTAs signed but not in force	14	1.7
Preferential between developing countries	54	6.6
Multiple FTAs for the same trade flow	52	6.3
Negotiations ongoing	95	11.6
Suspended negotiations	13	1.6
Failed negotiations	64	7.8
Total number of relationships	820	100

Note: Some categories are overlapping. Data sources: See Appendix Table A.2

had on average FTAs with 10.4. A first conclusion is therefore as follows: In spite of the fast spread of FTAs, three-fourth of the trade links are not yet covered by FTAs. Hence there is still a scope for the WTO, and there are many trade flows not ruled by FTAs. The prevalence of FTAs is surely higher in our sample than in the whole world; so the FTA coverage would be considerably lower if the whole world was included. According to WTO (2011), counting all FTAs worldwide, every WTO member was on average participant in 13 FTAs. If we assume that all these 13 were with different countries, the coverage ratio as of 2010 would be about 13/153 or 8.5%; that is, less than one out of ten links is covered by an FTA.

In addition to the agreements in force or completed, there were a number of negotiations (95) going on; either with new countries or with the purpose of updating or deepening existing agreements. Some agreements or negotiations were suspended and some failed. In the latter category, we have listed, for example, the TPP, since the USA would not ratify it. As seen by Appendix Table A.2, the USA has many failed negotiations in the past, limiting its number of FTAs.

The WTO uses a categorisation of agreements depending on the legal paragraph under which they are notified by the members. Per this, a "free trade agreement" or a "customs union" is for trade in goods and notified under Article XXIV of the GATT (General Agreement on Tariffs and Trade); an "economic integration agreement" is for trade in services and notified under Art. V of the GATS (General Agreement on Trade in Services); and a "partial scope agreement" is related to developing countries and notified under WTOs "enabling clause". Whereas an FTA under GATT Article XXIV must cover "substantially all the trade", a partial scope agreement may be more limited in coverage and tariff cuts. In practice, partial scope agreements span the whole range from very limited agreements to more or less full-fledged FTAs. In the classification we use here, we include some of the partial scope agreements as FTAs, but others—the more limited agreements—are classified as "preferential" in Table 3.2 above. There are many such agreements, covering more than 50 of the 820 bilateral relationships.

Which countries have been leading in the proliferation of FTAs? Figure 3.1 shows the number of bilateral relationships covered by FTAs

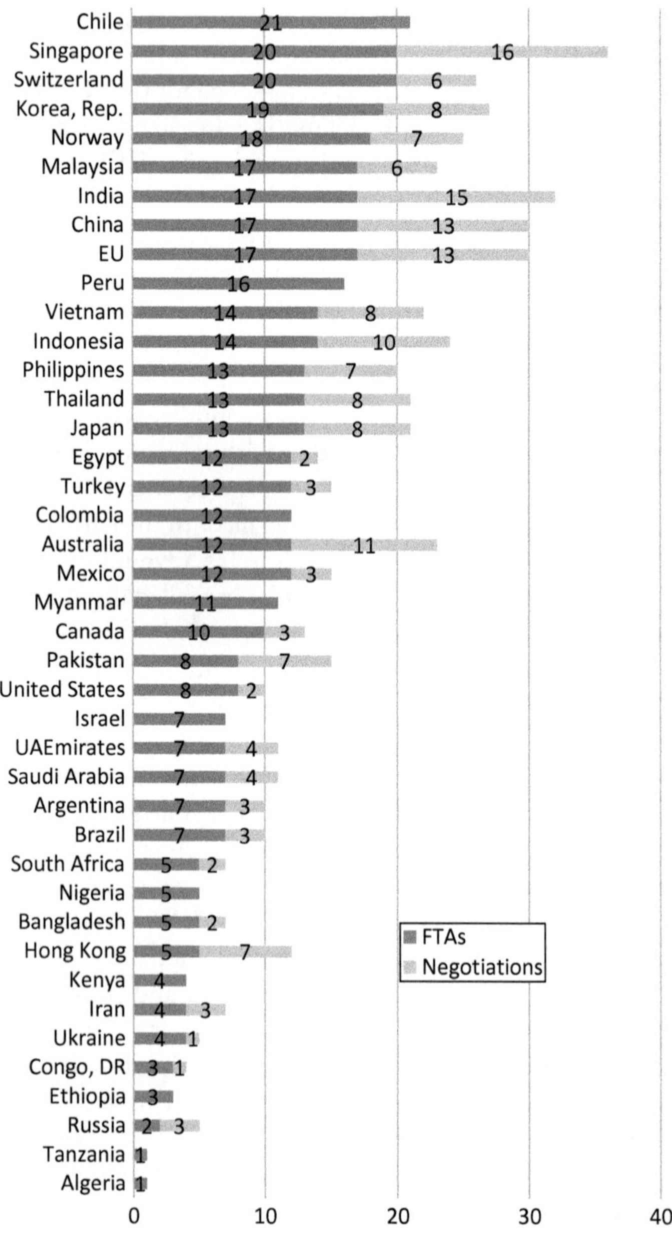

Fig. 3.1 Champions of the FTA race. Number of trade flows covered by FTAs or FTA negotiations among 40 countries and the EU. (Source: See Appendix Table A.2)

in force or completed, as of July 2017 and by country, in our sample of 41. As noted, the maximum obtainable number is 40. To the right, the number of ongoing FTA negotiations is also shown.

The small countries Chile, Singapore and Switzerland are the "champions of the FTA race"; on top of the ranking with 20–21 agreements. Among the giants, India, China and the EU all have 17 FTAs, whereas the USA (eight), Brazil (seven) and Russia (two) are in the lower half of the ranking. Near the bottom we also find most of the African countries in the sample; a first indication that poor countries are not strongly involved in the FTA race.

Figure 3.1 also shows that some countries are negotiating with several other countries in the sample to deepen current FTAs or to establish new ones. For example, Singapore, India, EU and China are all negotiating with 13–16 countries, and many other countries have several active negotiations processes. The African countries are again at the lower end, perhaps surprisingly joined by the USA with negotiations in August 2017 with only two of the 40 potential partners or Russia with three. If the USA changes its mind, re-enters TPP and activates the Transatlantic Trade and Investment Partnership (TTIP) negotiations or even FTAA (the Free Trade Area of the Americas), they can climb on the list. If FTAs are as good as they say, the USA loses from her limited participation in the FTA race. We revert to this issue in Chap. 7.

3.2 How Much Trade Is Covered by FTAs?

As another measure of the importance of FTAs, we may measure the share of world trade undertaken between countries that have an FTA. According to WTO (2011, 64), the share of world goods trade undertaken between countries with an FTA rose from 28% in 1990 to 51% in 2008. In the following, we undertake a similar calculation for the 41 countries (with EU as one) covered by our sample. Hence we measure the share of goods trade between countries that have an FTA. Figure 3.2 shows this for the sample of 41, during 1995–2015.

Within the group of 41, the share of goods trade covered by FTAs rose from 45% in 1995 to 59% in 2015. As noted before, the proportion of trade links covered was 26% in 2017, that is, much lower than the share

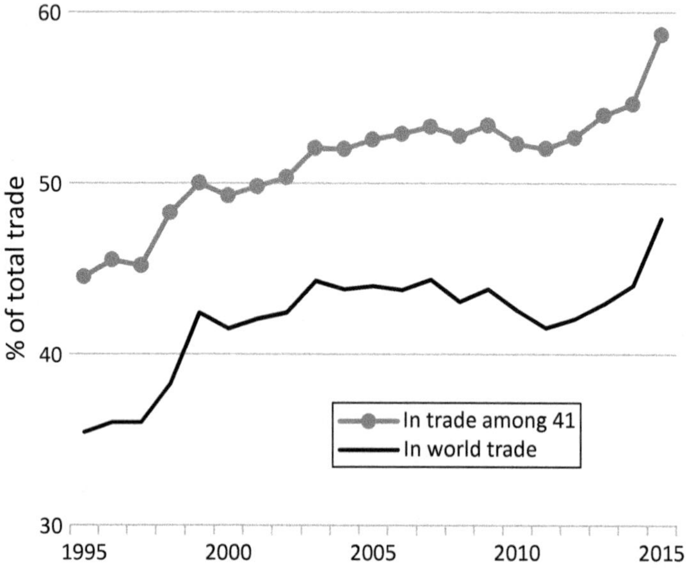

Fig. 3.2 Trade between pairs with FTAs among 41 countries; percentage of total goods trade. (Source: Own calculations based on data from the United Nations' trade database COMTRADE, retrieved using the World Integrated Trade Solution (WITS) software/search engine, and information about FTAs as shown in Appendix Table A.2)

of trade, and so FTAs tend to cover the larger trade flows. The proportion of trade links covered by FTAs rose from 5% in 1995 to 26% in 2017, also demonstrating the spread of FTAs.

Figure 3.2 also shows that, expressed as a share of total world trade, including all other countries and their trade, the share for FTA trade among the 41 rose from 35% to 48%. If we had added FTAs that are not within the sample, we would likely end up with a share of world trade covered by FTAs somewhat above 50%, in line with the WTO result referred to above.

Even if trade flows are between countries that have an FTA, trade barriers are not necessarily affected by the FTA: Tariffs could be zero for all countries, or some goods could be exempted from tariff cuts or other trade cost reductions within the FTA. WTO (2011, p. 74) undertook detailed tariff-line calculations for 20 countries and found that 29% of goods trade actually obtained tariff preferences in FTAs, or only 16% if intra-EU trade is excluded. This reservation also applies to the counting undertaken here.

Turning to the seven world regions examined in Chap. 2, Table 3.3 shows how much of the trade flows within the sample of 41 that are between countries with an FTA, for three different years. For some of the cells in the table, the sample of 41 covers all countries and trade; this is, for example, the case for North America and Western Europe. The coverage is also good for Asia and the Middle East. For the remaining three regions (Africa, Latin America and Eastern Europe), the coverage is limited and so the results should be interpreted with more caution. In the table, the intra-regional FTA coverage for Eastern Europe is underestimated for 1995 and 2005 due to the data and country sample (see e.g. Lynch 2010). With this reservation in mind, the table nevertheless shows some interesting patterns and trends.

Table 3.3 The share of trade covered by FTAs for major world regions (1995, 2005 and 2015)

	Year	North Am	Latin Am	West Europe	East Europe	Asia/ Pacific	Middle East	Africa
North Am	1995	100	1	0	0	0	27	0
	2005	100	19	5	0	11	32	0
	2015	100	56	8	0	17	29	0
Latin Am	1995		60	0	0	0	0	0
	2005		87	16	0	12	0	0
	2015		92	33	0	34	5	0
West Europe	1995			100	0	0	3	0
	2005			100	0	0	60	75
	2015			100	13	14	69	69
East Europe	1995				0	0	0	0
	2005				0	0	0	0
	2015				100	0	0	0
Asia	1995					13	0	0
	2005					35	0	0
	2015					79	11	2
Middle East	1995						0	3
	2005						31	2
	2015						53	7
Africa	1995							6
	2005							32
	2015							25

Source: Own calculations based on trade data from WITS/COMTRADE and data on FTAs as indicated in Appendix Table A.2. Average of calculations is based on export and import data

For trade within world regions, North America and Western Europe had full FTA coverage already in 1995, with Latin America at 60% at that time. For Latin America and other world regions, there was an increase in intra-regional FTA coverage over time. The Middle East and Africa have the most limited intra-regional integration within the sample; both regions have even stronger trade integration with Western Europe. The spread of FTAs is particularly impressive within the Asia region, with the share of intra-regional trade covered by FTAs rising from 13% to 79% of trade between the sample countries during the period. Figure 3.3 shows this spectacular rise, and that it started after the turn of the century. Expressed as a share of the total intra-Asian trade, the rise was from 10% to 65%. As for the lower curve in Fig. 3.2, this is a lower bound for the "FTA coverage" within the region, since FTAs beyond our sample are not included (e.g. some countries in Association of Southeast Asian Nations (ASEAN) are not in the sample).

For the inter-regional trade flows, Table 3.3 indicates that for the off-diagonal trades, the rule of FTAs is limited, save some exceptions. But there is a rising trend in some cases: Between North America and Latin

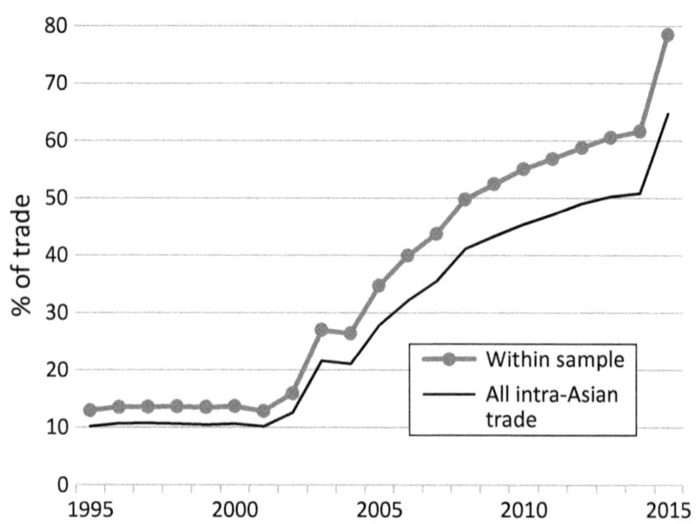

Fig. 3.3 Share (%) of intra-Asian trade between country pairs with FTAs. (Source: Own calculations based on trade data from WITS/COMTRADE. For information on FTAs from various sources, see Appendix Table A.2)

America; and between Western Europe and the Middle East plus Africa. Except for these cases, the FTA coverage for inter-regional trade flows is limited. TPP and TTIP could have meant a quantum leap for inter-regional trade integration, but with President Trump in power, these plans have been aborted or at least delayed.

We may conclude that the spread of FTA has led to next to universal FTA coverage for intra-regional trade in most world regions, with Africa lagging behind. For trade between world regions, the coverage of FTAs is still limited; albeit increasing and reaching significant levels for some of the inter-regional trade flows. More than half of world trade in goods is covered by FTAs, and the coverage of services trade has accelerated strongly.

Our conclusion and assessment is dual: There has been a rapid expansion of FTAs, but many trade flows in the world are not yet covered by FTAs and will remain so for a while. Even for the "FTA champions", many trade flows are not covered by FTAs. FTAs are also more prevalent for high or middle-income countries, while the poor countries in our sample are largely left behind. A global trade regime may therefore not only rely on FTAs, but needs strong global institutions to maintain jurisdiction also for the large number of countries down the income ladder.

Referring to our trade analysis in Chap. 2, FTAs are particularly prevalent for the intra-regional trade of industrial regions, but not exclusively so. Even the Middle East is keen on trade integration, and Latin America is stepping up trade integration with other world regions. This chapter shows that a number of commodity exporters have a revealed interest in FTA, and in Chaps. 6, 7 and 8 we will show that they have a reason to do so. In the later chapters, we shall therefore turn to the impact of FTAs for different types of traders.

This chapter has presented evidence on the spread of FTAs and their prevalence in the matrix of trade flows across world regions. Aiming to get beyond the simple counting of FTAs, we have examined a sample of 40 larger countries plus the EU, covering most of the world economy, showing not only who have FTAs but also where they are missing. Later, we have related FTAs to trade flows covering the whole 1995–2015 period. A limitation of the analysis is that it has counted FTAs without telling much about their content and depth. The following two chapters will therefore examine the content of the FTAs.

Notes

1. For country selection and for calculating these shares, we use data from the World Bank: World Development Indicators.

References

Acharya, R. (2016). Introduction. Regional Trade Agreements: Recent Developments. In R. Acharya (Ed.), *Regional Trade Agreements and the Multilateral Trading System* (pp. 1–17). Cambridge, UK: Cambridge University Press/World Trade Organization.

Dür, A., Baccini, L., & Elsig, M. (2014). The Design of International Trade Agreements: Introducing a New Database. *Review of International Organizations, 9*(3), 353–375.

Lynch, D. A. (2010). *Trade and Globalization. An Introduction to Regional Trade Agreements*. Lanham: Rowman & Littlefield Publishers..

WTO. (2011). *World Trade Report 2011. The WTO and Preferential Trade Agreements: From Co-existence to Coherence*. Geneva: World Trade Organization.

4

Tariffs: The Most and the Least Favoured Nations

Chapter 3 counted Free Trade Agreements (FTAs) without describing their content. However, this mere counting could be misleading since FTAs vary from deep and comprehensive to shallow and limited. For the analysis, it is therefore necessary to take another step and attempt to characterise the depth and nature of current FTAs. This chapter considers tariffs in FTAs. The classical FTAs were mainly about tariff discrimination; early economic theory on FTAs was often, especially in Europe, referred to as "customs union theory" and large parts of the curriculum were about tariff discrimination (Viner 1950; for overview and discussion, see e.g. Robson 1980 or Baldwin 2009).

In current trade policy debates, it is sometimes stated that tariffs have become so low that they do not matter much any longer—the key issues are about non-tariff barriers and their elimination. For example, in the USA-EU negotiations on TTIP (Transatlantic Trade and Investment Partnership), it was announced and perceived that non-tariff issues and regulatory cooperation were the most important issues (see e.g. Melchior 2016 for a discussion). There is some truth in this, but the argument should not be exaggerated: Tariffs matter, and deep cuts in non-tariff

A. Melchior, *Free Trade Agreements and Globalisation*,
https://doi.org/10.1007/978-3-319-92834-0_4

barriers are more difficult to achieve. Tariffs remain high in many countries and they vary across products—so countries with low average tariffs often have high tariffs for "sensitive goods". Furthermore, complicated rules of origin (see text box) may be a significant trade barrier, on top of administrative customs formalities—with large variation across countries. For example, if Brexit means leaving the EU customs union, there will be new customs formalities even if tariffs remain zero, and there is a vivid debate about how this is to be handled (see e.g. Pelkmans 2017).

If you are still not convinced that tariffs matter, have a look at recent FTA negotiations. For example, check the US tariff schedule in the Trans-Pacific Partnership (TPP) as of 2016, of no less than 386 pages (!), with differential treatment, transition periods, and tariff rate quotas, including a 30-year phase-out period for trucks from Japan (USTR 2016). Even for the USA, with a tariff average about 3%, 386 pages were needed to spell out the TPP tariff reforms. In TPP, there were some liberal countries with generally low tariffs (Australia, Chile, New Zealand and Singapore); three with a low average but high tariffs in some sectors (Canada, Japan and USA); and five emerging countries with higher tariffs (Brunei, Malaysia, Mexico, Peru and Vietnam) (Freund et al. 2016). This setting is representative, illustrating the variation in tariff levels as well as the complexity of FTA tariff negotiations.

In this chapter as well as Chap. 5, we review the achievements of FTA, with some new material but also drawing on a number of other sources. The aim is to arrive at an overall characterisation of FTAs. How deep is liberalisation in FTAs? Are the FTAs discriminatory or not? Do the FTAs go much deeper than the World Trade Organization (WTO)? In the field of tariffs, we will find that FTAs are generally ambitious and go beyond the WTO. The discriminatory impact is dampened by the proliferation of FTAs and other tariff preferences: A paradox is that sometimes most trade partners have some form of preferences, and so the "Most Favoured Nations" are actually the "Least Favoured Nations" (Melchior 2006a)!

4.1 Tariff Levels and Anomalies

Using the WITS/UNCTAD/WTO database, Table 4.1 shows average tariffs for 124 countries, or 151 if we count EU countries individually.[1] We have included only WTO members, in order to facilitate comparison between WTO tariffs and preferential tariffs (see text box for explanation of terms).

Table 4.1 is calculated from country tariff averages that are weighted; that is, each tariff line is weighted by the product's share of trade. Simple and weighted averages in the table, on the other hand, refer to how the average across countries is calculated; simple or weighted by each country's import value.

The simple average of bound tariff rates across countries is a high 38.5%, but the weighted average in the column to the right is much lower—at 11%. The reason is that the economically large and rich countries have lower tariffs. Hence bound tariffs are on average far from zero, and for developing countries, they are often high.[2] The next row shows the Most Favoured Nation (MFN)- applied tariff; that is, the standard tariff for imports from countries with no tariff preferences. For the MFN-applied tariffs, the simple and weighted averages across countries are 8.4% and 4.2%, respectively. Figure 4.1 shows the underlying country observations; it ranks countries from low to high according to their tariff levels.[3] The figure shows the 124 WTO members covered in Table 4.1 and (to the right) 40 non-members or WTO members with no bindings—these have no bound tariffs to show.

While MFN-applied tariffs vary from zero to about 40%, bound tariffs range from zero to 147. For the non-members or "non-binders" to the

Table 4.1 Average tariffs for 124 (151) countries

	Average all countries	
Type of tariff	Simple	Weighted
Bound	38.54	11.07
MFN applied	8.36	4.16
Preferential	2.69	1.24

Source: Calculated using tariff data from WITS/TRAINS/CTS (see endnote 1 in this chapter for explanation). At the country level, weighted tariff averages have been used

Tariffs: Some Key Concepts

Tariff lines—individual products in the list of tariffs. Here the Harmonised System (HS) of classification is applied. This is standardised internationally down to the six-digit level with about 5000 products (check World Customs Organization, www.wcoomd.org). Beyond this, countries may have even more detailed classifications with eight digits or even more; with more than 10,000 tariff lines in many cases.

A bound tariff is a legally binding upper limit for a tariff line, agreed in WTO negotiations. At the WTO, there are negotiations about which tariff lines should be bound, and the upper limit. In the Uruguay Round negotiations (1986–1993) that led to the establishment of the WTO, an aim was to improve radically the extent of binding. Most rich countries have bound all their tariffs, but for developing countries, the extent of binding is more variable. According to Melchior (2006b), 69% of tariff lines for non-agricultural goods were on average bound after the Uruguay Round of the WTO. The binding schedules are filed at the WTO, for every member country. In the context of Brexit, an issue is whether the UK can take over EU's WTO schedule of bound tariffs, in order to facilitate the process and avoid negotiating a new tariff schedule from scratch.

The **MFN (Most Favoured Nation)-applied tariff** is the tariff actually used by a country in practice and listed in the national tariff schedules. This is set by the national government, and for WTO members, it has to be at or below the bound rate. The MFN-applied tariff may be lower than the bound tariff, and in this case we say that there is "water in the tariff". At the WTO, negotiations are about bindings and bound tariffs, not the actually applied ones. A paradox is that WTO negotiations are partly about the "water"—agreeing on reforms that have no immediate real effect.

Rules of origin (RO) are used when tariffs vary across supplying countries; then rules are needed to avoid tariff-motivated transshipment and to define the origin of goods if value chains include more than one country. For example, a shirt is made from yarn, then fabric, then cut fabric and then sewing. The RO has to define what kind of transformation that has to take place if the shirt is to have origin for tariff purposes in the exporting country. A liberal RO might say that sewing is enough to obtain origin status; a more restrictive RO might say that even the fabric has to be made there; and the most restrictive would be to require that even the thread must be produced in the country of origin. ROs may be based on process rules like this, or classification changes, or thresholds for the share of value added in the exporting country (see e.g. Estevadeordal and Suominen 2008).

Preferential tariffs are of two types. WTO requires that tariffs should generally be non-discriminatory or MFN (= the same for all WTO partners), but two main exceptions are allowed: Article XXIV of General Agreement on Tariffs and Trade (GATT) allows preferential tariffs in FTAs, and the "enabling clause" dating from 1979 allows lower tariffs for imports from developing countries. The latter is implemented through the Generalised System of Preferences (GSP)—dating from 1971, whereby several WTO members (13, with the EU as one) unilaterally set lower tariffs for developing countries (or groups of developing countries). Beyond "ordinary" GSP, the EU has even more generous tariff preferences for the Least Developed Countries (LDCs) under the EBA (Everything But Arms) scheme. Similarly, the USA has GSP but also the CBI (Caribbean Basin Initiative) and the AGOA (African Growth and Opportunity Act), with additional benefits for some. Following a WTO recommendation from 2005, some developing countries also grant preferences for the LDCs. Differentiation across subgroups under GSP should build on objective and development-related criteria; arbitrary discrimination may be questioned. The word "Generalised" in GSP is about that—sometimes misspelled as "General"! This legal aspect may be a reason why the EU has transformed its preferences for ACP (Africa, Caribbean and Pacific) countries into EPA (Economic Partnership Agreements) with different subgroups. Compared to GSP-type preferences, FTAs offer more flexibility with respect to differentiation across partners. More information on GSP is available on UNCTAD's website (unctad.org).

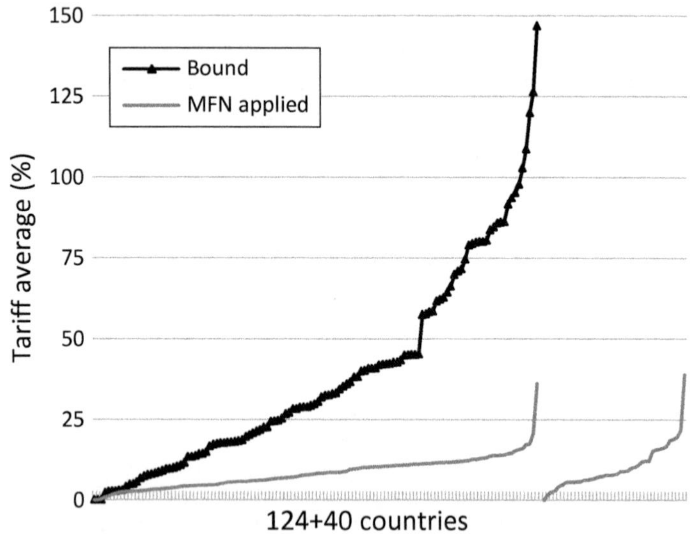

Fig. 4.1 Average tariffs for 124 WTO members and 40 non-members or WTO members with no bindings. (Data source: WITS/TRAINS/CTS)

right, the range for MFN-applied tariffs is comparable to that of the WTO members, in the 0–40 range. Table 4.1 and Fig. 4.1 both confirm beyond doubt that tariffs still matter, with high levels in many countries.

Tariff anomaly 1: Table 4.1 and Fig. 4.1 illustrate an important and challenging feature of the world trade system: MFN-applied tariffs are generally far below the upper limits set by the WTO; in the trade jargon we have considerable "water in the tariffs". On top of this gap, many WTO members have not even bound their tariffs. An implication of this anomaly is that future negotiations at the WTO are doomed to be in the air, to some extent: Negotiating cuts in bound tariffs that have no direct relevance for actual practices. With the current frequency of WTO negotiation rounds, it could take decades before some of the highest bound tariffs are cut to a level that affects actual practice. To some extent, this turns the WTO into a "paper tiger", negotiating virtual reforms with limited significance. As we shall see in Chap. 5, a similar disease has set in also for services.

Tariff anomaly 2: Another anomaly in the tariff scene is the excessive detail in classification. The WCO (World Customs Organization) urges all countries to have minimum about 5000 tariff lines (at the six-digit level), and many countries have 10,000 or more (at the ten-digit level or even more). The EU has a stunning 15,000 product categories![4] This is accepted as a state of nature by bureaucrats, traders and trade negotiators and trade researchers can enjoy the massive supply of detailed data, measuring every movement of at least 5000 products across the globe. Imagine that the VAT (value added tax) was implemented with a similar level of disaggregation: Every year a new "VAT schedule" with 10,000 products had to be decided and published, and in every shop we had to check that classification was right and we paid the right duty! This sounds absurd, but this is the practice in trade. The excessive disaggregation is a result of a hundred years of trade policy, where classification was tailor-made for protection and perhaps control purposes. It would make sense to reconsider and classify goods into much fewer and broader categories. This might be a radical reform, but it would simplify customs administration; relieve poor countries from excessive costs of customs administration, misclassification and corruption; and save resources for firms and governments all over the world. Such a proposal might be met with outrage from the trade establishment, and so some courage would be needed. Perhaps President Trump could add it to his list of demands?

For anomaly 1, a contribution would be to establish tariff bands for countries at different income levels: High-income countries may have tariffs between 0 and x%; middle income between 0 and y%; and low-income countries between 0 and z%, with z>y>x. Except for rich countries that generally have low average tariffs, there is large variation for countries at similar income levels (Melchior 2006c) and such bands would create a more equitable system. With upper tariff bounds, we could get rid of most of the water in the tariffs and reduce the "paper tiger" feature of the WTO.

Some tariff-cutting formulas automatically establish an upper limit for tariffs. The so-called Swiss formula, used in the Tokyo round of GATT negotiations in the 1970s, has the form:

$$t_1 = \frac{At_0}{A + t_0}$$

where t_0 is the original tariff, t_1 the tariff after the cut, and A is some constant. It is easily established that if t_0 becomes very large, the new tariff will approach A. Hence A is an upper limit for the new tariff. If WTO negotiations could end up using the Swiss formula with A differentiated across income groups, it would establish tariff bands for countries at different levels of development. It would also promote convergence by cutting the high tariffs more. This formula approach was actually at the bargaining table of the WTO in 2008, before the Doha Round negotiations came to a halt: The proposal was to have A=8% for developed countries and A in the range 20–25% for developing countries, depending on how many products they exempted from the tariff formula cuts (WTO 2008). This would have meant a strong reform in the world tariff system and the Doha Round was apparently close to making a significant step in the right direction. The bad news, however, was that only 40 WTO members (with the EU as one) would be subjected to the formula—the rest were exempted for various reasons. For some countries, a key issue was to increase the level of binding and the price to pay for this would be less tariff cuts for these. Second, a large number of developing countries were declared "small and vulnerable economies" and exempted from the formula. Then there were the RAMs: Recently acceded members, of which some were fully and others partly exempted. Finally there were the LDCs, also exempted. The paradoxical result would be a radical reform that would only apply to a minority of WTOs members.[5] Hence some patience will be required until all tariffs are bound at reasonable levels for all WTO members. But the Doha Round was somehow on the right track, and such reforms should be pursued in the future, hopefully with fewer exemptions.

4.2 Preferential Tariffs and FTAs: The Most and the Least Favoured Nations

Turning to preferential tariffs, Table 4.1 shows that their averages are about one-third of the MFN-applied levels. This includes preferences in FTAs as well as preferences for developing countries. Observe that MFN and preferential rates in Table 4.1 are not directly comparable since preferences apply only to a subset of partner countries, and the number of tariff lines covered by preferences may be lower than the total number of tariff lines. Table 4.1 is therefore just a rough indication that preferential tariffs are on average considerably lower than MFN tariffs. An accurate comparison has to use data for all tariff lines. Doing this for all countries is beyond the scope here, but we shall delve more into the EU and US tariff hierarchies, in order to illustrate the role of preferential tariffs.

Using data for 2014, we obtain EU preferential tariff rates for 43 different partners or partner groups, in addition to the MFN tariffs. Out of the 14,968 tariff lines of the EU in 2014, tariffs were zero in 3293 cases (22% of the total number of lines). For 1623 products, there were specific tariffs (e.g. x Euro per kg), but these are converted into ad valorem equivalents in the WITS/TRAINS database. We may therefore compare all tariffs and calculate averages. In the database, tariffs are aggregated to the six-digit level, with about 5200 categories. In the following, we present simple tariff averages of EU tariffs for all categories, for different trade partners. Figure 4.2 shows the "EU Christmas tree": The simple average tariff for each preferential regime reported in the database.

There is indeed tariff discrimination, spanning from zero for some trade partners at one end, to the EU's MFN level of 5.61% at the other end. The LDCs and EU's EPA (Economic Partnership Agreements) have the best terms, followed by a mixed group including some Mediterranean and Balkan partners and EEA (European Economic Area) countries. The ranking is however not always intuitive and this may depend on the role of "sensitive sectors"—agriculture, seafood, textiles and clothing—in each case. Ordinary GSP is at an intermediate level, with an average at 60% of the MFN level.

Figure 4.3 shows a similar ranking for US tariff preferences in 2016.

The USA has fewer distinct arrangements and a somewhat more "dualistic" pattern with fewer intermediate cases. Western European countries have more generous tariff preferences for the poorest countries. Figure 4.3 shows that in the FTAs, US tariff cuts are generally deep.

How deep are tariff cuts in FTAs more generally? Are the EU and USA cases representative? For tariffs, GATT's Article XXIV requires that tariffs and other restrictions should be "eliminated on substantially all the trade" (see www.wto.org, Art. XXIV.8 of GATT 1947). Furthermore, this should happen "within a reasonable length of time". How these two

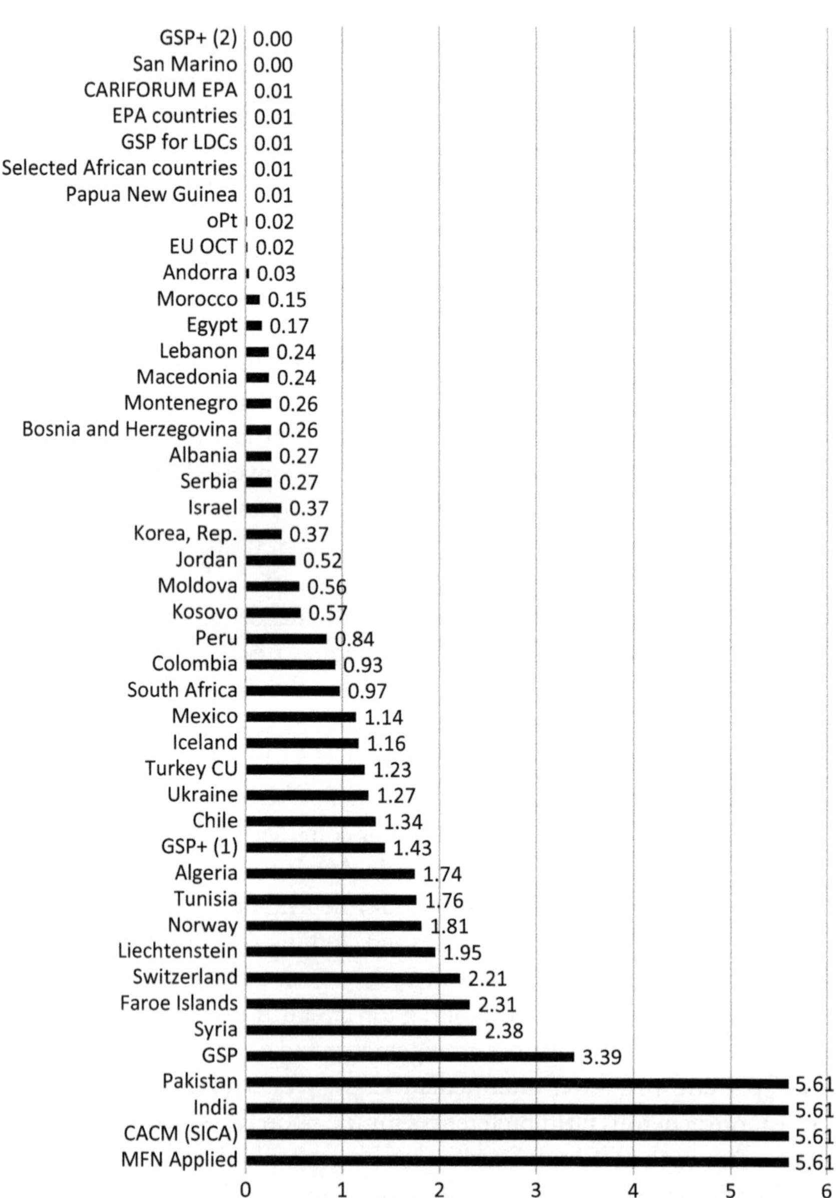

Fig. 4.2 The EU tariff Christmas tree (2014). Simple tariff averages for different EU trade agreements and regimes. (Data source: Own calculations based on data from WITS/TRAINS/IDB. OCT = Overseas Countries and Territories. oPt = Occupied Palestine Territories. EPA = Economic Partnership Agreements. CACM/SICA related to Central America. For more detailed information, see the EU Commission website ec.europa.eu/trade.)

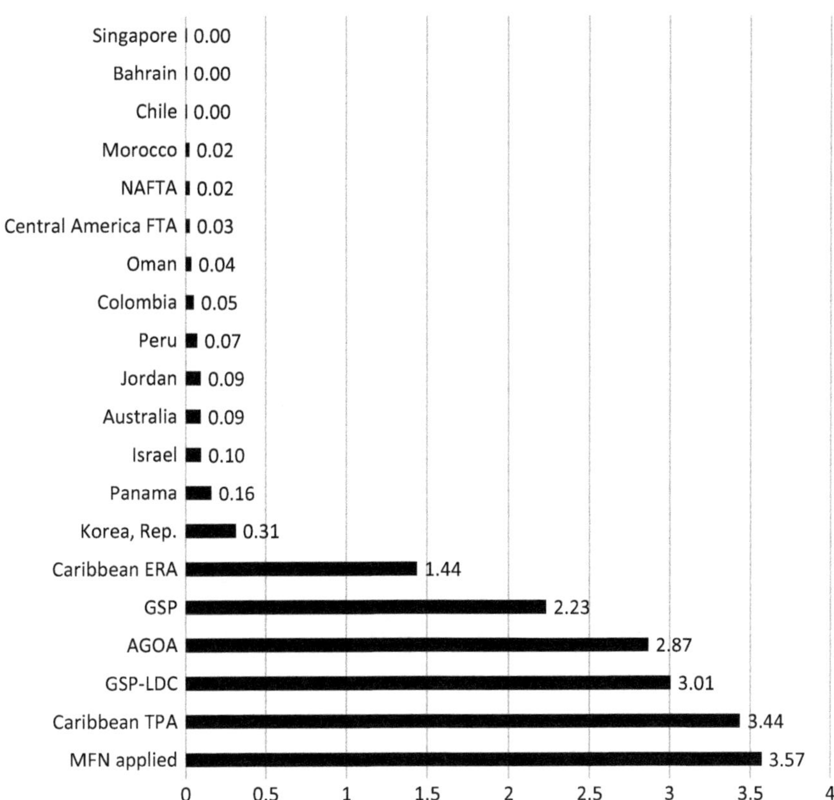

Fig. 4.3 The US hierarchy of trade preferences (2016). Simple tariff averages (%) for different US trade agreements and tariff regimes. (Data source: Own calculations based on data from WITS/TRAINS/IDB). (AGOA is the African Growth and Opportunity Act. The Caribbean Basin Initiative (CBI) comprises, inter alia, the Caribbean Basin Economic Recovery Act (CBERA) and the Caribbean Basin Trade Partnership Act (CBTPA), named Caribbean-ERA and Caribbean-TPA in the diagram. CBERA covered 17 beneficiaries in 2016, of which eight were also beneficiaries under CBTPA (WTO 2016). The WITS/TRAINS database also contains tariff data for the Canada-US Auto Pact (giving a tariff average of 0.14) but this is not included in the figure since we have no information on the continued existence of this agreement.)

requirements should be interpreted is not carved in stone and there is a debate, but actual practice points in the direction of a threshold at about "90 % of the tariff lines within 10 years" (Estevadeordal et al. 2009b). Ninety per cent also holds for the value of trade (ibid.). A relatively high level of ambition is therefore mandatory for tariffs in FTAs. Crawford (2016) examined 253 FTAs and found that on average, 91% of the tariff lines were fully liberalised when the agreements had been fully implemented. Transition or phase-out periods are common and the share of agricultural tariff lines liberalised is lower (72%). Textiles, clothing and footwear are also often less liberalised (Estevadeordal et al. 2009b). For sensitive sectors, tariff rate quotas and other restrictive measures are also relatively common, and the discipline is therefore less strict for "other restrictive measures" (ibid.). In spite of this, we may conclude that on the whole, FTAs are ambitious in the tariff area and lead to substantial tariff cuts. Crawford (2016, p. 33) also found that tariff cuts in FTAs generally start from MFN-applied levels rather than bound rates so liberalisation is meaningful and not just cuts in the 'water'.

For agreements between developing countries that are not notified under Article XXIV, a more modest liberalisation is also acceptable at the WTO. Out of the 297 FTAs notified to the WTO and examined in Chap. 3, 23 were so-called PSAs (Partial Scope Agreements, notified under WTO's enabling clause). The PSAs span a wider range, from relatively deep to more shallow agreements.

An issue is whether tariff preferences have become economically less significant over time due to "preference erosion". Preference erosion may happen in two ways: Either because MFN-applied rates are lowered so that the preference becomes numerically smaller, or because FTAs become less exclusive since the number of FTAs has increased. For industrial countries, it is clearly the case that tariff levels have declined over time and this tends to reduce the impact of preferences. For some time, the story circulated widely that industrial countries had tariffs at 40% after the second world war, and these were reduced to below 5% at the time when the WTO was established (1995). As shown by Bown and Irwin (2015), the figure in 1947 was 22% rather than 40, and so the decline over time is somewhat less dramatic. As shown in this chapter, many countries have high tariffs also today, and so the preference margins vary across countries.

It is also true that the value of former tariff preferences is eroded by the proliferation of new FTAs. For developed countries, GSP also plays a significant role, as illustrated by Fig. 4.2 for the EU. The EU is perhaps the most extreme example of tariff discrimination via FTAs and GSP, by having agreements and regimes for so many countries and groups. As noted my Melchior (2006a), the "Most Favoured Nations" are sometimes only a handful of countries, and so they are actually the "Least Favoured Nations"! For some countries, especially in Europe, this is a paradox of trade policy: The majority of trade partners have preferences, and using the MFN-applied tariffs is the exception rather than the rule.

For the economics of FTAs, it is useful to observe that the if only one trade partner obtains a preference, the effect for this partner is much larger than if tariffs were reduced for all partners (see text box). The extent of "exclusivity" is therefore an important determinant for the economic impact.

Overall, we may conclude that FTAs lead to significant tariff preferences and FTAs have been successful in the tariff area. It is a kind of irony that the WTO is a main driver behind this success, through the mandatory depth and coverage of tariff cuts stipulated by Article XXIV. In a way, the WTO undermines itself by requiring that tariff cuts in FTAs should be deep and comprehensive!

FTA Economics and Trade Elasticities: The Value of Being the Only One

Consider a standard two-level demand system:

At level 1, consumers choose between aggregates (food, cars, clothing, etc.). Related to this choice we have, say for clothing, the demand function

$$X_c = aP_c^{\alpha}$$

where X_c is the quantity of clothing demanded, with P_c as the corresponding price or price index, a is a constant and α is the level 1 demand elasticity. If the underlying utility function is Cobb-Douglas, this demand elasticity is minus one.

At level 2, consumers choose between clothing from different supplying countries. Assume a CES (constant elasticity of substitution) sub-utility function for this choice. The elasticity of substitution σ measures how the ratio of demand from two suppliers (x_{ci}/x_{cj})

responds to a change in the price ratio (p_{ci}/p_{cj}). σ is a positive number (so we have to add a minus for a normal price response), and we assume that its absolute value is higher than the level 1 demand elasticity. The reason is that we switch more easily between two suppliers of clothing than between, say, clothing and cars. From empirical research on international trade, a typical value of the elasticity of substitution is five (Head and Mayer 2014). The level 1 elasticity, on the other hand, is likely much lower, perhaps in a range around minus one. If there are many small suppliers and one of them changes its price, a standard result with CES is that the price elasticity of demand is equal to the elasticity of substitution. If, on the other hand, one supplier has the whole market, or all suppliers change their prices in the same proportion, the elasticity at level 1 would have to apply. In general, the observed demand elasticity will be between these two limits. The exact relationship depends on the form of competition (see e.g. Smith and Venables 1988 for a discussion), but under some conditions, the observed demand elasticity for supplier i will be a function of the level 1 demand elasticity α and the level 2 substitution elasticity σ, as follows:

$$\varepsilon = -\sigma + s_i * (\sigma + \alpha)$$

where s_i is the market share of supplier i.

If the market share is one, so that the price change applies to the whole market for clothing, we have $\varepsilon = \alpha$. If, on the other hand, the market share is close to zero, we approach $\varepsilon = -\sigma$. So the observed demand elasticity varies between the level 1 demand elasticity and the (negative of) the elasticity of substitution at level 2, depending on the market share.

Applied to FTAs and using the relationship above as illustration, consider a situation where $\sigma = 5$ and $\alpha = -1$, and we have ten supplying countries with equal market shares:

- If the tariff is reduced by 1% for all ten suppliers, demand would increase by 1% for all of them.
- If the tariff is reduced by 1% for one supplier only, demand for this supplier would increase by 4.6% (using the formula).
- If the tariff is cut by 1% for five of the suppliers, demand for these suppliers would increase by 3%.

This illustrates that an exclusive tariff preference has a stronger demand impact than a preference that applies to many suppliers. This simple mechanism will be present in more complex models used in the analysis of economic integration, including the one used in Chaps. 6, 7 and 8 of this book.

Notes

1. The number of countries is less than the number of WTO members (164) due to data availability, or because some WTO members have no bindings. Data is for 2015 in about three-fourth of the cases, and other years during 2010–2016 for the rest, except three observations with tariff data before 2010. Trade Analysis Information System (TRAINS) is a tariff and trade database of United Nations Conference on Trade and Development (UNCTAD). WTO-CTS is the Consolidated Tariff Scedules database of the World Trade Organisation (WTO). IDB is the Integrated Data Base of the WTO. All the databases are accessible through the World Integrated Trade Solution (WITS) software/search engine.
2. Observe that not all tariffs are bound and therefore the bound and MFN-applied tariff averages are not strictly comparable. Since non-bound products tend to have higher MFN-applied tariffs, Table 4.1 may understate the extent of water in the tariffs.
3. Bound and MFN-applied tariffs are ranked separately to show the ranges, and so countries generally have different ranks for bound and applied tariffs.
4. The figure is approximate. For 2014, the figure was 14,968, based on data from the WITS/TRAINS database.

5. See WTO (2008) for more detail or Melchior (2006c) (in Norwegian!) for a discussion of different tariff-cutting formulas and other aspects of the WTO tariff proposals.

References

Baldwin, R. (2009). Big-Think Regionalism: A Critical Survey. In Estevadeordal, A., Suominen K. & Teh, R. (Eds.). (2009a), Chapter 2, pp. 17–95.

Bown, C. A. & Irwin, D. A. (2015). *The GATT's Starting Point: Tariff Levels Circa 1947*. National Bureau of Economic Research, NBER Working Paper 21782, http://www.nber.org/papers/w21782

Crawford, J. (2016). Market Access Provisions on Trade in Goods in Regional Trade Agreements. In R. Acharya (Ed.), *Regional Trade Agreements and the Multilateral Trading System* (Chapter 1, pp. 21–57). Cambridge, UK: Cambridge University Press/World Trade Organization.

Estevadeordal, A., & Suominen, K. (2008). *Gatekeepers of Global Commerce. Rules of Origin and International Economic Integration*. Washington, DC: Inter-American Development Bank (IDB).

Estevadeordal, A., Suominen, K., & Teh, R. (Eds.). (2009a). *Regional Rules in the Global Trading System*. Cambridge, UK: Cambridge University Press, in Cooperation with the Inter-American Development Bank (IDB) and the World Trade Organization (WTO).

Estevadeordal, A., M. Shearer & Suominen, K. (2009b). *Market Access Provisions in Regional Trade Agreements* (Chapter 3, pp. 96–165). In Estevadeordal et al. (Eds.). (2009a).

Freund, C., Moran, T., & Oliver, S. (2016). Tariff liberalization. In *Peterson Institute for International Economics, Assessing the Trans-Pacific Partnership, Volume 1: Market Access and Sectoral Issues* (Chapter 2, pp. 31–40). Washington, DC: PIIE, PIIE Briefing 16–1, February 2016.

Head, K. & Mayer, T. (2014). Gravity Equations: Workhorse, Toolkit, and Cookbook. In G. Gopinath, E. Helpman and K. Rogoff (Eds.), *International Economics Volume 4* (Chapter 3, pp. 131–195). Amsterdam: North-Holland/Elsevier, Handbooks in Economics.

Melchior, A. (2006a). *The Most and the Least Favoured Nations: Norway's Trade Policy in Perspective. The World Economy, 29*(10), 1329–1346.

Melchior, A. (2006b). *Tariffs in World Seafood Trade*. Rome: FAO (Food and Agriculture organization), FAO Fisheries Circular No. 1016.

Melchior, A. (2006c). WTO-forhandlingene om markedsadgang for industrivarer og fisk (NAMA). Oslo: Norwegian Institute of International Affairs, NUPI Paper No. 698.

Melchior, A. (Ed.). (2016). *TTIP and Norway: Impact and Trade Policy Options.* Oslo: Norwegian Institute of International Affairs, NUPI Report No. 9/2016. With Contributions from from Alvik, I., Bekkedal, T., Felbermayr, G., Theie, M. G., Grünfeld, L. A., Medin, H., Mittenzwei, K., Pettersen, I. & Veggeland, F. At https://brage.bibsys.no/xmlui/handle/11250/2425477

Pelkmans, J. (2017). *The Brexit Customs Vision. Frictions and Fictions, 22 August 2017.* Brussels: Centre for European Policy Research, CEPS Commentary. At https://www.ceps.eu/system/files/CEPS%20Commentary%20Pelkmans%20BrexitCustomsUnion.pdf

Robson, P. (1980). *The Economics of International Integration.* London: George Allen & Unwin. Studies in Economics 17 (Ed. C. Carter).

Smith, A., & Venables, A. (1988). The Costs of Non-Europe. An Assessment Based on a Formal Model of Imperfect Competition and Economies of Scale. Chapter 5. In EC Commission (Ed.), *Studies on the Economics of Integration. Research on the "Cost of Non-Europe". Basic Findings* (Vol. 2, pp. 287–338). Brussels: Commission of the European Communities.

USTR. (2016). Tariff Schedule of the United States (HS 2012). Downloaded 20 March 2018 at https://ustr.gov/sites/default/files/TPP-Final-Text-US-Tariff-Elimination-Schedule.pdf

Viner, J. (1950). *The Customs Union Issue.* Washington, DC: Carnegie Endowment for International Peace.

WTO. (2008). *Draft Modalities for Non-agricultural Market Access,* Fourth Revision. Geneva: World Trade Organization, WTO Document TN/MA/W/103/Rev. 3, 6 December 2008.

WTO. (2016). *Trade Policy Review. Report by the Secretariat. United States.* Geneva: World Trade Organization, Trade Policy Review Body, Document WT/TPR/S/350, 14 November 2016.

5

Non-tariff Issues in FTAs

Chapter 4 showed that on tariffs for trade in goods, Free Trade Agreements (FTAs) go deeper than the World Trade Organization (WTO), and they are overall ambitious. Furthermore, tariff preferences are discriminatory across trade partners, even if the discriminatory impact is eroded by general tariff cuts and the proliferation of FTAs. In this chapter, we ask: Are the qualitative assessments similar for non-tariff issues in FTAs? Are FTAs ambitious? Do they go beyond the WTO? And are they discriminatory? As we will see, the conclusion is often "not so much" on all three questions. In several areas, FTAs are mostly non-discriminatory and give limited privileges to the FTA partners. The lack of discrimination may be because FTAs just confirm or legally bind measures that were introduced in a non-discriminatory fashion for political reasons or it may be because discrimination is infeasible or impractical. For example, in the presence of a food standard or a qualification threshold for business services, substandard import rules for food or lower qualification thresholds for business services are not plausible "preferences" within an FTA.

In most non-tariff areas, there is a dual conclusion: The "no, no, no" verdict above applies to many, but not all. A handful of FTAs are deep; they go far beyond the WTO; and they are discriminatory. Who is in this

A. Melchior, *Free Trade Agreements and Globalisation*,
https://doi.org/10.1007/978-3-319-92834-0_5

"top league" varies across themes. But the EU and the EEA (European Economic Area) are often there, with comprehensive harmonisation, common rules and institutions and jurisdiction based on a court system overruling national systems in the relevant areas.

The field covered by this chapter is enormous and numerous volumes could be filled with details on the "spaghetti bowl" of the several hundred FTAs. This is out of the scope here: The aim is to provide a compact interpretative survey where we ask some key questions that are essential for understanding FTAs. When attempting to characterise the FTA landscape, we draw on earlier research; for example, the theme-by-theme examinations of FTAs undertaken in Estevadeordal et al. (Eds., 2009); and in particular Acharya (Ed., 2016). These volumes examine to what extent FTAs go further than the WTO—with considerable detail in each area. Baldwin and Low (Eds., 2009) examine the relationship between FTAs and the WTO with a focus on the extent of discrimination in FTAs and whether FTA rules may be "multilateralised". A useful source is the DESTA (Design of Trade Agreements) database (Dür et al. 2014), classifying and ranking the depth of FTAs along selected dimensions. A comprehensive overview of many trade agreements and their making is Lynch (2010). On trade agreements in Asia, Kawai and Wignaraja (2013) provide a useful overview. In the following, we draw on these and other sources to provide a bird's eye view on the non-tariff issues in FTAs.

In the following, the analysis is selective by focusing on some key issues, about the depth of commitments and the extent of discrimination in the various non-tariff areas. There is plenty of detail behind in each area, but the aim here is to simplify and for the interested reader, the references contain more detailed and useful information in all areas. In spite of the aim to simplify, the field covered is vast and the chapter cannot avoid some technicalities. We therefore apologise to the readers that the chapter has to include a fair amount of trade-technical terms!

5.1 Services and Investment in FTAs

As noted in Chap. 2, about one-fourth of world trade is in services. This, however, is mainly cross-border trade and does not include services delivery from affiliates abroad; that is, in Mode 3 according to the

WTO—"commercial presence". According to the WTO Secretariat (WTO 2015), Mode 3 constitutes the largest component of world services trade, representing 55% of world services trade in 2014, compared to 30% for Mode 1—cross-border trade. This composition is however hard to measure and there is some uncertainty about the magnitudes, due to issues of comparability and different data sources across modes. A large-scale database is currently under construction, and some first evidence for the EU using this database shows an even higher share for Mode 3: According to Rueda-Cantuche et al. (2016), 69% of EU services exports in 2013 were in Mode 3.

The high share for Mode 3 in global services trade is one reason why we discuss investment and services jointly. Trade policy in services is partly trade policy for investment, and so there is a clear overlap between the two areas. Another reason to consider investment and services jointly is the important role of the Organisation for Economic Co-operation and Development (OECD) in both areas. For OECD countries, including Western Europe, North America and parts of Asia/Pacific including Japan, Australia and New Zealand, the OECD Codes of Liberalisation of Capital Movements and Current Invisible Operations are legally binding and promote liberalisation in both areas (OECD 2008, 2017).[1] These are best-endeavours commitments but OECD has led a process over more than 50 years with progressive liberalisation. For capital, the liberalisation lists have been expanded over time to comprise practically all capital movements. Coverage of cross-border trade in services by the Current Invisibles Code is large, but not quite as comprehensive. Major sectors covered are banking and financial services, insurance and private pension services, professional services, maritime and road transport and travel and tourism. Even if the OECD Codes are binding, OECD liberalisation is unilateral and not a result of give-and-take negotiations. OECD has a strong commitment to the Most Favoured Nation (MFN) principle, but regional integration beyond OECD is to some extent accepted, with the precondition that new barriers cannot be introduced by any of the countries involved. For example, if country A is very liberal in some area and country B is very restrictive, they cannot make a regional pact that makes country A more restrictive. Financial services is an example of regional integration that goes deeper than the OECD; the "single passport" of the EU financial market is not extended to non-EU countries in the OECD.

The far-reaching investment liberalisation in the OECD implies that Mode 3 in services is also liberalised for a large part of the world economy. On top of this, the EU and the European Economic Area have their four freedoms with liberalisation of services beyond the OECD. Some Central European countries, for example, have more extensive reservations for services in the OECD, but they have committed to liberalisation vis-à-vis many OECD members within Europe.

The OECD Codes partly "carve out" investment, Mode 3 services provision and, selectively, cross-border services trade from the agenda of FTAs between OECD countries. For example, if the USA and the EU negotiates Mode 3 commitments in services, that is already liberalised for many sectors. This may be one reason why the General Agreement on Trade in Services (GATS)-type approach to services is rarely used between developed countries (Latrille 2016, p. 429). It also means that the TISA (Trade in Services Agreement) negotiations will mainly have an impact in areas that are not already liberalised through unilateral measures. Unilateral liberalisation may also promote a "paper tiger" effect if liberal countries introduce bindings in GATS or other trade agreements that are more restrictive than their practice on the ground, in order to safeguard their leverage in negotiations with less liberal countries.

An issue is whether the MFN provision of the OECD is in practice generalised beyond the OECD. If an OECD country commits unilaterally to liberalise investment or some cross-border services trade, will it do so in general or with a clause that market access applies only to the OECD? A full-scale examination of this is beyond the scope here, but our maintained hypothesis is that the answer is no: Liberalisation is often generalised and applies to the whole world. A prominent example is the EU: Capital movements is the only one of the four freedoms of the EU internal market that is extended globally. Article 63 of the TFEU (Treaty of the Functioning of the European Union says: "… all restrictions on the movement of capital between Member States and between Member States and third countries shall be prohibited." There are exemptions for some "sensitive" sectors (notified before 1993), and for tax, prudential, security, anti-terror and some other reasons, but investment in the EU is essentially liberalised on an MFN basis.

For services, such a multilateralisation of OECD commitments is all the more likely since the GATS has an MFN clause that requires the multilateralisation of services commitments. Such multilateralisation implies that OECD liberalisation often apply to the whole world on an MFN basis. To the extent this is the case, OECD has a strong footprint in the FTA landscape—it means that many FTA commitments on services may be replications of unilateral commitments that already exist. Hence the OECD as well as the GATS have MFN obligations that promote the multilateralisation of services liberalisation commitments. On top of this, some FTAs in services have so-called non-party MFN clauses saying that if one of the parties grant better treatment to a third party, this should be extended to the other parties in the FTA. In their analysis of 66 services FTAs, Miroudot et al. (2010, p. 26) found that 22 agreements (39%) had Non-Party MFN clauses with respect to new FTAs with third countries, and 12 agreements (22%) had such clauses applying to any agreement with third parties. Hence such clauses represent a third legal driver for the multilateralisation of services FTA commitments.

Another reason why services liberalisation in FTAs may be less discriminatory than for goods is that rules of origin for services are often liberal. For goods, ROs define how much of the physical good is made in the exporting country, and this is possible to measure in various ways (see text box, Chap. 4). For services, it is generally the nationality or origin of the service provider that matters. From their examination of services provisions in FTAs (using the term Regional Trade Agreements (RTAs)), Fink and Jansen (2009, p. 237) conclude that "the great majority of existing RTAs adopt liberal rules of origin as they pertain to companies: preferential treatment is extended to all service suppliers that are established and have substantial business operations in at least one RTA party, regardless of who owns and controls them." The "substantial business operations" (SBO) criterion is a requirement in GATS Article V on FTAs (see e.g. Miroudot et al. (2010) for a discussion). Latrille (2016)—examining 122 FTAs in services—found that 80% of the agreements relied on the SBO criterion. More restrictive ROs are implemented in some FTAs, but the majority of agreements are liberal and use SBO. The implication is that firms from third countries may obtain market access within an FTA by establishing business operations in one of the FTA countries. As also concluded by Fink and Jansen (2009, p. 258) and supported by Roy et al. (2007), liberal ROs is a key element reducing the discriminatory impact of FTAs in services.

In empirical research on services and investment provisions in FTAs, we find more evidence supporting the interpretation that FTAs in services are not very discriminatory: Analysing 66 FTAs in services, Miroudot and Sheperd (2014) found that trade costs were only slightly lower due to these agreements. In addition, the trade cost reductions tended to take place before the agreement had been signed. The authors interpret this as consistent with countries using FTAs as a way of "locking in" reforms, and conclude that regionalism in the case of services seems relatively non-discriminatory and does not lead to substantial trade preferences. Miroudot et al. (2010, p. 28) also conclude that for services FTAs, "trade liberalisation often resembles unilateral liberalisation that is bound through regional agreements."

The discussion above helps the interpretation of services liberalisation commitments in FTAs. Counting commitments on services in FTAs, there is no doubt that the FTAs go further than the WTO. The results of Roy et al. (2007) as well as Miroudot et al. (2010) confirm beyond doubt that sectors covered as well as the depth of commitments in services FTAs go well beyond the GATS. It is much more difficult to assess to what extent real liberalisation has taken place within GATS or in FTAs beyond the GATS. Given unilateral liberalisation in rich countries, one could look for liberalisation in agreements with non-OECD partners or in sectors not covered by the OECD. Roy et al. (2007), for example, found that the USA obtained significant improvements in their market access from their FTA partners (many of these are in the Americas). While Roy et al. (2007) observe that "binding the status quo" is common in GATS and services FTAs, Miroudot and Pertel (2015, p. 28) found that current services trade policies are in fact much more open than what countries have committed in the GATS. It seems therefore that in services, the WTO has created another "paper tiger" parallel to what we have seen for goods tariffs (Chap. 4). Current services negotiations are therefore partly about the "water in the GATS".

While the discussion here suggests that investment and services liberalisation in FTAs has to a large extent been non-discriminatory, there are several exceptions and in some areas, discrimination is possible and existing. For example, the origin of services suppliers is sometimes defined in a more restrictive way than by the SBO criterion. In other areas, for example, on qualification requirements, standards are generally universal so what may be discriminatory is their implementation. In this respect, services have some aspects that are similar to technical barriers or food standards: The standards are universal but cooperation may take place in the form of mutual recognition, procedures for approval and testing and so on. We revert to such issues in the discussion on non-tariff barriers in Chap. 9.

While we have emphasised the role of OECD in the liberalisation of investment and services, there is considerable variation across OECD countries with respect to how liberal they actually are. This dispersion is evident, for example, from the OECD Services Trade Restrictiveness Index (STRI). So even if OECD countries have liberalised as a result of the OECD Invisibles Code and process, there is a considerable policy space left where the FTA can make a difference. While our interpretative survey has focused on some main characteristics of the investment and services FTA regime, there are many detailed provisions where rules are differentiated and there is an "institutional space" for FTAs. FTAs, for example, allow the "customisation" of investment rules in order to take into account the difference between developed and developing countries (Kotschwar 2009).

Some services sectors are "regulation-intensive" in the sense that their operation rely on regulations and standards. An interesting example is the financial sector, where, for example, the development of the EU common financial market is a long and arduous process with considerable complexity. Following the financial crisis in 2007–2008, the EU has set up a new financial market system with three supervisory authorities operative from 2011 (for banking, securities and pensions), in addition to the European Systemic Risk Board for macro-prudential regulation. Evidently, the European Central Bank and the key EU institutions also play important roles. In spite of the free movement of capital in EU for some decades, many barriers to a seamless financial market still exist (European Commission 2017). The current EU plans for the EU Capital Market Union aims to overcome existing barriers, in order to obtain a seamless financial market with efficient allocation of capital across member states.

Observe how capital flows and financial markets are closely intertwined. EU has three levels of legislation in the areas: Primary legislation include directives on banking capital requirements, insurance, financial instruments, financial infrastructure, insurance capital requirements, and more.[2] Secondary legislation is decided by the European Commission and may be on details or implementation. At the third level, the financial supervisory authorities can issue recommendations or guidelines on implementation and practice.

The EU common financial market is therefore a complex mechanism with several institutions and a large volume of legislation. An interesting illustration is obtained if we consider how the EU financial market is implemented in European Free Trade Association (EFTA) states. The European Economic Area (EEA) Agreement stipulates how EU legislation is integrated into national law in EFTA countries. Most of the EU legislation is integrated, and regulations (that apply directly to all EU citizens) are generally integrated word by word, so-called incorporation. For directives, some local adaptation is possible. In Norway, the Government writes "position papers" on new legislation, with information and recommendations. As a test, we search for position papers on "Banks and other credit institutions" and find 114 papers, of which 33 were from 2017. Hence the EU financial market is a stream of new legislation.

How should the EU approach negotiations in GATS or the WTO on financial regulation? With such a complex legislative process at the heart, it is evident that, for example, free movements for financial derivatives cannot be traded against the tariffs for vegetables. There are some virtues of issue linkages at the WTO, but a process that is detached from the regulatory process will likely have limited value. International liberalisation could more meaningfully ask how EU regulations should relate to international standardisation and bodies such as the Basel Committee for Banking Supervision, IOSCO (International Organization of Securities Commissions), IAIS (International Association of Insurance Supervisors), FSB (Financial Stability Board) and FATF (Financial Action Task Force); we could also add the OECD and its extended process for 54 countries in its Freedom for Investment Process.[3] The aim would be to create global traffic rules that facilitate the coexistence of national and regional regulatory systems. Trade policy in the financial area should be taken away from the tit-for-tat diplomatic table and transferred to institutions that have the expertise to work for a better global system. In this endeavour, there would be a difficult political border area including themes such as taxation, crisis management, firms versus consumers, state versus market and so on. Similar issues of regulation, politics and complexity appear in a number of other areas, from food standards to chemicals, energy markets and others. Should investment dispute settlement be there only to protect firms or also to protect states and consumers?

While the WTO has a services agreement (the GATS), there is no global investment regime. The WTO has GATS Mode 3 and the TRIMS (Trade-Related Investment Measures) agreement, with the latter regulating local content requirements and other trade-related investment measures. Beyond this, there is a large number of BITs (Bilateral Investment Treaties), 2363 in force as of March 2018.[4] Many BITs include an Investor-State Dispute Settlement (ISDS) mechanism whereby investors may sue states if they are unduly treated. For a discussion of the international investment regime (or the lack thereof), see Kotschwar (2009).

For investment and services, we have a system that has evolved from the "rich man's club": OECD countries have until recently been leading investors and services exporters. With unilateral liberalisation of investment and services undertaken already in the OECD context, it is difficult to generalise the regime to emerging and developing countries. That is a main reason why the proposed MAI (Multilateral Agreement on Investment) failed in the mid-1990s, and one reason why the tangible results of GATS in terms of real liberalisation are limited. Gradually, however, former developing countries have become larger investors and services exporters. As shown by Loungani et al. (2017), the share of emerging markets in world services exports has increased substantially over the last two decades, so middle-income countries have a growing interest in market access for services. Outward investment from emerging countries is also on the rise, with China as a key player. In this setting, the unilateral approach of the OECD may be out of date, and there is a need for a more balanced regime, with stronger reciprocity. In Chaps. 7 and 8, we examine further the need for reciprocity in trade agreements.

5.2 Other FTA Issues: Brexit Hierarchies

For other non-tariff issues in FTAs, currently available evidence indicates that in several areas, *most* agreements do not go very much further than the WTO. The typical pattern is that most FTAs are relatively shallow, not very discriminatory, and they do not go much beyond the WTO. But most does not mean all; a minority of the FTAs are deep, discriminatory and go far beyond the WTO. In the following, we review some areas where this dichotomy is visible. We call it "Brexit hierarchies": This is the menu that the UK faces in its search for new trade agreements across the globe. Should it be deep FTAs with extensive regulatory cooperation and binding jurisdiction, or more simple inter-governmental agreements where matters are addressed in negotiations as they may arise?

5.2.1 Jurisdiction in FTAs

A key feature of FTAs is their jurisdiction: How binding are the rules and how are disputes settled? For jurisdiction in FTAs, the hierarchy is, according to Chase et al. (2016):

- Political/diplomatic, where disputes are settled through inter-state consultations between the states involved;
- Quasi-judicial, where conflicts are resolved via ad hoc third-party adjudication and based on legal interpretations; and
- Judicial; where adjudication is not *ad hoc* but undertaken by more permanent and independent courts or court-like institutions.

In 2012, only 10 out of 226 FTAs (4%) used the judicial model, while 147 (65%) solved disputes using quasi-judicial approaches and 69 (31%) relied on political/diplomatic consultations (ibid.). Over time, the quasi-judicial model has been on the rise, and so jurisdiction in FTAs has become more formalised. But these agreements do not really go much further than the WTO; Chase et al. (2016, p. 610, using the term Dispute Settlement Mechanism (DSM)) conclude "Our examination of the 226 RTAs notified to the WTO until the end of 2012 also finds that the degree of innovation in their design of DSMs is limited...

With few exceptions, the level of institutionalization of RTA-DSMs is far lower than that of the WTO dispute settlement mechanism." In the context, it should be recalled that the WTO dispute settlement system is a unique achievement: Global governance and binding dispute settlement between nations are not easy to establish, but the WTO made it. The USA was a driver underlying this success in 1995, and it is a paradox that in 2018, the USA is challenging the DSM by blocking the appointment of new members of the WTO Appellate Body.[5]

Referring to the earlier analysis of intra- versus extra-regional FTAs, the ten FTAs with judicial dispute settlement are all intra-regional, within our seven world regions.[6] An observation is that the level of jurisdiction is not fully coinciding with the depth of agreements in the economic sense: Some relatively deep agreements use the political/diplomatic DSM mode (e.g. ANZCERTA, the Australia-New Zealand Closer Economic Relations Trade Agreement) and some use the quasi-judicial approach (e.g. NAFTA, the North American Free Trade Agreement).

5.2.2 Trade Remedies

"Trade remedies" in FTAs include:

- Safeguards, that is, trade restrictions for imports that threaten domestic industry. At the WTO, safeguards are allowed under GATT Article XIX and the related Safeguard Agreement.
- Anti-dumping (AD), where tariffs are introduced for imports at prices below normal, according to specific criteria. AD is allowed under Article VI of the WTO, and its use is widespread, particularly for homogeneous goods such as steel.
- Countervailing duties (CD), where tariffs are introduced to compensate for subsidies in the exporting country. CD is allowed under WTOs Articles VI and XVI; its application is common but less frequent than AD since the burden of proof is more challenging.

Such measures often use tariffs to restrict imports but we include them here since the depth of FTAs depends on qualitative aspects or regimes rather than the height of tariffs.

For trade remedies, the FTA hierarchy is as follows (see e.g. Rey 2016; Teh et al. 2009):

- Shallow: No FTA rules at all, and so the WTO rules apply.
- Intermediate: FTA partners are exempted from trade remedy measures, subject to specific conditions that may be vague (e.g. best endeavours) or precise (e.g. more lax criteria for determining AD).
- Deep: FTA partners are exempted from trade remedy measures, wholly or for specific products. For example, AD is fully eliminated in the EU internal market. In the EEA (European Economic Area), this is also the case for manufacturing, but the legal right to use AD is retained for agriculture (and fisheries), since this sector is not fully integrated in the internal market regime.

Since FTAs have limited rules on state subsidies and the WTO does not bite too hard either, there is limited FTA jurisdiction on CD. But, for example, the EU/EEA includes extensive regulation of subsidies and so this is possible and exists in some FTAs. CD and AD measures are by nature discriminatory; they are applied to specific exporting countries. Exemption from AD and CD therefore means that the instruments are not used against FTA partners. By contrast, safeguards should be applied on a non-discriminatory (MFN) basis towards all suppliers, and the WTO explicitly states that the use of safeguards should be non-discriminatory. But there is some legal uncertainty (Crawford et al. 2016), and some FTAs explicitly exempt partners from safeguards. Also for AD, there is some legal uncertainty but WTO panels have ruled that if AD investigations are initiated for all partners and FTA partners are later excluded without due reason, it is a violation of the MFN principle (Teh et al. 2009, p. 236ff.; see also Rey 2016). This could be a consideration when Trump in March 2018 introduced steel tariffs as a security measure and not AD; the exclusion of NAFTA partners could have been disputed under the AD regime of the WTO. In the NAFTA agreement, AD is not excluded as such (Rey 2016, pp. 175, 208). According to Rey, only a minority of FTAs legally exclude the use of AD. Some very deep agreements such as the EU/EEA and ANSZCERTA (Australia-New Zealand, acronym expanded above)—again intra-regional FTAs—fundamentally change AD patterns, but for the majority of agreements, the impact of FTAs on AD is less visible. Out of 253 FTAs studied, only about 10% had rules limiting the use of AD between the FTA partners (ibid.). For safeguards, Crawford et al. (2016) find that only a couple of FTAs fully exclude the use of safeguards among partners, but about a quarter of the agreements provided for the possible exclusion of safeguards, subject to certain criteria. The reasons underlying this "shallowness" in the field for the majority of FTAs could be legal or political. Legally, the potential conflict with WTO rules could limit the spread of "deep" FTAs excluding trade remedies. The political argument may be simply trade remedies, particularly AD, if the "holy grail" of protectionism that is not surrendered so easily by its users—and they are many! Within NAFTA, there have been several AD disputes, with the recurring USA-Canada conflict on timber as a prominent example.

On trade remedies, we have thereby found the same dichotomy as for jurisdiction: The majority of FTAs are shallow, but some are deep and the latter are mostly intra-regional.

5.2.3 TBT (Technical Barriers to Trade) and SPS (Sanitary and Phytosanitary Measures)

TBT and SPS are often referred to as "non-tariff barriers" but the related standards or regulations normally have a positive motivation and could be welfare-enhancing. SPS may safeguard animal or human health, and TBT enhances efficiency or safety in the field of technical regulations. TBT and SPS may however also act as trade barriers and be abused for protectionist purposes. That is why the WTO establishes "traffic rules" in the two areas, with separate WTO agreements in both fields. The SPS Agreement of the WTO includes transparency and notification requirements; a necessity criterion—measures should not be unduly restrictive in the light of their purpose; a science criterion—measures should be based on scientific evidence unless they are based on international standards; and non-discrimination—measures should not discriminate against imports or between trade partners. TBT also aims to prevent that technical rules unduly restrict trade, with similar notification, necessity and non-discrimination criteria. TBT focuses more on process, promoting transparency and accessibility for national procedures for approval and testing and coordination or mutual recognition across borders.

For SPS and TBT, the FTA hierarchy is somewhat less clear-cut but we may depart from a standard "triad";

- FTAs with no provisions on SPS and TBT;
- FTAs with provisions but not going much beyond the WTO; and
- FTAs with provisions and going beyond the WTO.

On this scale, Molina and Khoroshavina (2016) conclude on TBT that "the frequency and level of detail of TBT provisions in RTAs have increased significantly over time." Out of the 238 FTAs covered, 171 had at least one TBT provision, and recent FTAs all included TBT. But at the same time, "only a minority of RTAAs differ from the TBT Agreement by using more stringent wording and imposing broader commitments seeking to facilitate trade between the parties" (ibid., 407).

On (SPS), Jackson and Vitikala (2016, p. 362) similarly find that "typically the majority of RTAs with SPS provisions do not go beyond the rights and obligations detailed in the WTO SPS Agreement".

For SPS and TBT, observe that the WTO does not harmonise standards and regulations, but promotes harmonisation and coordination. Alternative to harmonisation, there could be;

- Equivalence: This means that a country unilaterally declares that the standards or regulations of another country fulfil the requirements of its own regulation.
- Mutual recognition agreements (MRA): This means that countries mutually agree to recognise the each other's regulation or standard as equivalent or fulfilling the requirements of its own rules.

Harmonisation, equivalence and mutual recognition may apply to standards or regulations, or to conformity assessment or testing procedures. In an FTA, there could be MRAs on testing procedures; even if standards are not harmonised or mutually recognised. The question is then: To what extent have FTAs developed such cooperation, and what is it worth? For TBT, Molina and Khoroschavina (2016, p. 406ff) found that out of 238 FTAs, 5–6% included either harmonisation equivalence or MRAs on conformity assessment. For SPS, Jackson and Vitikala (2016, p. 327) similarly found that only eight out of 253 FTAs included harmonisation beyond the WTO, and about 20 agreements had provisions on equivalence beyond the WTO.

For an assessment of the depth of FTAs in this field, an issue is how the different measures compare and how strong are their effects. The survey of empirical research by Ronen (2017) presents a mixed picture, but tends to suggest that harmonisation and common standards have a strong trade-promoting effect whereas the impact of MRAs is more ambiguous. Crivelli and Gröeschl (2016) found that SPS barriers act as an entry barrier and interpret this as evidence of sunk costs; on the other hand, firms that entered had a gain and so SPS had a trade-promoting effect for the entrants. The authors also found evidence on large implementation costs related to MRAs. A study of MRAs by Correia de Brito et al. (2016) concludes "The weak impact of MRAs on trade can also be explained by the relatively small costs gains, as a share of the total costs of TBTs. Most of the costs of TBTs are caused by regulatory divergence and by definition that is not touched by traditional MRAs." Surprisingly, Cadot and Gourdon (2016) find stronger trade effects of MRA than harmonisation, at least for TBT, and so we may say that the jury is still out.[7] A look at past Trans-Atlantic trade integration reveals that several MRAs were never implemented; and the agreements on equivalence were not the greatest success (Melchior (Ed.), 2016, Chap. 7).

5.2.4 Trade Facilitation

UNECE (United Nations Economic Commission for Europe), a key agency in the field, defines trade facilitation as "the simplification, standardization and harmonization of procedures and associated information flows required to move goods from seller to buyer and to make payment."[8] According to OECD (2009) the cost related to these procedures is considerable but somewhat uncertain, with estimates varying from 15% to less than 1% of the trade value. Given the magnitude of goods trade, even the smallest estimate amounts to a huge overall cost, and so trade facilitation measures may give significant economic gains. The WTO concluded its Trade Facilitation Agreement (TFA) in 2013, with entry into force in 2017. The TFA focuses on customs procedures and the handling of goods.

In some of the fields examined in this chapter, we have seen that discrimination is technically or practically feasible even if policies are often non-discriminatory. This applies to investment and services market access. For SPS and TBT, standards and rules are mostly non-discriminatory by nature, but procedures could be discriminatory, with special treatment of FTA partners. Some trade facilitation measures are inherently non-discriminatory by nature; for example, contact points and provision or facilitation of information. If customs procedures become more efficient and corruption is eliminated, it will likely benefit all trade partners. But also in this case, there could be discrimination: Fast lanes, better templates, self-declaration or other simplifying procedures for FTA partners.

An illustration of FTAs and trade facilitation are the customs procedures on non-EU members of the EEA (European Economic Area). The EEA is not a customs union but a "Free Trade Agreement" in the WTO sense—external tariffs are not harmonised. Rules of origin therefore matter more, and customs procedures are more extensive than within the customs union (the EU). EFTA members of the EEA have many third-country FTAs beyond Europe, and so there is a considerable "spaghetti bowl" of tariffs and rules of origin. As an illustration, the Norwegian customs uses the same form for all FTAs. Traders may fill in the forms themselves, but that majority of traders use brokers to handle the customs clearance. Customs clearance does not only handle tariffs, but also value added tax (VAT), and payment systems (and procedures for VAT refund when applicable) are important. For trade with EEA partners, customs handling is facilitated by common pan-Euro-Mediterranean rules of origin (EU Council 2010) and common templates used in the whole area. Customs handling is efficient and mostly electronic, but there is a cost that the firms have to incur themselves or by paying brokers. It appears that customs handling is largely non-discriminatory, but with additional facilitation for intra-EEA trade due to common rules and procedures. Given the large volume of trade with the EEA, traders and brokers could also be more familiar with the EEA rules than the rules for other FTAs.

In her examination of the content on trade facilitation provisions in FTAs, Neufeld (2016) emphasises the inherently non-discriminatory nature of many trade facilitation measures. Park and Park (2016) examined empirically the trade impact of FTAs with trade facilitation provisions. They found that the trade facilitation provisions in existing FTAs are "non-discriminatory by generating more intra- and extra-bloc trade in general". Current evidence therefore seems to indicate that trade facilitation measures matter, but are not strongly discriminatory. To the extent that FTAs promote trade facilitation, it could therefore benefit all trade partners.

5.2.5 X Factor: Institutional Similarity and Regulatory Clubs

For financial services, we have seen broad liberalisation for investment-driven services trade, but at the same time, the emergence of complex regulatory systems. The common EU system increases the regulatory burden, but at the same time eliminates the extra costs from a "spaghetti bowl" of national European systems. While the reduction of this extra cost is also to the advantage of the non-EU firms, it could be the case that third-country firms face higher costs because they are less familiar with the European system.

Hence there could be a cost of "regulatory distance", and this could be relevant in a number of areas. For example, in several areas of SPS and TBT, regulation is becoming more extensive and more complex. For food standards, the demand for food security is rising with income, but even emerging nations follow suit and develop their regulatory systems. A considerable body of research confirms the vulnerability of poor countries with respect to SPS and TBT standards (Ronen 2017).

In addition to "vertical" regulatory distance (high/low and developed/developing), there could be "horizontal" differences in the sense that regulations or standards are different even if they are at a similar level. Using the OECD STRI (Services Trade Restrictiveness Index) database related to trade in services, Nordås (2016) developed measures of institutional similarity across countries and found that regulatory similarity promotes services trade.

The USA-EU Transatlantic Trade and Investment Partnership (TTIP) negotiations illustrated how regulatory distance as an obstacle to an agreement. The parties promised the gold standard, but it was still not in sight when the process was put on halt in 2016 (Melchior (Ed.), 2016). On food standards, the epic battle about the "precautionary principle" has, for example, split the world into Genetically Modified Organisms (GMO)-free and GMO-using world regions, and an EU-USA compromise is not in sight, not now and not in TTIP. Scientific change may soften the fronts over time, but as of 2018 it is hardly possible. On chemicals (see text box), the EU established its REACH (Registration, Evaluation, Authorisation of Chemicals) regulatory system in 2006–2007. It was characterised as the most complex bill in EU history,[9] and took seven years to pass. At the other side of the Atlantic, the USA finally amended and modernised its Toxic Substances Control Act (TCSA) in 2016, after decades of discussion. With difficult processes underlying legislation on both sides, TTIP could not harmonise regulations, but negotiate only on less spectacular forms of cooperation or mutual recognition. Chemicals illustrate how regulatory distance between the EU and the USA limits the scope for a deep FTA across the Atlantic.

The regulatory gaps between the EU and the USA has also to some extent created "agreement clubs" among the FTAs, mainly because these countries are leaders with stronger influence on the approaches chosen. In several areas, there is an American versus a European model of FTAs:

- Services and investment: The American model has a separate investment chapter but no GATS-type Mode 3 in services, and a "negative list" (everything is liberal unless it is listed) approach. The European model is more often GATS-based or hybrid (Roy et al. 2009; Latrille 2016). As of 2009, US agreements were also more ambitious on services market access (Roy et al. 2009).
- SPS and TBT: Harmonisation is more often used in the European model, but not in the American style (Piermartini and Budetta 2009).

On food standards, some third countries have been converging to European standards.
- Jurisdiction: The judicial approach is not used in the American approach (cf. discussion above).
- On intellectual property rights (IPR), Valdes and McCann (2016) show that a majority of FTAs have IPR provisions, but especially US agreements go further the WTO in terms of detail and enforcement.

These differences may be a result of economic interests as well as historical accident. To the extent that FTAs are non-discriminatory and shallow, this "club divergence" will have only a modest economic impact.

Regulatory Distance: Chemicals in USA and the EU

The chemicals sector represents 11% of world trade in goods and includes four of the nine sectors that were chosen as priorities for regulatory cooperation in the TTIP negotiations (chemicals, cosmetics, pesticides and pharmaceuticals). Some chemicals involve important health risks and many countries have therefore developed extensive regulations. As shown by Ecorys (2009), chemicals are subject to a large number of various rules and regulations in the EU and the USA; some sector-specific and some general. Chemicals are an example of the complexity of regulatory cooperation.

In the EU, the REACH (registration, evaluation, authorisation and restriction of chemicals) regulation adopted in 2006 is the major pillar in chemicals regulation. A basic principle is "no data, no market" and so REACH requires the firms to present considerable information about production, use, classification, labelling, chemical content and toxicological properties before it is approved for sale. REACH is based on the precautionary principle, which means that a product may be restricted if there is a potential risk, even if there is scientific uncertainty. In addition to REACH, the regulation on classification, labelling and packaging (CLP) is another main pillar of EU's regulation of chemicals.

In the USA, chemical regulation rests on several legal pillars and procedures (Elliott and Pelkmans 2015) but a key piece of legislation has been the Toxic Substances Control Act (TSCA). The original law from 1976 was widely considered as obsolete, but it was replaced in 2016 by a modernised version—a major step in US environmental legislation. The new TSCA strengthens and expands procedures for risk evaluation and data collection. This law also strengthens the Federal level, which is important since practices may vary across states. The TSCA reform brings US legislation closer to REACH, but still with more conditionality on data collection and less comprehensive testing and approval procedures.

If the EU and the USA want to set the "gold standard" for chemical regulation, they could sort out the differences related to the precautionary principle and search for a middle ground, allowing but limiting the use of the precautionary approach (e.g. related to the nature of scientific evidence, the duration of measures, etc.). This is however politically difficult and a "rapprochement" between the two systems is not in sight.

Useful reviews of regulatory issues related to TTIP and chemicals are provided by Ecorys (2009), Kommerskollegium (2013), Elliott and Pelkmans (2015), and Ecorys (2016). Some international regulatory issues are also addressed in OECD (2010) and OECD (2013).

5.3 Summing Up: The Non-tariff Content of FTAs

The broad pattern emerging from this overview is that in many areas, FTAs are beyond tariffs not discriminatory and they do not go much beyond the WTO in most cases. In several areas, however, there is a minority of agreements that are deeper and go further.

The deepest agreement of all is the EU, with common jurisdiction through its institutions and court system, with harmonisation of standards and regulations in most areas of the internal market and an extensive regulatory process.

The analysis in this chapter provides a backdrop for the economic analysis of FTAs and provides signals about methodology, economic proportions and policies:

On methodology, the economic FTA literature rests on the assumption that integration in FTAs is discriminatory. Beyond tariffs, this chapter suggests that many FTAs and not very discriminatory; liberalisation in some areas is non-discriminatory. For some non-tariff measures (NTMs), we have also seen that the "sign is reversed": Regulations create a "regulatory burden" and sunk costs, but the firms that enter gain market shares and the NTM may have a trade-promoting impact—contrary to the tariff case.

On economic proportions, the analysis has shown that while tariff cuts are ambitious and deep, NTM reforms are lightweight in the majority of agreements. But also for NTMs, some agreements are deep and sometimes discriminatory, and these are mainly within rather than between world regions.

On trade policy, we have seen that the WTO has become a "paper tiger" for tariffs and services, with "water in the tariffs" and a similar slack for services. This turns trade negotiations into a virtual game, risking a loss of credibility. For investment and services, we have argued that trade negotiations should be taken away from the diplomat tit-for-tat negotiations and related more closely to the regulatory field and its institutions.

Notes

1. See http://www.oecd.org/investment/investment-policy/codes.htm for information.
2. For an overview of EU law, see https://ec.europa.eu/info/law/law-topic/eu-banking-and-financial-services-law_en.
3. On OECD, see http://www.oecd.org/investment/investment-policy/foi.htm.
4. According to UNCTAD's web page on investment, see http://investmentpolicyhub.unctad.org/IIA.

5. For a discussion, see Melchior (2017) (in Norwegian!).
6. The ten judicial FTAs are, according to Chase et al. (2016): Two in the Americas (Andean Community and CARICOM); five in Africa (CEMAC/Central Africa, COMESA/Southern Africa, East African Community, ECOWAS/West Africa and WAEMU/West Africa), two in Western Europe (EU and EFTA) and one in the former Soviet area (Eurasian Economic Community—now Union, EAEU).
7. Cadot and Gourdon (2016) use the data set of Piermartini and Budetta (2009) and a potential caveat is the dichotomisation of all indicators, with values of zero or one. This dichotomisation also applies to the DESTA database of Dür et al. (2014). On TBT, also Dür et al. (2014) partly relies on Piermartini and Budetta (2009). Having a closer look at EUs agreements and TBT in DESTA (downloaded from the DESTA website March 2018), we find a score of zero on all seven TBT indicators for EC 1957, EC Single European Act, EC Amsterdam, EC Lisbon, EC Maastricht and EC Nice. The European Economic Area (EEA) gets a score of one for only one out of the seven TBT indicators, whereas EFTA as such as well as many of EFTAs FTAs with third countries get positive scores on more indicators. This overall ranking is not plausible, and so there could be some devils in the details of the regression data. For example, TBT measures could be in secondary legislation that is not visible in the main text of FTAs such as EEA.
8. See http://tfig.unece.org/, Introduction to trade facilitation.
9. See https://euobserver.com/economic/24169.

References

Acharya, R. (Ed.). (2016). *Regional Trade Agreements and the Multilateral Trading System*. Cambridge: Cambridge University Press/World Trade Organization.

Baldwin, R., & Low, P. (Eds.). (2009). *Multilateralizing Regionalism. Challenges for the Global Trading System*. Cambridge: Cambridge University Press, in cooperation with the World Trade Organization (WTO).

Cadot, O., & Gourdon, J. (2016). Non-tariff Measures, Preferential Trade Agreements, and Prices: New Evidence. *Review of World Economics, 152*, 227–249. https://doi.org/10.1007/s10290-015-0242-9.

Chase, C., Yanovich, A., Crawford, J., & Ugaz, P. (2016). Mapping of Dispute Settlement Mechanisms in Regional Trade Agreements—Innovative or

Variations on a Theme? In R. Acharya (Ed.), *Regional Trade Agreements and the Multilateral Trading System* (Chapter 10, pp. 608–702). Cambridge: Cambridge University Press.

Correia de Brito, A., Kauffmann, C., & Pelkmans, J. (2016). *The Contribution of Mutual Recognition to International Regulatory Co-operation* (OECD Regulatory Policy Working Papers, No. 2). Paris: OECD Publishing. https://doi.org/10.1787/5jm56fqsfxmx-en

Crawford, J., McKeagg, J., & Tolstova, J. (2016). Mapping of Safeguard Provisions in RTAs. In R. Acharya (Ed.), *Regional Trade Agreements and the Multilateral Trading* System (Chapter 5, pp. 230–315). Cambridge: Cambridge University Press

Crivelli, P., & Groeschl, J. (2016). The Impact of Sanitary and Phytosanitary Measures on Market Entry and Trade Flows. *The World Economy, 39*(3), 444–473.

Dür, A., Baccini, L., & Elsig, M. (2014). The Design of International Trade Agreements: Introducing a New Database. *Review of International Organizations, 9*(3), 353–375.

Ecorys. (2009). *Non-tariff Measures in EU-US Trade and Investment—An Economic Analysis.* Rotterdam: ECORYS Nederland BV (authors Berden, K. G., Francois, J., Thelle, M., Wymenga, P., & Tamminen, S.). Brussels: Final Report for the European Commission, Directorate-General for Trade Reference: OJ 2007/S 180-219493.

Ecorys. (2016, May). *Trade SIA in the Transatlantic Trade and Investment Partnership (TTIP) between the EU and the USA* (Draft Interim Technical Report). Brussels: European Commission/Ecorys.

Elliott, E. D., & Pelkmans, J. (2015). *Greater TTIP Ambition in Chemicals: Why and How.* Brussels: CEPS (Centre for European Policy Studies), Paper No. 10 in the CEPS-CTR project 'TTIP in the Balance' and CEPS Special Report No. 114 / July 2015.

Estevadeordal, A., Suominen, K., & Teh, R. (Eds.). (2009). *Regional Rules in the Global Trading System.* Cambridge: Cambridge University Press, in cooperation with the Inter-American Development Bank (IDB) and the World Trade Organization (WTO).

EU Council. (2010, June 18). *Regional Convention on Pan-Euro-Mediterranean Preferential Rules of Origin.* Brussels: Council of the European Union, Legislative Acts and Other Instruments, Document 9429/10; Interinstitutional File: 2010/0092 (NLE).

European Commission. (2017, March). *Accelerating the Capital Markets Union: Addressing National Barriers to Capital Flows.* Brussels: European Commission,

Report from the Commission to the Council and the European Parliament, COM, 147 final.
Fink, C., & Jansen, M. (2009). Services Provisions in Regional Trade Agreements: Stumbling Blocks or Building Blocks for Multilateral Liberalization? In R. Baldwin & P. Low (Eds.), *Multilateralizing Regionalism: Challenges for the Global Trading System* (Chapter 6, pp. 221–261). Cambridge: Cambridge University Press.
Jackson, L. A., & Vitikala, H. (2016). Cross-Cutting Issues in Regional Trade Agreements: Sanitary and Phytosanitary Measures. In R. Acharya (Ed.), *Regional Trade Agreements and the Multilateral Trading System* (Chapter 6, pp. 316–370). Cambridge: Cambridge University Press.
Kawai, M., & Wignaraja, G. (2013). *Patterns of Free Trade in Asia* (Policy Studies No. 65). East-West Center.
Kommerskollegium (National National Board of Trade). (2013). *Regulativt samarbete och tekniska handelshinder inom ramen för Transatlantic Trade and Investment Partnership (TTIP)*. Stockholm: Kommerskollegium.
Kotschwar, B. (2009). Mapping Investment Provisions in Regional Trade Agreements: Towards an International Investment Regime. In A. Estevadeordal et al. (Eds.), *Regional Rules in the Global Trading System* (Chapter 7, pp. 365–407). Cambridge/New York: Cambridge University Press.
Latrille, P. (2016). Services Rules in Regional Trade Agreements: How Diverse or Creative Are They Compared to the Multilateral Rules? In R. Acharya (Ed.), *Regional Trade Agreements and the Multilateral Trading System* (Chapter 8, pp. 421–493). Cambridge: Cambridge University Press.
Loungani, P., Mishra, S., Papageorgiou, C., & Wang, K. (2017). *World Trade in Services: Evidence from a New Dataset* (IMF Research Department Working Paper WP/17/77). Washington, DC: International Monetary Fund.
Lynch, D. A. (2010). *Trade and Globalization. An Introduction to Regional Trade Agreements*. Lanham: Rowman & Littlefield Publishers, Inc.
Melchior, A. (Ed.). (2016). *TTIP and Norway: Impact and Trade Policy Options* (NUPI Report No. 9/ 2016). Oslo: Norwegian Institute of International Affairs. With contributions from Alvik, I., Bekkedal, T., Felbermayr, G., Theie, M. G., Grünfeld, L. A., Medin, H., Mittenzwei, K., Pettersen, I., & Veggeland, F. At https://brage.bibsys.no/xmlui/handle/11250/2425477
Melchior, A. (2017). *Handelspolitikken Under Trump* (Working Paper No. 879). Oslo: Norwegian Institute of International Affairs. In Norwegian.
Miroudot, S., & Pertel, K. (2015). *Water in the GATS: Methodology and Results* (OECD Trade Policy Papers, No. 185). Paris: OECD Publishing. https://doi.org/10.1787/5jrs6k35nnf1-en

Miroudot, S., & Sheperd, B. (2014). The Paradox of 'Preferences': Regional Trade Agreements and Trade Costs in Services. *The World Economy, 37*(12), 1751–1772.

Miroudot, S., Sauvage, J., & Sudreau, M. (2010). *Multilateralising Regionalism: How Preferential Are Services Commitments in Regional Trade Agreements?* (OECD Trade Policy Papers, No. 106). Paris: OECD Publishing. https://doi.org/10.1787/5km362n24t8n-en

Molina, A. C., & Khoroshavina, V. (2016). Technical Barriers to Trade Provisions in Regional Trade Agreements: To What Extent Do They Go beyond the WTO TBT Agreement? In Acharya (Ed.), *Technical Barriers to Trade Provisions in Regional Trade Agreements: To What Extent Do They Go beyond the WTO TBT Agreement?* (Chapter 7, pp. 371–420). Cambridge: Cambridge University Press.

Neufeld, N. (2016). Trade Facilitation under the RTA Umbrella. In R. Acharya (Ed.), *Regional Trade Agreements and the Multilateral Trading System* (Chapter 3, pp. 111–156). Cambridge: Cambridge University Press.

Nordås, H. K. (2016). *Services Trade Restrictiveness Index (STRI): The Trade Effect of Regulatory Differences* (OECD Trade Policy Papers No. 189). Paris: OECD Publishing. https://doi.org/10.1787/5jlz9z022plp-en

OECD. (2008). *OECD Codes of Liberalisation. User's Guide 2008*. Paris: OECD.

OECD. (2009). *Overcoming Border Bottlenecks. The Costs and Benefits of Trade Facilitation*. Paris: OECD, OECD Trade Policy Studies.

OECD. (2010). *Cutting Costs in Chemical Management. How OECD Helps Government and Industry*. Paris: OECD. http://www.oecd.org

OECD. (2013). *International Regulatory Co-operation. Addressing Global Challenges*. Paris: OECD. http://www.oecd.org

OECD. (2017). *OECD Code of Liberalisation of Capital Movements, 2017*. Paris: OECD.

Park, I., & Park, S. (2016). Trade Facilitation Provisions in Regional Trade Agreements: Discriminatory or Non-discriminatory? *East Asian Economic Review, 20*(4), 447–467.

Piermartini, R., & Budetta, M. (2009). A Mapping of Regional Rules on Technical Barriers to Trade. In A. Estevadeordal et al. (Eds.), *Regional Rules in the Global Trading System* (Chapter 5, pp. 250–315). Cambridge/New York: Cambridge University Press.

Rey, J. (2016). Do Regional Anti-dumping Regimes Make a Difference? In R. Acharya (Ed.), *Regional Trade Agreements and the Multilateral Trading System* (Chapter 4, pp. 157–229). Cambridge: Cambridge University Press.

Ronen, E. (2017). Quantifying the Trade Effects of NTMs: A Review of the Empirical Literature. *Journal of Economics and Political Economy, 4*, 263–274.

Available as MPRA Paper No. 83730, at https://mpra.ub.uni-muenchen.de/83730/

Roy, M., Marchetti, J., & Lim, H. (2007). *Services Liberalization in the New Generation of Preferential Trade Agreements: How Much Further than the GATS?* (World Trade Review 6/2007), reprinted in A. Estevadeordal et al. (Eds.). (2009). Chapter 6, pp. 316–364.

Rueda-Cantuche, J. M., Kerner, R., Cernat, L., & Ritola, V. (2016, November). *Trade in Services by GATS Modes of Supply: Statistical Concepts and First EU Estimates*. Brussels: European Commission, DG Trade, Chief Economist Note Issue 3 (editor: Lucian Cernat). ISSN 2034-9815.

Teh, R., Prusa, T. J., & Budetta, M. (2009). Trade Remedy Provisions in Regional Trade Agreements. In A. Estevadeordal et al. (Eds.), *Regional Rules in the Global Trading System* (Chapter 4, pp. 166–249). Cambridge/New York: Cambridge University Press.

Valdés, R., & McCann, M. (2016). Intellectual Property Provisions in Regional Trade Agreements: Revision and Update. In R. Acharya (Ed.), *Regional Trade Agreements and the Multilateral Trading System* (Chapter 9, pp. 497–607). Cambridge: Cambridge University Press.

WTO. (2015). *Trade in Services. The Most Dynamic Segment of International Trade*. Geneva: WTO, brochure at https://www.wto.org/english/thewto_e/20y_e/services_brochure2015_e.pdf

6

How Important Is Trade? Estimates from a World Trade Model

In the first half of this book, we have examined trade, trade agreements and trade policy. In the second half of this book, we analyse the economic impact of trade and trade agreements. In this chapter, we present a numerical model of world trade that will be a main tool of the analysis. As a first test of the model, we use it to estimate the value of trade: We compare the current world economy with a situation where all trade is eliminated. On average, countries lose 27% of their income when trade is no longer possible. We compare this to the importance of human and physical capital endowments, and natural resource endowments, for real income differences across countries, and find that trade is the second most important determinant of income levels. But physical and human capital is even more important than trade, and we argue that for Brexit, factor market effects could be as least as important as trade effects.

The model has 110 countries and regions and we use data for 2014 in the base scenario. It is a complete mathematical model for the world economy, with a unique solution. For each model scenario, we obtain a complete "synthetic world" where wages, prices, production, trade and welfare are determined with great precision for the 110 countries and regions. We examine trade and trade policy by changing trade costs or

A. Melchior, *Free Trade Agreements and Globalisation*,
https://doi.org/10.1007/978-3-319-92834-0_6

country/region characteristics and simulating the model. Comparing to the base scenario, we can derive the predicted impact of trade policy or other changes.

The model replicates true income levels with a high correlation, and so we can use it examine how rich and poor countries fare in global trade. As a key feature, the model includes a commodity sector, and so we may analyse how commodity exporting countries are affected by trade policy. According to the analysis of world trade in Chap. 2, more than half the world's countries are commodity exporters and our analysis fills a gap in the trade policy literature by taking this into account.

6.1 Model Overview

Figure 6.1 shows the sectors and factor endowments for a region or country in the model. For simplicity, we drop the country/region subscript here. In the numerical model we have countries and regions; in the following, we use the term country, for brevity. The complete mathematical structure of the model is presented in Appendix B, as well as the technical implementation and the data inputs. Data tables and results are presented in

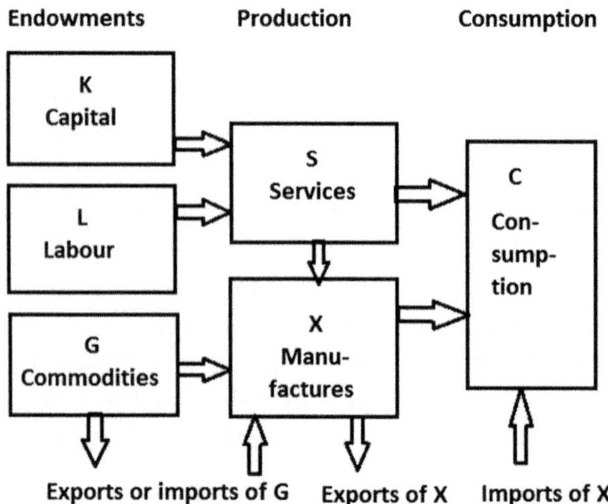

Fig. 6.1 Overview of the model

Appendix C. In the following, we provide an overview of key features and the underlying motivation.

There are two production sectors S and X; for simplicity, we call them services and manufactures, even if empirically, both could include goods as well as services. Services are non-traded, and used in the production of manufactures X, and partly in domestic consumption. Manufactures are differentiated goods produced with economies of scale and imperfect competition. For X, there are exports as well as imports, and so there is intra-industry trade in manufactures.

Countries use their endowments of physical and human capital K and "raw labour" L to produce services. In the model, the capital-labour ratio is a key feature that determines the productivity of a country—countries with higher K/L are more productive and richer. For the numerical model, we have data on L and we use per capita income levels to generate K, drawing on growth research. Following Caselli (2005), we use the strong observed correlation between per capita income levels and capital-labour ratios to derive the latter, also using evidence from the growth accounting literature. The resulting variable is a strong determinant of a country's real income level. We assume that K and L are fully utilised, and so there is no unemployment and the quantity of services produced follows directly from the endowments of K and L, given the production function.[1] The price of services, on the other hand, is endogenous and affected by markets and trade.

The commodity sector G is constructed in a stylised way to make the model tractable. G is an endowment that is used in the production of X but can also be traded. If the country uses more (less) than its commodity endowment G in the manufacturing sector, it will import (export) commodities. Commodities or natural resources are homogeneous and traded internationally with zero cost. Due to costless trade, there is a common world market price for G (except in the case of autarky). The assumption of zero trade cost for commodities is a simplification for the sake of tractability, but still resembles reality if we think of oil, that has a common world market price and relatively low transport costs.

The bottom line in Fig. 6.1 shows the trade flows. There is two-way trade in X and one-way trade in G, and for each country total trade must be balanced. If a country exports (imports) G, it will have a trade deficit (surplus) for X.

In the numerical model, we use the commodity price g as numeraire (so we set g = 1). With factor endowments, production and consumption functions and trade costs given, the model has an exact solution, with all prices and values expressed in terms of g. The endogenous variables determined are then as follows:

- The wage levels that vary across countries. From the wage levels, we also obtain the capital rent, the price of services, the costs in manufacturing and nominal Gross Domestic Product (GDP) or total income.
- The number of manufacturing firms is endogenous and so the industrial structure of the country depends "on everything". Countries with a large commodity endowment can be deindustrialised with zero manufacturing production. When some countries are deindustrialised, the model solution is different but also well-defined and tractable. Trade flows in manufactures are exactly determined for every bilateral trade flow and for every firm, with or without complete specialisation in some countries. Trade in G is determined on aggregate for every country.[2]

The model presented is a general equilibrium model that is solved numerically. In the baseline scenario with 110 countries and regions and data for 2014, the real income per capita levels are correlated with observed income levels with a coefficient of 0.96, and bilateral trade flows are correlated with bilateral manufacturing trade flows with a coefficient of 0.65.[3] Hence the model resembles reality, and inputs and parameter values are based on data and research. It is however still "theory with numbers" in the sense that the results are not empirical and their truth depends on the model properties.

There are different motivations underlying our approach: First, we want to make economic theory more realistic; rather than abstract predictions in unrealistic settings, we derive predictions for true countries and regions. The impact of trade policy depends on location and country characteristics, and the model aims to capture these differences. Our prediction is not "trade is good for all, at all times" but how does trade or trade policy changes affect Germany, UK, USA or others.

Second, it is of interest to construct empirically anchored general equilibrium models to examine principal issues and qualitative questions without the huge data requirements and lesser transparency involved in large-scale CGE (Computable General Equilibrium) models. For example, the GTAP model (Global Trade Analysis Project, see https://www.gtap.agecon.purdue.edu/) has 57 sectors and 140 countries and therefore huge data requirements for the model construction itself and for most policy simulations. A motivation underlying this paper is that some broader questions could be analysed with less detail and greater simplicity and transparency in smaller-scale CGE models. Our aim is to obtain qualitative knowledge about trade, welfare and industrial development, not "the number for chemicals".

Compared to some recent "new quantitative trade models" such as Caliendo and Parro (2015) or Felbermayr et al. (2018), the approach here differs, for example, by the way commodities are included, and by having imperfect competition in the manufacturing sector, with endogenous determination of the number of firms. These other models build on the "Ricardian" trade model of Eaton and Kortum (2002), with probabilistic determination of productivity levels and perfect competition in manufacturing where the lowest-cost supplier is chosen for each product. Contrary to this "winner-takes-all" mechanism, our model determines the number of manufacturing firms in each country, with intra-industry trade in addition to commodity trade. Eaton and Kortum (2002, 1742) argue "We think that our model best describes trade in manufactures among industrial countries." The model used here fills a gap by including commodity trade, making it suitable for global trade policy analysis including the large number of countries relying on commodity exports.

For global models of economy and trade, an issue is how models should be "calibrated" to real-world data. For example, the extent to which predicted bilateral trade flows are equal to their empirically observed counterparts depends on taste parameters, trade elasticities (how trade flows respond to changes in trade costs) and the magnitude of trade costs. While some CGE models have relied heavily on taste parameters (e.g. scrutinised by Hillberry et al. 2005), another approach is to estimate trade elasticities first and then "calibrate" trade barriers using these elasticities (Kee et al. 2008, 2009) in the chosen model. In the "new quantitative trade theory" approach (see e.g. Felbermayr et al. 2018), parameter estimation and model prediction is (with some exceptions) undertaken with the same data set. Different options are possible, but the aim is often that the model should be calibrated to fit the data perfectly for selected components. Contrary to this, we take for granted that our model is not able to fully explain the world, and we do not calibrate elasticities or trade barriers to make the model replicate data. The macro-approach here also deviates from a "wedges" approach (e.g. trade barriers as wedges) as illustrated by Egger and Nigai (2016) and Chari et al. (2007). We use trade elasticities based on earlier research and other inputs based on available data.[4]

In current research, there is a growing interest and focus on global value chains (GVCs, see e.g. Timmer et al. 2014). In the model used here, manufactures are not used as inputs, and so we do not capture this component of GVCs. On the other hand, we capture the most ancient and probably most important of value chains: Between manufactures and commodities. While raw materials have continuously been important in world trade, economic research on international trade has during recent decades focused increasingly on trade in differentiated manufactured goods. Following the observation by Grubel and Lloyd (1975) that a large part of international trade was intra-industry trade in differentiated products, models with imperfect competition were introduced (e.g. Krugman 1980) and gradually took over the stage. These new models have led to important new insights about trade, industrial agglomeration and economic geography, but in this paper, we ask whether trade in raw materials (in the following, we use the term commodities for goods based on natural resources) has been forgotten in this new world view. In the Handbook of International Economics Volume 1 (Jones and Kenen 1984), commodities were still on the agenda but Kemp and Long (1984) maintained that even at that time, the standard theories of trade neglected this key component of world trade. In the later corresponding handbooks (Grossmann and Rogoff 1995, Gopinath et al. 2014), natural resources are no longer addressed. While theories of intra-industry trade are valuable tools in general and especially for understanding trade between rich countries, a considerable part of world trade is in commodities such as oil, gas, metals, minerals, timber and more. Hence in the study of industrial development and trade at the global level, we should address intra-industry trade and commodity trade jointly. This is a key motivation underlying our model. As seen from Chap. 2, more than half the world's countries rely on commodity exports.

This paper is also a contribution to "global economic geography" by including geography and spatial trade costs; it is a "geographical economics" world trade model building on Melchior (2010, 2011) and adding commodity trade. As witnessed by, for example, the gravity model of international trade (see e.g. Head and Mayer 2014), economic transactions are strongly affected by distance. The combination of spatial trade costs (related to distance) and non-spatial transaction costs such as tariffs creates a geographical footprint that affects production, trade, income levels and welfare. Each configuration of trade costs has a particular footprint, and in this paper we study how this interacts with other aspects that affect production and trade. Given this interest in global economic geography, we do not treat Luxemburg and China in the same way; large countries are decomposed into regions whereas some countries are aggregated into country groups. Seven countries (USA, Canada, Brazil, Russia, Kazakhstan, India and China) are divided into altogether 47 regions (Appendix Table C.2). On the other hand, some countries were aggregated into regions in order to reduce the dimensionality of the model (Appendix Table C.3). With the use of MATrix LABoratory (MATLAB) software, the model solution could be derived relatively fast with up to about 110 countries or regions. In the numerical model used in this book, we therefore have 44 individual countries, 47 subnational regions and 19 country aggregates (comprising 101 countries).

Contrary to some of the "new economic geography" models that have relied on labour migration (Krugman 1991) or vertical linkages between input- and output-producing firms (Krugman and Venables 1995), the model we present does not have "cumulative causation". Spatial effects are however strongly present, and with the trade model we use, there is no "catastrophic agglomeration" (all industry located in one place, see Bosker et al. 2010) or multiple equilibria. For the simulation with 110 countries/regions, tractability is an important issue, and we chose to use a model without externalities. Unlike, for example, Allen and Arkolakis (2014), we maintain imperfect competition in the tradables sector, with endogenous number of firms. Instead of the "numeraire" sector used in some new economic geography models, commodity trade allows unbalanced trade in the tradables sector.

While the model is static, the results are also relevant for the literature on trade and growth by quantifying the drivers of cross-country income differences. In this paper, we assess the relative importance of trade compared to factor endowments including natural resources. While the growth accounting literature relies on cross-country regressions (see e.g. Frankel and Romer 1999; or Caselli 2005), the model captures the complete global pattern of economic interactions. Henderson et al. (2011) show that functional form and non-linearities are important for the results from growth regressions, and a global model with geography should be able to capture this in a better way. In line with Noguer and Siscart (2005) and Wacziarg and Welch (2008), the model suggests that trade is good for income and provides a framework to examine why this is the case and how important it is. An important feature is that the model captures term-of-trade effects, which are crucial for commodity exporters.

6.2 World Contest: What Determines National Income Levels?

As a first test of our model, we ask: What are the most important drivers of cross-country differences in income levels? Given the book's theme, trade is obviously a candidate. The experiment we undertake is to simulate production and consumption in autarky with no trade between countries. By comparing to the base scenario, we can see how much countries lose if they cannot trade.

In our contest, trade has to compete with two other key determinants of income and welfare. The first of these is technology or productivity, reflected in the K/L ratio. As noted in the introduction, K/L is an expression of productivity, and K includes physical as well as human capital. L is therefore "raw labour"—not accounting for skills. While the growth accounting literature has tried to measure the relative contributions of human and physical capital and the residual element "total factor productivity" (Hsieh and Klenow 2010), we make no distinction here. In the analysis, physical and human capital are merged and may be said to represent a country's technology level. Spolaore and Wacziarg (2013) provide some support for the notion of a long-run and deep-rooted "national technology level". The experiment undertaken for productivity is to simulate that the world capital stock is redistributed across countries and regions, so that all have the same K/L ratios, equal to the weighted world average in the base scenario.

Commodities or natural resources constitute the third contender in our global competition: Many countries rely heavily on natural resources as a source of income. In our contest, the third experiment is to reallocate the global stock of natural resources in the same way as for capital; that is, proportional to the labour force L. In this way, some countries luckily receive a new source of wealth, whereas others are deprived of their national treasures.

The three experiments serve as counterfactuals: By comparing to the base scenario, we can see how the changes in K or G or the elimination of trade affects production, trade, income and welfare for each of the 110 countries and regions. The contest also serves to illustrate key properties of our model. As said, this is not the truth but "theory with numbers", and the model properties affect the results. The experiments here therefore serve as a backdrop for the later analysis of trade policy scenarios, and the interpretation of results. In Appendix B, Sects. B.6 and Appendix Table C.1, some small-scale simulations also shed light on the model's properties.

6.2.1 Reallocation of Natural Resources ("Commodity Scenario")

On commodity trade, Corden and Neary (1982) showed, in a model for a small open economy facing given prices, how a booming energy sector could lead to deindustrialisation and "Dutch disease". This could occur either through a spending (demand) effect whereby costs and prices increase and lead to a contraction of the traded manufacturing sector, or through a resource movement effect whereby the energy sector pulls resources out of manufacturing. In the stylised model we construct here, we sacrifice the resource movement effects for the sake of model tractability, but there is a strong spending effect: Natural resource endowments are good for income levels and welfare, but leads to a contraction of manufacturing. In conformity with this prediction, Harding and Venables (2013) show empirically (using data for 1970–2006) that resource booms raise imports and have a strong negative impact on non-resource exports.

The model we present suggests that natural resources are a blessing as well as a curse, if we perceive deindustrialisation as the curse. In the literature on the so-called resource curse, it is maintained that resource abundance may, for some reason, lead to slower growth and thereby also eliminate the blessing. If there are positive externalities of some kind in the manufacturing/traded sector, deindustrialisation caused by a resource boom could reduce growth. The model presented here is static and generates no such "curse". While we do not reject the possibility of such externalities, their existence is an empirical issue. According to the survey of van der Ploeg (2011), the empirical evidence in favour of the resource curse hypothesis is mixed. Some recent contributions (e.g. Arezki and van der Ploeg 2011) provide support for this hypothesis, whereas others (e.g. Brunnschweiler 2008; Alexeev and Conrad 2009) find that natural resource abundance actually promotes economic growth. According to one line of research (see e.g. Mehlum et al. 2006), it depends on the quality institutions whether the effect is positive or negative.

When the total world endowment of G is reallocated proportionally to the labour force L, there are large changes in the country level G. These changes in G are shown in Appendix Table C.7. The changes in welfare per capita and the share of tradables in GDP are shown in Appendix C.8.

In the baseline scenario, there are 12 regions with complete specialisation; that is, no manufacturing production. Key variables and results in the baseline scenario are shown in Appendix Table C.6. When G is redistributed so that all countries have the same G/L ratio, all the world's regions become diversified, with some manufacturing/tradables production. Recall that G is freely traded and so the physical access to commodities is exactly the same as before, but the allocation of natural resource income is dramatically changed.

The reallocation of natural resources implies large changes in the share of natural resource rents in GDP. Figures 6.2 and 6.3 plot this change against the change in real income per capita (Fig. 6.2) and the share of tradables in GDP (Fig. 6.3).

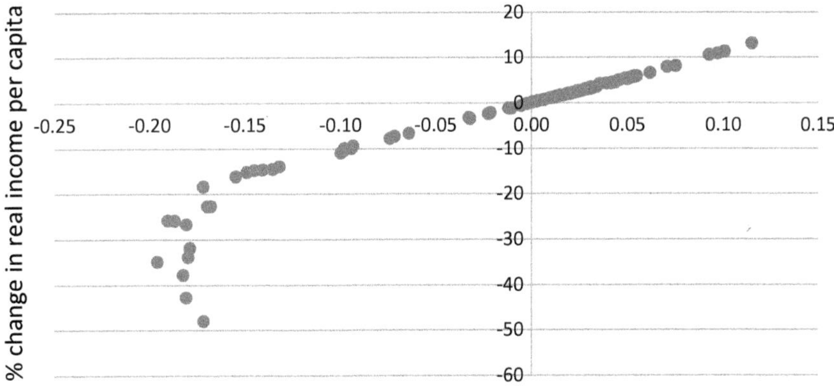

Fig. 6.2 Commodity scenario: changes in natural resource rents versus changes in real income per capita. (Source: Own calculations. Results from numerical simulation)

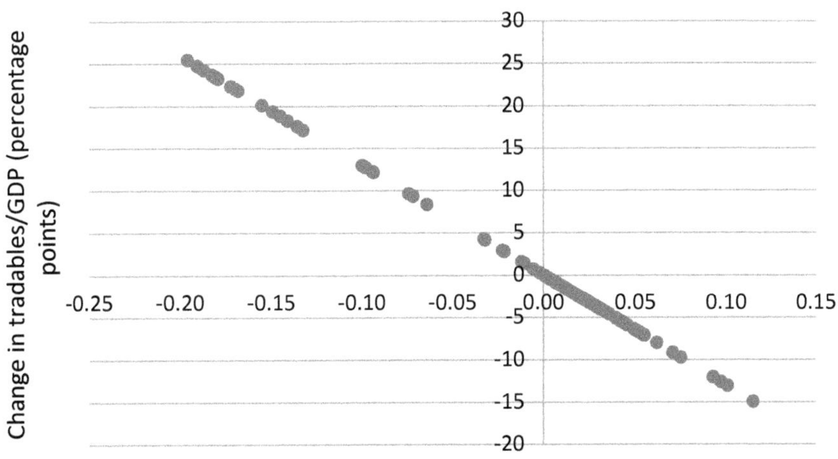

Fig. 6.3 Commodity scenario: changes in natural resource rents versus changes in the share of manufacturing in GDP. (Source: Own calculations. Results from numerical simulation)

Figure 6.2 shows that losing natural resources is equivalent to losing income in most cases. Figure 6.3 shows a linear relationship between commodity reliance (measured as natural resource rents/GDP) and the share of manufacturing in GDP. The results mimic the small-scale simulation results in Sect. B.6 and show that natural resource endowments are indeed a blessing and a curse; more natural resource wealth raises real income but the spending effect of Corden and Neary (1982) has a strong adverse impact on competitiveness in manufacturing. This is not only a statistical artefact (since more commodity rents raise GDP) but is also reflected in trade patterns.[5]

6.2.2 Reallocation of the Capital Stock ("Productivity Scenario")

As a second experiment, we treat capital the same way; an unchanged global capital stock is reallocated proportionally to the labour force. The changes in K or the K/L ratio are shown in Appendix Table C.7, and the real income and tradables/GDP changes are shown in Appendix Table C.8. The world average K/L ratio is 2.23 but the initial country levels vary from 0.5 to 15.8, and so the reallocation is dramatic. Figures 6.4 and 6.5 show the changes in real

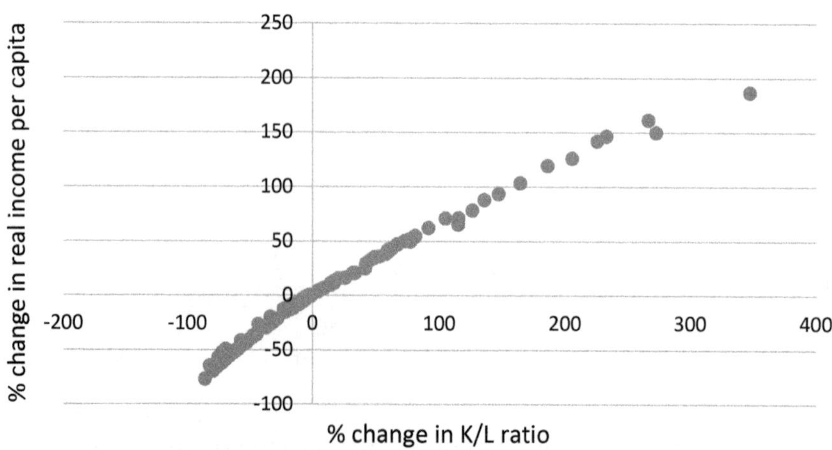

Fig. 6.4 Productivity scenario: changes in K/L ratios versus changes in real income per capita. (Source: Own calculations. Results from numerical simulation)

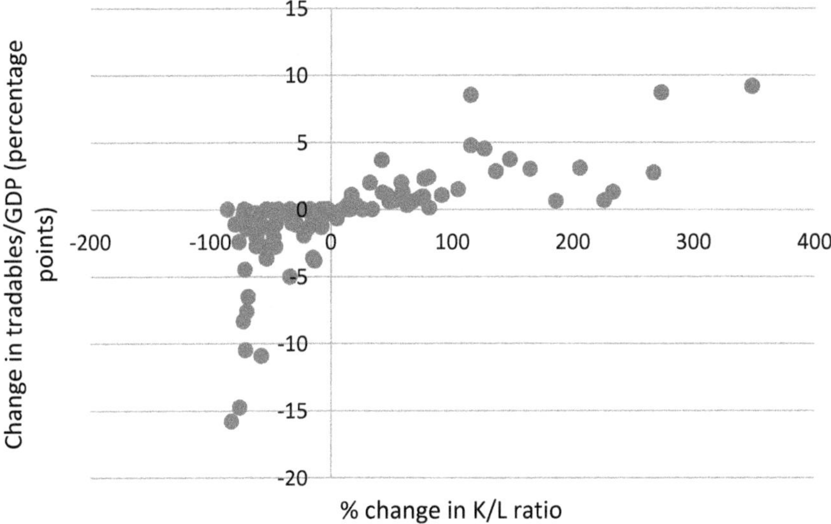

Fig. 6.5 Productivity scenario: changes in K/L ratios versus changes in the share of manufacturing in GDP. (Source: Own calculations. Results from numerical simulation)

income per capita and manufacturing/GDP, respectively, this time plotted against the percentage change in the K/L ratio.

As we might expect, there is clearly a positive relationship in both cases; almost linear for welfare and a bit more mixed with respect to X production. Changes in welfare are large in the productivity scenario; with average percentage changes (positive or negative) at 42% on average.

6.2.3 Trade: The Case of Autarky

A third candidate with a potentially large impact on welfare and production patterns is trade. Using the analytical results in Appendix B, Sect. B.5, we therefore include autarky among the scenarios. The results, shown in Appendix Table C.8, demonstrate that trade is indeed a positive contributor to real income levels. In our context, it may be recalled that the use of CES (constant elasticity of substitution) demand functions in the demand for manufactured goods (Eq. 16, Appendix B) generate a taste for variety and so when countries are not allowed to enjoy imported varieties any more, it has a considerable negative impact on welfare. In addition, autarky reduces production efficiency, since specialisation based on comparative advantage is no longer possible. In autarky, commodities cannot be traded anymore, and so countries without natural resources will have a problem in manufacturing production, and resource-rich regions will face low commodity prices due to their abundance.

The results in Appendix Table C.8 show that all countries lose in autarky, with losses ranging from 12% to 61%. Correlation analysis confirms our expectation that small countries lose much more; typically it is Iceland that loses the most. Eaton and Kortum (2002) also found that small countries gain more from trade. In line with the argument of the preceding paragraph, we find that the welfare loss in autarky is the largest for those with very little or very much natural resources. This is illustrated in Fig. 6.6.[6]

Countries with very high G/L ratios can no longer gain from exporting these to the world and face severe welfare losses. At the other end, countries with little natural resources can no longer import commodities from the world market, causing inefficient production and large welfare losses.

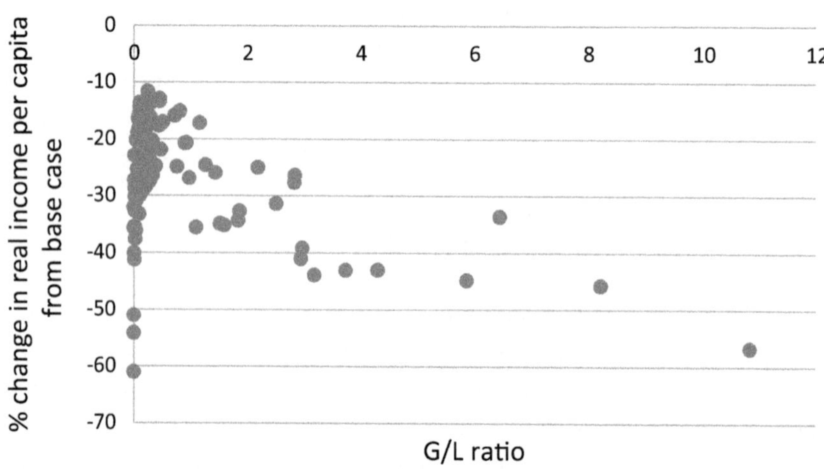

Fig. 6.6 Autarky welfare loss (compared to base scenario) versus G/L ratio. (Results from numerical simulation)

6.3 Ranking of Real Income Determinants: The Medal Awards

While changes in autarky are all in one direction, the impact in the commodity or productivity scenarios is positive or negative, depending on the change from baseline. As a measure of the relative importance of each factor, we may use the average absolute percentage change in per capita real income for the three scenarios. The result is shown in Fig. 6.7.

The gold medal is clearly going to the productivity scenario; with a mean change of 42% from the base case if resources were distributed equally. Trade is on second place, with an average contribution of 27%. Commodities get the bronze medal; it is also a major determinant of real income according to the model, but less important than the other two.

The counterfactual simulations suggest that natural resource abundance is a blessing and a curse at the same time; it adds to real income levels but the "spending effect" of Corden and Neary (1982) generates

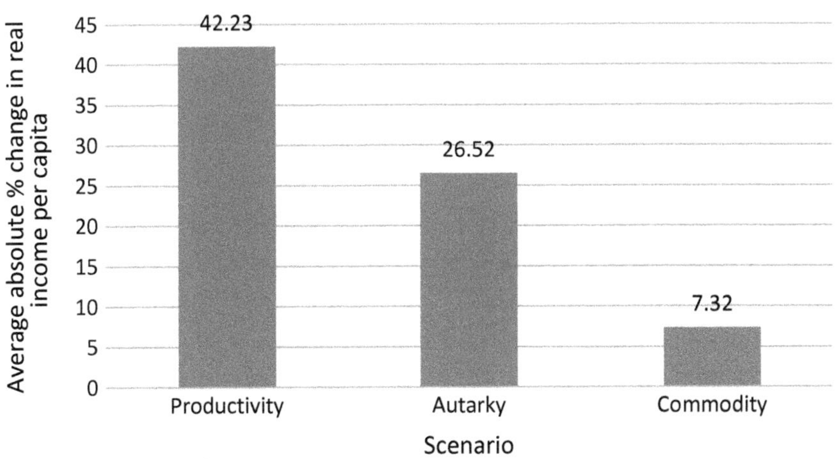

Fig. 6.7 Main drivers of real income differences across 110 countries/regions. (Averages based on results from numerical simulation. Own calculations)

systematic deindustrialisation at the same time. We have shown that natural resources are the third most important determinant of real income levels, with productivity/capital endowments and trade ranked above. While the growth accounting literature rests on cross-country comparison, our model takes into account all the interactions and interdependency in the world economy.

In the following chapters, the model will be used for more detailed analysis of trade policy. While not examined in detail here, the model captures terms-of-trade effects that are highly important, especially for commodity exporters. Given that large countries are split into regions, the model is also a tool for examining the intra-national trade of large countries.

The model provides an interesting tool for analysis but also has its shortcomings. For the sake of tractability, key simplifications were made; for example, one tradable sector only (fixing the wage/rental ratio); assuming costless trade in commodities (also using the commodity price as numeraire); no processing of commodities (thereby dropping the "resource use" effect); and a fixed commodity supply. The model is static and abstracts from commodity price fluctuations, which are important (Newbury and Stiglitz 1981). In future applications, the empirical foundation of the model can also be improved; for example, on trade costs where real data are used but the scaling of different components is uncertain and ad hoc in the current model version (see Appendix B for details).

6.4 How Important Is Trade Versus Factor Markets? Brexit Implications

The analysis above suggests that trade is important, but factor endowment changes are even more important. This is relevant in the context of Brexit, where migration and capital flows may be affected, in addition to trade flows. As an illustration of this, we may compare the economic impact of changes in trade costs and trade on one side, and changes in factor stocks on the other. Using the model, we run the following four stark scenarios:

- Trade Brexit: Trade costs are raised by 20 percentage points for exports from the UK to the EU, but remain unchanged in the other direction.
- Trade Brexit two-way: Trade costs are raised by 20 percentage points between the UK and the EU, in both directions.
- Capital Brexit: The UK stock of human and physical capital is reduced by 5%.
- Labour Brexit: The UK stock of "raw labour" is reduced by 5%.

These scenarios are crude and we make no attempt to quantify Brexit; the aim is to illustrate the relative importance of trade versus factor market effects in the model. The capital stock may be affected by capital and knowledge flows, and the labour stock (compared to what it would have been otherwise—we do not say that the UK will throw out 5% of the workers) by migration policies. The assumed trade cost changes are high, but serve to illustrate the proportions of trade versus factor markets.

Figure 6.8 shows the impact for the UK in the four scenarios.

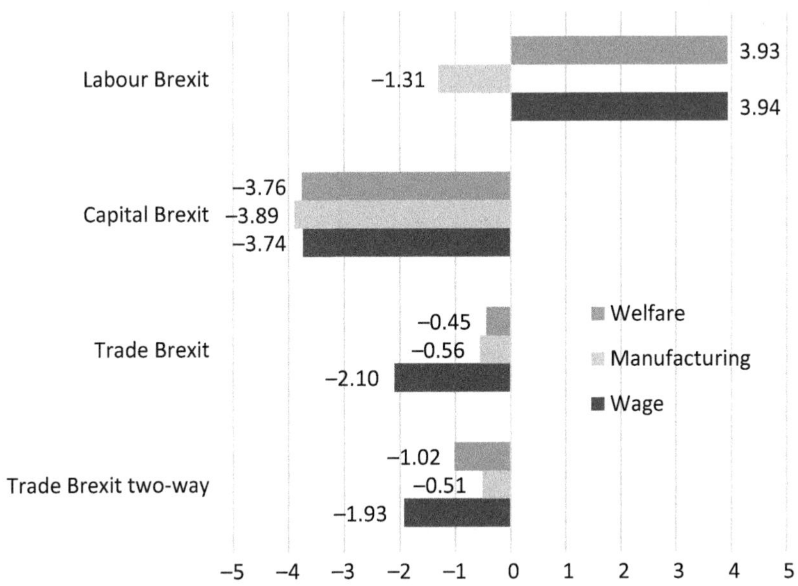

Fig. 6.8 Brexit—the importance of trade versus factor market changes. Changes for the UK from the base scenario. (Source: Own calculations. Results from numerical simulation)

As we would expect, Trade Brexit reduces welfare, manufacturing production and nominal wages in the UK. The welfare loss is more than doubled if the UK "retaliates" (Trade Brexit two-way), but this added protection has no positive impact on UK manufacturing.

Compared to Trade Brexit, the changes in factor stocks have larger quantitative effects. Since the K/L stock determines productivity in the model, the loss of capital leads to a considerable reduction in welfare, manufacturing production and wages. Conversely, a reduction in L leads to a higher K/L ratio that has a positive impact on wages and welfare, in spite of some loss of manufacturing production.

What this means in practice, depends on the scale of changes that might be involved. Within the EU, the span from top to bottom for the capital-labour ratio is about 3:1, and so 5% change is in this perspective not very large or "out of scope". The message from our indeed stylised scenarios is therefore that in the context of Brexit, trade matters but factor market effects could be quantitatively important. As noted, we make no attempt here to quantify the changes in trade costs or factor market repercussions of Brexit; we just repeat the point that trade is important, but not all that matters!

Notes

1. Since K and L are fully utilised in the production of S, there is no K/L factor substitution across sectors. Alternatively, we might drop K and use a production function of the type aL, where a is a productivity parameter. We keep K and L for better correspondence with data; in particular, the correspondence between K/L and GDP per capita found in the growth literature (see Appendix B). The model can also be extended to allow K/L factor substitution.
2. The bilateral trade flows in G are not determined; for example, a commodity importer could buy a little from every commodity exporter or all from one. This is however not a problem or limitation.
3. This correlation is for the trade of the individual countries among the 110 countries and regions, since we do not have bilateral trade data for the subnational regions.

4. Some model components may be developed further in future research. For example, geography is represented here as a scaling of distance but a future aim is to include better data on transport modes and trade costs, bringing it closer to the new quantitative trade theory in later applications.
5. For brevity, more detailed results are not reported but these are available upon request.
6. The correlation between the change in welfare per capita and country size measured by L (the labour stock) is 0.55; and with natural resource abundance measured by G/L the correlation is −0.49. Fishery resources are not included in the World Bank natural resource data and so Iceland is twice unlucky here!

References

Alexeev, M., & Conrad, R. (2009). The Elusive Curse of Oil. *The Review of Economics and Statistics, 91*(3), 586–598.

Allen, T., & Arkolakis, C. (2014). Trade and the Topography of the Spatial Economy. *The Quarterly Journal of Economics, 129*(3), 1085–1139.

Arezki, R., & van der Ploeg, F. (2011). Do Natural Resources Depress Income Per Capita? *Review of Development Economics, 15*(3), 504–521.

Bosker, M., Brakman, S., Garretsen, H., & Schramm, M. (2010). Adding Geography to the New Economic Geography: Bridging the Gap between Theory and Empirics. *Journal of Economic Geography, 10*(6), 793–823. https://doi.org/10.1093/jeg/lbq003.

Brunnschweiler, C. N. (2008). Cursing the Blessings? Natural Resource Abundance, Institutions, and Economic Growth. *World Development, 36*(3), 399–419.

Caliendo, L., & Parro, F. (2015). Estimates of the Trade and Welfare Effects of NAFTA. *Review of Economic Studies, 82*(1), 1–44.

Caselli, F. (2005). Accounting for Cross-Country Income Differences. In P. Aghion & S. N. Durlauf (Eds.), *Handbook of Economic Growth* (Vol. 1A, Chapter 9, pp. 679–741). Amsterdam/New York: North-Holland. https://doi.org/10.1016/B978-0-444-53538-2.00012-5

Chari, V. V., Kehoe, P. J., & McGrattan, E. R. (2007). Business Cycle Accounting. *Econometrica, 75*(3), 781–836.

Corden, M., & Neary, P. (1982). Booming Sector and De-industrialisation in a Small Open Economy. *The Economic Journal, 92*(368), 825–848.

Eaton, J., & Kortum, S. (2002). Technology, Geography, and Trade. *Econometrica, 70*(5), 1741–1779.
Egger, P., & Nigai, S. (2016). *World-Trade Growth Accounting* (CESIfo Working Paper No. 5831). Munich: Center for Economic Studies and Ifo Institute.
Felbermayr, G., Gröschl, J., & Heiland, I. (2018). *Undoing Europe in a New Quantitative Trade Model* (Ifo Working Paper No. 250). Munich: Ifo Institute, Leibniz Institute for Economic Research at the University of Munich.
Frankel, J. A., & Romer, D. (1999). Does Trade Cause Growth? *American Economic Review, 89*(3), 379–399.
Gopinath, G., Helpman, E., & Rogoff, K. (Eds.). (2014). *Handbook of International Economics, Volume 4* (pp. 1–740). Amsterdam: North-Holland.
Grossmann, G. M., & Rogoff, K. (Eds.). (1995). *Handbook of International Economics* (Vol. 3, pp. 1243–2107). Amsterdam: North-Holland.
Grubel, H. G., & Lloyd, P. J. (1975). *Intra-industry Trade. The Theory and Measurement of International Trade in Differentiated Products.* London: Macmillan.
Harding, T., & Venables, A. J. (2013). *The Implications of Natural Resource Exports for Non-resource Trade* (OxCarre Research Paper No. 103). Oxford University, Department of Economics, Oxford Centre for the Analysis of Resource Rich Economies.
Head, K., & Mayer, T. (2014). Gravity Equations: Workhorse, Toolkit, and Cookbook. In G. Gopinath, E. Helpman, & K. Rogoff (Eds.), *Handbook of International Economics* (Vol. 4, Chapter 3, pp. 131–195). Amsterdam: North-Holland/Elsevier.
Henderson, D. J., Papageorgiou, C., & Parmeter, C. F. (2011). Growth Empirics without Parameters. *The Economic Journal, 122*, 125–154. https://doi.org/10.1111/j.1468-0297.2011.02460.x.
Hillberry, R. H., Anderson, M. A., Balistreri, E. J., & Fox, A. K. (2005). Taste Parameters as Model Residuals: Assessing the 'Fit' of an Armington Trade Model. *Review of International Economics, 13*(5), 973–984.
Hsieh, C., & Klenow, P. J. (2010). Development Accounting. *American Economic Journal: Macroeconomics, 2*(1), 207–223.
Jones, R. W., & Kenen, P. B. (Eds.). (1984). *Handbook of International Economics, Volume 1, International Trade* (pp. 1–623). Amsterdam: North-Holland.
Kee, H. L., Nicita, A., & Olarreaga, M. (2008). Import Demand Elasticities and Trade Distortions. *Review of Economics and Statistics, 90*(4), 666–682.
Kee, H. L., Nicita, A., & Olarreaga, M. (2009). Estimating Trade Restrictiveness Indices. *The Economic Journal, 119*(1), 172–199.

Kemp, M. C., & van Long, N. (1984). The Role of Natural Resources in Trade Models. In R. W. Jones & P. B. Kenen (Eds.), *Handbook of International Economics, Volume 1, International Trade* (Chapter 8, pp. 367–417). Amsterdam: North-Holland.

Krugman, P. (1980). Scale Economies, Product Differentiation, and the Pattern of Trade. *American Economic Review, 70*(5), 950–959.

Krugman, P. (1991). Increasing Returns and Economic Geography. *Journal of Political Economy, 99*, 483–499.

Krugman, P. R., & Venables, A. J. (1995). Globalization and the Inequality of Nations. *Quarterly Journal of Economics, 110*(4), 857–880.

Mehlum, H., Moene, K., & Torvik, R. (2006). Cursed by Resources or Institutions? *World Economy, 29*(8), 1117–1131.

Melchior, A. (2010). Globalisation and the Provinces of China: The Role of Domestic Versus International Trade Integration. *Journal of Chinese Economic and Business Studies, 8*(3), 227–252.

Melchior, A. (2011). East-West Integration: A Geographical Economics Approach. In M. Dabrowski & M. Maliszewska (Eds.), *EU Eastern Neighborhood. Economic Potential and Future Development* (Chapter 2, pp. 23–44). Heidelberg: Springer.

Newbery, D. M. G., & Stiglitz, J. E. (1981). *The Theory of Commodity Price Stabilization. A Study in the Economics of Risk.* Oxford: Oxford University Press.

Noguer, M., & Siscart, M. (2005). Trade Raises Income: A Precise and Robust Result. *Journal of International Economics, 65*, 447–460.

Spolaore, E., & Wacziarg, R. (2013). How Deep Are the Roots of Economic Development? *Journal of Economic Literature, 51*(2), 325–369.

Timmer, M. P., Erumban, A. A., Los, B., Stehrer, R., & de Vries, G. J. (2014). Slicing Up Global Value Chains. *Journal of Economic Perspectives, 28*(2), 99–118.

Van der Ploeg, F. (2011). Natural Resources: Curse or Blessing? *Journal of Economic Literature, 49*(2), 366–420.

Wacziarg, R., & Welch, K. H. (2008). Trade Liberalization and Growth: New Evidence. *The World Bank Economic Review, 22*(2), 187–231.

7

Trade, USA and the Rise of China: Pains and Gains

The growth of Asia and particularly China is the most dramatic event in the world economy during the last 50 years. As shown in Chap. 2, the share of Asia in world trade has grown spectacularly. Chapter 3 showed that Asia's participation in trade agreements followed suit. But the rise of Asia and China also causes painful industrial adjustment in the incumbent manufacturing nations and, in 2018, frictions in trade policy. In this chapter, we address some issues. We show that the US trade deficit is a generic issue that is not mainly caused by the trade practices of China. After 1990, China has added to this deficit but this is because of China's growth rather than a worsening of USA's relative position.

Using the world trade model presented in Chap. 6 and Appendix B, we simulate the impact in the world economy of China's growth from 1990 to 2014. According to the results, all other countries and regions gain from China's growth in terms of welfare, but there is also a pain in the form of manufacturing contraction and a downward pressure on wages. There is large variation across countries and regions. Commodity exporters gain from terms-of-trade effects and so their gains as well as pains are larger. Countries close to China have larger gains and smaller pains. For North America and Western Europe, the welfare gains are

A. Melchior, *Free Trade Agreements and Globalisation*,
https://doi.org/10.1007/978-3-319-92834-0_7

modest and the pains larger, except for commodity countries/regions such as Norway and Alaska.

The analysis supports the hypothesis that reciprocity in trade policy matters; if trade barriers for exports to China are higher than for imports from China, it means cheaper imports but fewer manufacturing firms. Chapters 4 and 5 illustrated that there is some lack of reciprocity in global trade policy. But Free Trade Agreements (FTAs) contribute to more reciprocity and are therefore part of the solution and not the problem. Simulating the impact of US trade integration with various regions of the world, we find that reciprocal trade integration may be good for welfare as well as manufacturing jobs in the USA. For the USA, integration with Asia and Europe may bring considerable gains, if successful. Due to the rise of Asia, trade integration with Asia has also become important, and the Trans-Pacific Partnership (TPP) is (as of April 2018) an important opportunity lost for the USA.

In this chapter, we run stylised scenarios and make no attempt to quantify how large reductions in trade costs are feasible in real negotiations. The results should be interpreted in this light. If deep integration is not feasible across continents, the ranking will change and integration within world regions may remain on top of the ranking.

7.1 The US Trade Deficit

In the universe of President Trump, the US trade deficit is to a large extent caused by unfair competition from abroad; especially China. In Navarro and Autry (2011), Trump's key trade policy advisor Peter Navarro attacks China for its "weapons of job destruction" that kill American manufacturing jobs. According to this narrative, foreign nations are practising unfair competition and this is a key driver of the US trade deficit. The USA is a victim of these practices and a main role for trade agreements is to secure a level playing field and re-establish fair competition.

In the following, we show that if the narrative of Navarro is to be right, almost the whole world has to be cheaters and crooks: China has contributed to the US trade deficit but is hardly the main driver. As an illustration, we show the US trade balance in goods with the world and the world without China. For the purpose, we calculate simple *net export ratios* (sometimes called Balassa indexes) of the form $100 * (x - m)/(x + m)$, where x is exports and m imports. This index varies between minus 100 (only imports) and 100 (only exports). Using trade data from the United Nations Commodity Trade Statistics Database (COMTRADE), retrieved using the World Integrated Trade Solution (WITS) software, Fig. 7.1 shows the index for US trade with the world, with and without China.[1]

The two curves in Fig. 7.1 coincide fully until 1990; later there is some divergence. After 1990, China contributed to a larger trade deficit, but the major trend over time is similar with and without China. This illustrates that the US trade deficit cannot be caused generally or mainly by unfair trade practices by China, it is a common trend that applies to US trade in general. For example, the "Reagonomics" of the 1980s (tax cuts and large defence spending) made the USA spend too much and increased the deficit (see e.g. Chinn et al. 2011). The dollar's role as a reserve

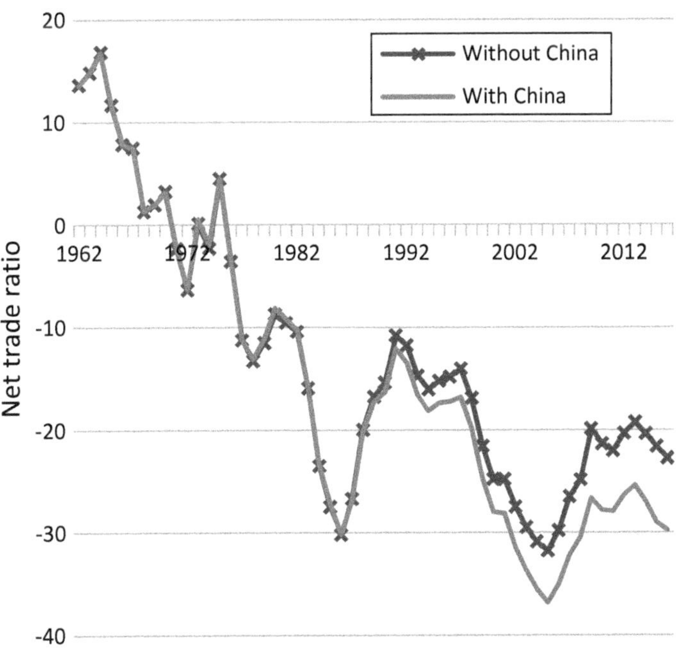

Fig. 7.1 The US trade balance in goods 1962–2017, with and without China. Net trade ratios. (Data source: WITS/COMTRADE)

currency is also a key issue (see e.g. Blinder 1996). Since current account deficits must be matched by capital account surpluses, capital movements and macroeconomic developments are important (see e.g. Gourinchas and Rey 2014). The US trade deficit is more an exchange rate and macroeconomic issue than a trade policy issue (see e.g. Bergsten and Gagnon 2017).

Figure 7.2 presents the same data from a slightly different angle, showing similar net export ratios for the USA goods trade with China (the lower curve) and the world except China (the upper curve) during 1990–2016.

The striking parallelism of the two curves in Fig. 7.2 suggests that there were common drivers behind the deficit that were not specific to China or other individual countries. A Navarro-type explanation would be that the whole world became more "crooked" during 1990–2005, but this is an unlikely explanation—with the World Trade Organization (WTO) entering the scene in 1995 and tightening trade disciplines.

Why does China add to the deficit in Fig. 7.1 while the relative deficit in Fig. 7.2 does not change so much? The simple reason is China's growth:

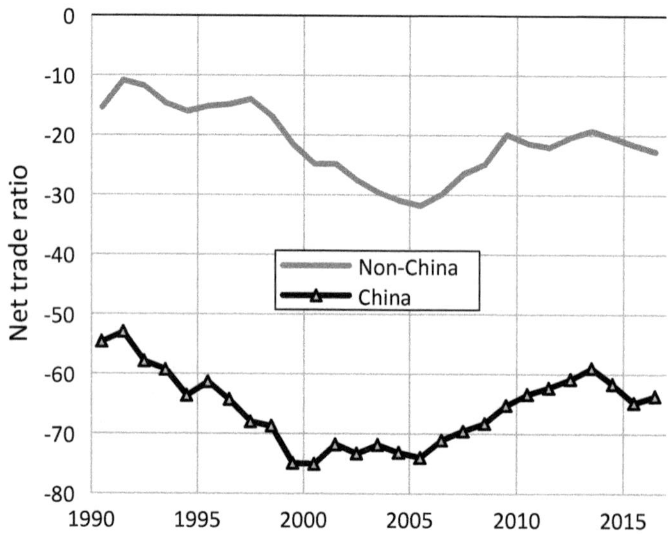

Fig. 7.2 The US trade balance in goods during 1990–2016 with China and the world except China. Net trade ratios. (Data source: WITS/COMTRADE)

It was mainly the changing size of China that led to a larger deficit, not a deterioration in the relative position of the USA. Since 1990, China has grown rapidly and become more productive. The growth of China is the course of history and not the result of trade agreements with China, even if market access has played a role. WTO membership and market access were of importance to China, but Chinese growth was mainly driven by more fundamental aspects such as massive investments in productive capacity and infrastructure (for a discussion, see e.g. World Bank 2013). China's growth has eliminated poverty on a large scale and has been good for the world.

In trade with China, there are certainly some real issues about intellectual property rights (IPR); the rule of law versus communist leadership; the practices and capital access of state-owned companies and so on. We do not consider these as irrelevant but show above that these were hardly the main reasons underlying the US trade deficit. Trade agreements also provide instruments for settling conflicts in these areas in a peaceful way; for example, the WTO has its TRIPS (Trade-Related Intellectual Property Rights) agreement, which is exactly what is needed to address IPR issues with China. As noted, the trade deficit is more of an exchange rate and macroeconomic issue than a trade policy issue, and so trade war is hardly the best medicine.

7.2 The Impact of China's Growth: The Pains and the Gains

In order to gain more knowledge on the impact of China's growth on the world economy, we use the model presented in Chap. 6 and Appendix B. As an experiment, we shrink China to its 1990 level, while the rest of the world stays like in 2014. This is historically not realistic since the rest of the world also changed during this period, but it allows us to isolate and shed light on the impact of China's growth. We have data for China (at the province level) back to 1990 for key variables, and that is the reason for choosing this period. From 1990 to 2014, China's labour force grew by 26%; the natural resource stock increased about five-fold and the capital stock increased six-fold. Hence there was some "extensive growth", but the predominant change was the increase in the non-labour endowments. For China, natural resource rents as a share of Gross Domestic Product (GDP) were at 3% in 1990, and increased to 4% in 2014. In the light of China's fast growth, there was a rapid growth also in its commodity sector even if China is a net importer of commodities.

Comparing the artificial scenario with China shrunk to its 1990 level to the base scenario, we reverse the signs and so we express the impact of China's growth. The complete results for all the 110 regions are shown in Appendix Table C.9. Figure 7.3 shows the impact of China's growth, aggregated for world regions (Asia is this time without China) for some main variables: The number of manufacturing firms; nominal wages; and real income per capita. For constructing the world region averages, nominal wages are weighted by the labour force, and welfare is weighted by population.

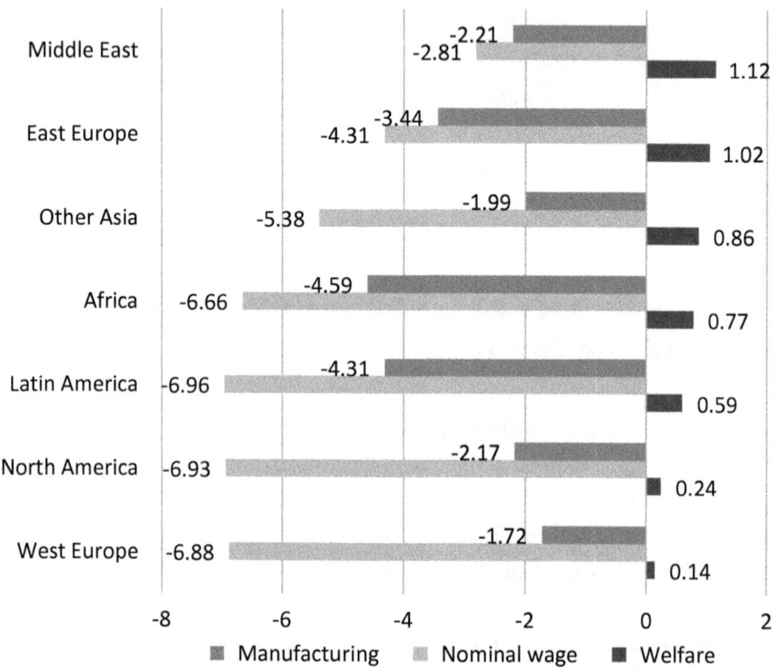

Fig. 7.3 The impact of China's growth on other world regions. Changes from base scenario for manufacturing, wages and welfare. (Source: Own calculations. Results from numerical simulation)

Figure 7.3 suggests there was a gain but also some pains: All other regions have a gain in welfare (real income per capita). At the same time, all regions face a downward pressure on nominal wages and a reduction in the number of manufacturing firms. Because of China's growth, the global number of manufacturing firms increases by 16%, but all of this growth and more is taken by China—almost quadrupling its number of manufacturing firms (285% growth). For the rest of the world, there is a 2.4% reduction in the number of manufacturing firms.

Why does the impact across world regions vary so much? A closer look reveals that *commodity abundance* and *proximity to China* are the most important drivers.

Commodity exporters obtain a larger welfare gain than others, but also face stronger decline in manufacturing production. On the other hand, the downward pressure on wages is more limited, the higher is the share of natural resource rents in GDP. Chinese growth bids up commodity prices and the "spending effect" in commodity-reliant countries bids up their wages, relative to the rest. An example is Norway: Even Western Europe has a bleak performance according to Fig. 7.3; Chinese growth creates a welfare gain for Norway at 0.93%—compared to 0.14% for Western Europe as a whole. In North America, Alaska tops the ranking for gains as well as predicted manufacturing decline. This variation across regions and countries for North America and Europe is shown in Figs. 7.4 and 7.5, respectively. In the USA, the eastern regions and US lakes have the least to gain from China's growth. In Europe, we find all the large nations except Poland at the bottom of the list.

Hence natural resource abundance is a key determinant of the China impact. The second key driver is proximity to China: Countries far from China face a larger wage decline and gain less in welfare or nominal GDP from China's growth. In this way, the model and results provide an underpinning of "growth spillover effects" that are empirically supported in the growth literature (Roberts and Deichmann 2011): If your neighbour grows, your own growth will also increase. This also illustrates the properties of the model. Advantages in market access can show up in trade effects and specialisation (net exports of scale-based goods, as in Krugman 1980) or in wage effects (higher wages in regions with better location, see Melchior 2009 for a discussion). According to Head and Mayer (2004),

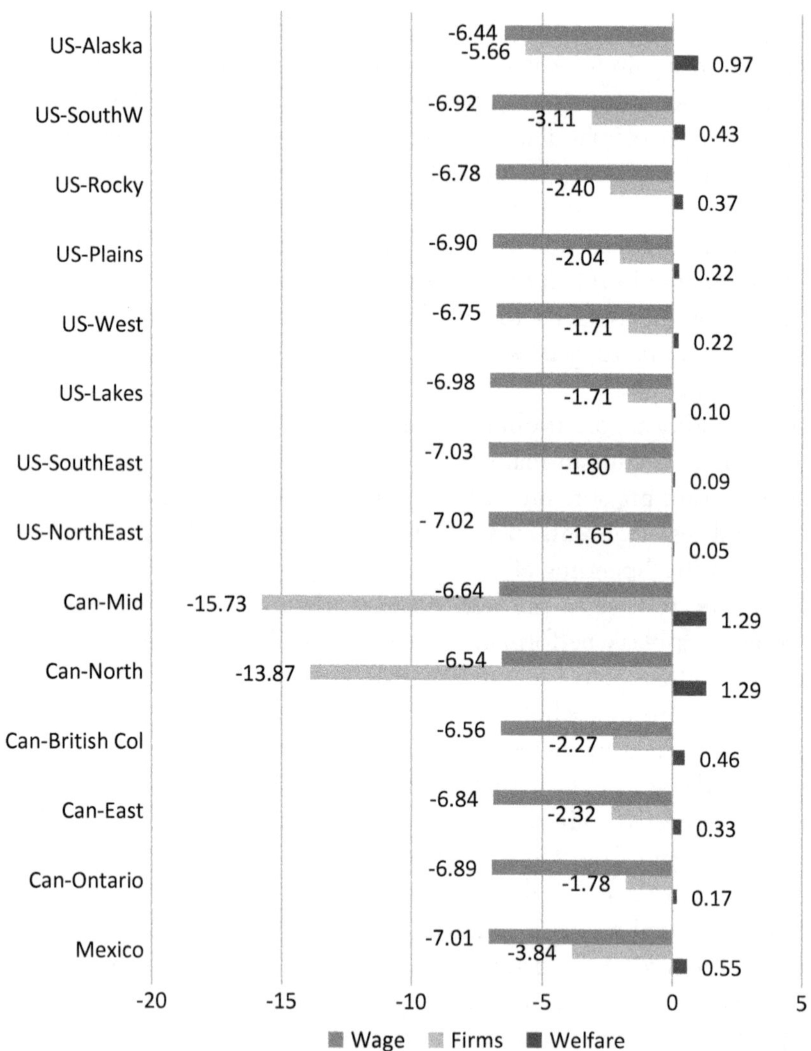

Fig. 7.4 The impact of China's growth on North American regions. (Source: Own calculations. Results from numerical simulation)

the empirical support is stronger for wage effects. Our model combines specialisation effects between commodities and manufacturing, and terms-of-trade and wage effects driven by all interactions in the model. When China grows, it is a locational advantage to be closer to this, and

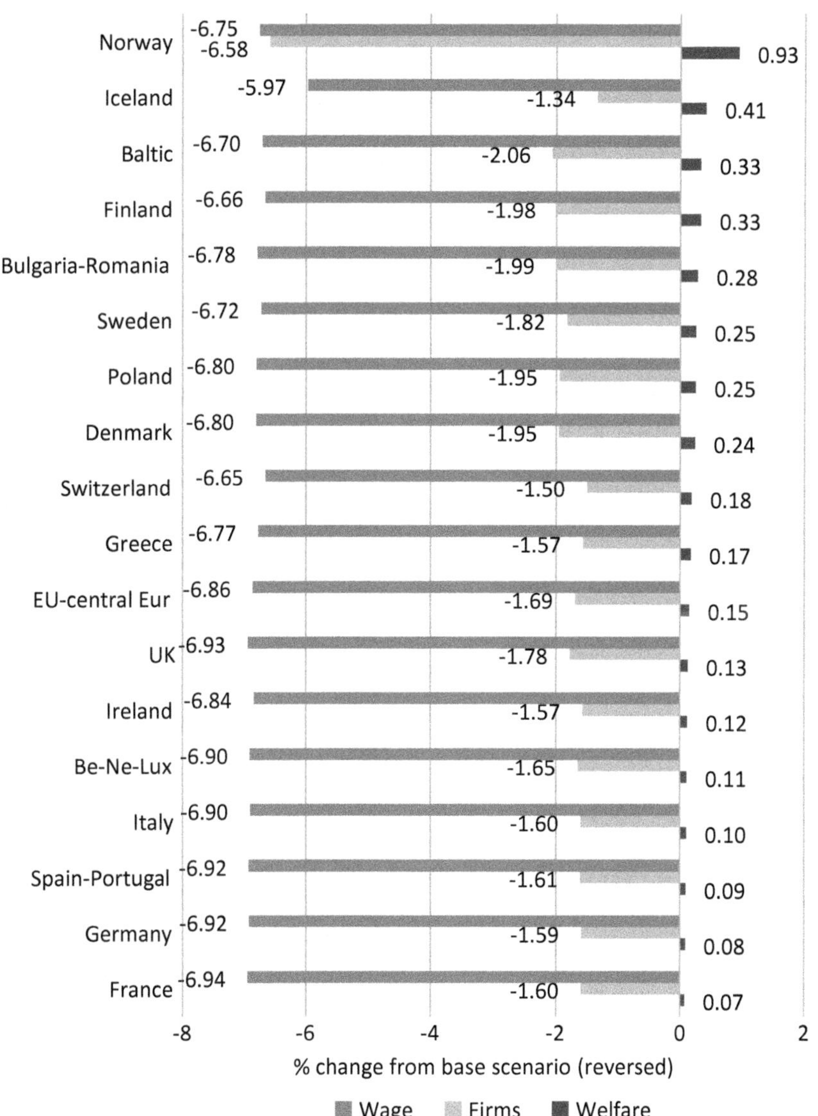

Fig. 7.5 The impact of China's growth on European countries. (Source: Own calculations. Results from numerical simulation)

the model suggests that there is such a growth spillover effect; and not a "crowding out" effect in manufacturing for countries close to China.

In order to check the drivers underlying the China impact more systematically, we regress the predicted changes for some endogenously determined variables on country/region characteristics. The results are shown in Table 7.1.

Natural resource abundance is measured by the G/L ratio and the strong impact of this variable is confirmed; negative for manufacturing and positive for wages, nominal GDP and welfare. For distance to China, there is no significant impact for manufacturing, but a negative effect for wages, GDP and welfare. Hence countries close to China gain more welfare from China's growth and have a weaker negative impact on wages and nominal GDP.

The K/L ratio is included to check whether Chinese manufacturing growth "crowds" out richer countries that have larger manufacturing production. We do not find any such effect; on the contrary, there is a slight positive impact of China's growth for manufacturing. The K/L variables have no measurable impact on the wage, GDP and welfare effects from China's growth. We also included country size, measured by the labour stock L, but this variable was insignificant in all regressions and was dropped.

Table 7.1 also includes "Trade cost reciprocity", which is measured as the difference between trade costs for exports to China, minus trade costs

Table 7.1 What determines the impact of China's economic growth?

Independent variables: country/region characteristics	Dependent variable (change from 1990 to 2014, according to model simulations)			
	Wage	GDP	Welfare	Manufacturing
K/L ratio	0.01	0.01	0.00	0.48*
G/L ratio	0.83***	0.85***	0.22***	−7.39***
Distance to China (in logs)	−1.24***	−1.09***	−0.36***	−1.17
Trade cost reciprocity	−2.68*	−3.33**	−1.27***	4.66
Adjusted R^2	0.70	0.74	0.66	0.44
Observations	102	102	102	91

Source: Own calculations based on results from numerical simulation

Note: The number of observations is lower when Manufacturing is a dependent variable, since 11 regions/countries are fully specialised. *, ** and *** indicate significant at the 10%, 5% and 1% levels, respectively; entries with no asterisks are statistically not significant

for imports from China (average for the eight Chinese regions in the model). Rich countries have lower tariffs and better infrastructure, and so they tend to have higher costs for exports to China than for imports from China. From the results, we found that trade cost reciprocity matters; countries with more non-reciprocity have lower welfare gains from China's growth, and that they face a stronger downward pressure on wages and nominal GDP. So Trump may have a point on the lack of reciprocity; however, it is by no means due to trade agreements since the majority of countries have no FTAs with China. On the contrary, FTAs with China may contribute to more reciprocity, by reducing tariffs in China as well as non-tariff barriers. China's WTO membership also led to a considerable trade reform in China, with lower tariffs and market opening. According to this, one should search for more trade agreements and not less, in order to eliminate the lack of reciprocity.

Beyond these drivers, the variation across countries is affected by "idiosyncratic" aspects—especially related to the characteristics of neighbour regions. For example, if your neighbour is deindustrialised due to China's growth, it will be good for your own manufacturing production since it creates a new market opportunity. Because of such "contextual" phenomena and interactions, there is considerable variation in the China effect across individual countries or regions. For example, in North America, the China boost of Alaska may affect the outcome for Northern and Western parts of Canada and be an explanation for why they come out on top for Canada in Fig. 7.4.

Our model simulations therefore suggest that the world has benefited from China's growth and experienced a welfare gain. But there is also a pain, and for major industrial nations the gains are small but the pains larger. Our model therefore also shed some light on the "fear of China" observed in some Western countries, and why it may be more pronounced in some countries and regions.

7.3 The Impact of Trade Integration: Simulation Results for the USA

We argued above that there is some basis for President Trump's "fear of China", but it is a fallacy that "trade agreements" is the culprit. On the contrary, trade agreements could actually be part of the solution, adding welfare as well as jobs in the traded sector. In order to examine more systematically whether this is the case, we present in the following some simulation results for US trade integration with various world regions. Using the same model as before, we undertake the following experiment: Trade costs in manufacturing are reduced by ten percentage points between the USA and five selected regions, one after the other: North American Free Trade Agreement (NAFTA), EU, European Free Trade Association (EFTA), South America and Asia/Oceania. We also run a scenario where such a reduction in trade costs is undertaken between the USA and all these regions at the same time. Finally, we also show a scenario where trade liberalisation is non-reciprocal: Trade costs are reduced by ten percentage points for imports into the USA from all these five regions, but there is no reduction in the other direction. This scenario illustrates the importance of reciprocity, or the lack thereof, in international trade relations—following up on the discussion in Sect. 7.2.

Observe that the scenarios do not rest on assumptions about what is feasible and not, or whether it applies to the past or the future. We make no attempt to quantify the magnitude of trade barrier reduction in neither NAFTA nor Transatlantic Trade and Investment Partnership (TTIP), we just ask: If cuts are equivalent to ten percentage points, what is the impact? The model captures the role of geography, country size, whether countries are rich or poor, and whether they are commodity exporters or not. In order to interpret the results, observe that in such a model with imperfect competition in manufacturing, regional integration has a "production-shifting" effect from third countries (Baldwin and Venables 1995). This is a main reason why trade integration in most cases not only gives a real income gain, but also an increase in manufacturing production.

Figure 7.6 shows the change in real income and the number of manufacturing firms for the USA in the seven scenarios. Figure 7.6 shows the corresponding changes for the trade partners involved in integration in each scenario. In Appendix Tables C.10 (real income) and C.11 (manufacturing), we show the results for all the 110 countries and regions. In Fig. 7.6, we have aggregated results for all the eight US regions. The same applies to Canada-NAFTA in Fig. 7.7.

For all cases with reciprocal trade integration, there is a gain in welfare as well as manufacturing production. The welfare gain is due to higher income, lower trade costs, lower prices and greater diversity in consumption.

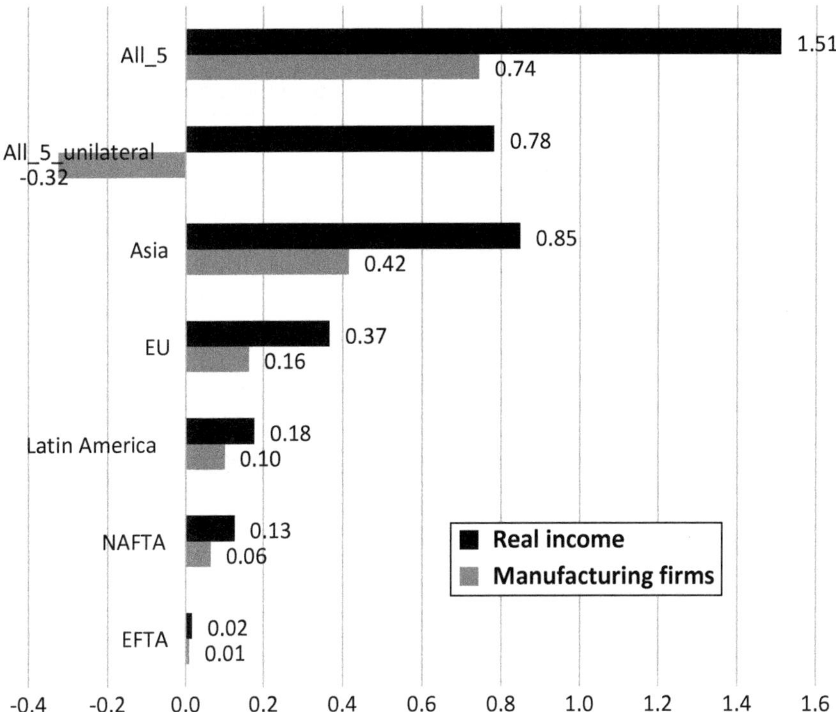

Fig. 7.6 Impact for the USA of trade integration with other world regions. Percentage change from base case. (Source: Own results based on numerical simulation)

Improved market access and production shifting from third countries contribute to larger manufacturing production.

The partners also gain from trade integration with the USA, especially the smaller trading nation—EFTA is included to show this size asymmetry: Smaller countries gain more from integrating with large partners. The more FTAs matter for the USA, the less they matter for the trade partners involved. According to the model, there is therefore a size asymmetry effect in trade policy. Only TTIP (the USA-EU integration scenario) is balanced in this sense, with equal interest on both sides. For NAFTA, the model provides a potential rationale for the revised US bottom line under President Trump. For small countries, it would be a bad thing if trade policy becomes big power politics.

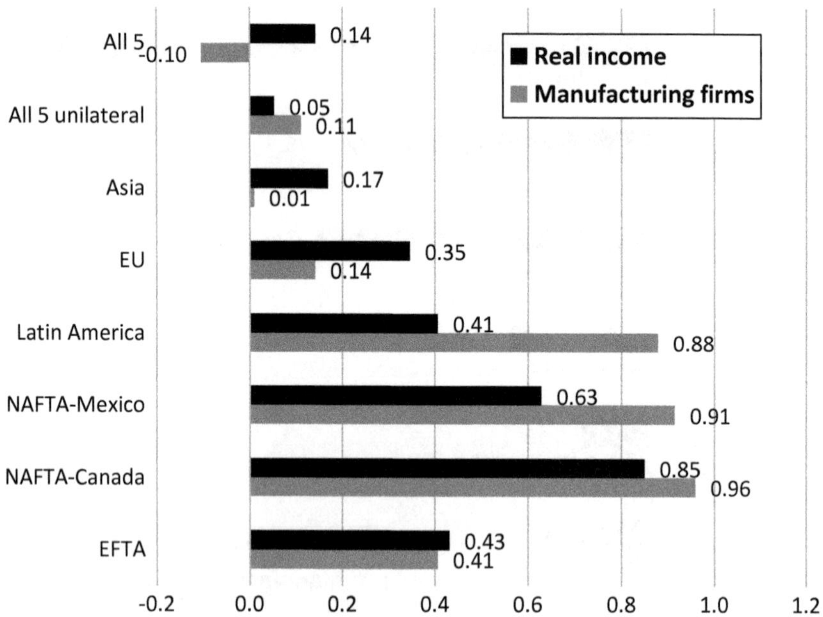

Fig. 7.7 Impact of US trade integration with other world regions, for the trade partners involved. Percentage change from base case. (Source: Own results based on numerical simulation)

According to the simulation results, reciprocity in liberalisation is a precondition for manufacturing growth. In the case with unilateral US liberalisation, there is a contraction in US manufacturing. Non-reciprocal trade liberalisation has an impact similar to China's growth (shown in Sect. 7.2): Cheaper shirts and fewer manufacturing firms. But if trade agreements are reciprocal, as they normally are, they are part of the solution and not the problem. Future trade agreements can make trade policies more reciprocal: For example, the USA has lower tariffs than China (or Mexico before NAFTA), and so an FTA would create more reciprocity.[2]

Observe also that due to the growth of Asia, this is now the most important region in trade policy. This is shown by the ranking across scenarios in Fig. 7.5. Integration with Asia could promote welfare as well as jobs in the traded sector, and should not be feared as long as it is reciprocal. Asia is potentially much more important than NAFTA (if a similar level of integration can be achieved); the results also indicate that NAFTA is less beneficial (but still positive) for US manufacturing production. While Caliendo and Parro (2015) find a welfare loss for Canada due to NAFTA and a larger welfare gain for Mexico than for the USA, the model used here suggests that trade integration with the USA should be positive for Canada as well as Mexico. Observe that the simulations here just quantify the impact of a certain level of trade cost reduction, without assessing what level of trade cost reduction that has actually been undertaken or may be undertaken in the future. Transatlantic trade integration between the USA and the EU would also have a significant positive impact if it succeeds; larger than what the USA would obtain from integrating with all of Latin America (beyond Mexico). EFTA is small in this context and seen from the US side the gains from trade integration are small, but for EFTA countries, integration with the USA could provide a significant welfare gain, in the range of 0.4–0.6% of GDP.

The idea that unfair trade practices is a key explanation of the US trade deficit, and that the problem can be fixed by more restrictive trade policies, is therefore not supported by our analysis. On the contrary, trade agreements with reciprocal liberalisation are beneficial to the USA and therefore "part of the solution". It should also be recalled that if the USA drops out of the "FTA race", other countries might instead benefit from the "production shifting", and even more US jobs will get lost. With the cancellation of TPP membership, the USA lags behind in the global race for FTAs (Chap. 3), and its modest number of FTAs with key trade partners could be part of the explanation for the industrial decline of the USA.

Notes

1. Data source: United Nations Commodity Trade Statistics Database (COMTRADE). Observe that import data include cost, insurance and freight, while export data do not. When trade is balanced, the net trade ratio will therefore be slightly negative. This should be observed but is not a problem here since we focus on the trend over time and the comparison of the two curves.
2. We also run simulations of unilateral US liberalisation in NAFTA. Also in this case there was a welfare gain but contraction in US manufacturing. For brevity, these results are not reported here.

References

Baldwin, R., & Venables, A. J. (1995). Regional Economic Integration. In G. M. Grossmann & K. Rogoff (Eds.), *Handbook of International Economics* (Vol. 3, pp. 1243–2107, Chapter 31, pp. 1597–1644). Amsterdam: North-Holland.

Bergsten, C. F., & Gagnon, J. E. (2017). *Currency Conflict and Trade Policy: A New Strategy for the United States*. Washington, DC: Peterson Institute for International Economics.

Blinder, A. S. (1996). The Role of the Dollar as an International Currency. *Eastern Economic Journal, 22*(2), 127–136.

Caliendo, L., & Parro, F. (2015). Estimates of the Trade and Welfare Effects of NAFTA. *The Review of Economic Studies, 82*(1), 1–44.

Chinn, M. D., Eichengreen, B., & Ito, H. (2011). *A Forensic Analysis of Global Imbalances* (National Bureau of Economic Research Working Paper 17513). http://www.nber.org

Gourinchas, P., & Rey, H. (2014). External Adjustment, Global Imbalances, Valuation Effects. In G. Gopinath, E. Helpman, & K. Rogoff (Eds.), *Handbooks in Economics, International Economics* (Vol. 4, Chapter 10, pp. 583–645). Amsterdam/Oxford: North-Holland/Elsevier.

Head, K., & Mayer, T. (2004). The Empirics of Agglomeration and Trade. In J. V. Henderson & J. Thisse (Eds.), *Handbook of Regional and Urban Economics. Volume 4, Cities and Geography* (Chapter 29, pp. 2609–2669). Amsterdam: Elsevier.

Krugman, P. (1980). Scale Economies, Product Differentiation, and the Pattern of Trade. *American Economic Review, 70*(5), 950–959.

Melchior, A. (2009). *European Integration and Domestic Regions. A Numerical Simulation Analysis*. Warsaw: CASE Studies and Analyses No. 378/ 2009.

Navarro, P., & Autry, G. (2011). *Death by China. Confronting the Dragon—A Global Call to Action*. Upper Saddle River: Pearson Education.

Roberts, M., & Deichmann, U. (2011). International Growth Spillovers, Geography and Infrastructure. *The World Economy, 34*(9), 1507–1533.

World Bank. (2013). *China 2030. Building a Modern, Harmonious, and Creative Society*. Washington, DC: World Bank/Development Research Center of the State Council, the People's Republic of China.

8

Global Versus Local Integration and Europe's Options

The counting of Free Trade Agreements (FTAs) in Chap. 3 showed that more and more FTAs span across continents or world regions and not only within these regions. Chapter 4 showed that for goods tariffs, FTAs are generally ambitious—even the inter-regional ones. Chapter 5, on the other hand, showed that beyond tariffs, the majority of FTAs are relatively shallow. A minority of FTAs are deep also in the non-tariff areas, but these are mainly within world regions. The analysis thereby suggests that deep integration beyond tariffs is feasible within regions but more difficult beyond, in spite of the proliferation of FTAs across continents.

In this chapter, we ask: How much is there to gain from FTAs across world regions, compared to intra-regional integration? In Chap. 7, we saw that with an equal reduction in trade costs in all cases, the USA could gain more from integrating with Asia or Western Europe, compared to integration with its partners in the North American Free Trade Agreement (NAFTA). Is that because Canada and Mexico constitute a relatively small part of the world economy? Will a similar conclusion apply to Europe? Should Europe reach out to the world rather than search for even deeper intra-European integration? Are the "Brexiteers" on the right track here—aiming for FTAs across the globe?

A. Melchior, *Free Trade Agreements and Globalisation*,
https://doi.org/10.1007/978-3-319-92834-0_8

As in Chap. 7, we do not attempt to measure what is feasible or not; we compare the impact of a certain reduction in trade costs. The results should be interpreted in the light of the findings in Chaps. 3, 4 and 5 and to what extent deep integration is feasible or not. Comparing this chapter with evidence from earlier chapters, there is an emerging "globalisation paradox": Global integration is rewarding and perhaps necessary, but a "high hanging fruit" that is not always feasible. But if integration across world regions is feasible, this chapter shows that it can be more rewarding than intra-regional integration. Intra-regional integration is also welfare-enhancing, and we find that Asia, and surprisingly Africa, are the world regions that have the most to gain from intra-regional economic integration. The commodity regions have relatively less to gain from integration in their neighbourhood. Commodity trade is more global than manufacturing trade (Chap. 2), and this chapter shows that commodity-exporting countries and regions, for example, Russia, should "go global" also in trade policy. Global trade integration contributes to industrial diversification in commodity-exporting countries, and it makes sense for them to engage in FTAs. Small countries have more to gain from global trade integration than other countries, and poor countries have no reason to fear free trade but should participate.

Along with Chap. 7, we show that non-reciprocal trade integration may contribute to a "cheap shirts, fewer jobs" problem: If Europe lowers its trade barriers but not their trade partners, there may be a welfare gain from the cheaper imports, but a loss of manufacturing. In earlier chapters, we have seen that this is a result of history: Rich countries have liberalised more than the rest. We give President Trump one point for raising the issue of reciprocity in trade policy, and the analysis here supports some of the worries. On the other hand, FTAs are not the problem: They are part of the solution. Most FTAs contribute to convergence of trade costs between partners; whereas the lack of trade agreements allows non-reciprocity. Some lack of reciprocity in trade policy is deliberate and allowed by the World Trade Organization (WTO), as a measure to support developing countries. We argue that poor countries also gain from trade liberalisation, and so the best treatment is actually not to be exempted from all trade rules.

8.1 The Impact of Global Trade Liberalisation

As a platform for interpreting FTAs and regional integration scenarios later, it is instructive to consider a globalisation scenario where all trade barriers in the world are reduced in the same proportion. Assuming that all trade barriers between our 110 countries and regions are cut by 30%, Appendix Table C.12 shows results for the main variables. Observe that trade costs include tariffs, export/import costs, infrastructure costs and transport costs, and all these are reduced. The percentage point reduction in trade costs will be higher if initial trade costs are large, and this affects the outcome.

With global integration, we do not have the trade diversion and production-shifting effects of regional integration that we observed in Chap. 7. Global integration is more equitable than selective FTAs, and we find that all countries in the world gain from global liberalisation, in the range of 1.7–3.8%. There is a modest redistribution of manufacturing production, with a maximum reduction of 1% and a maximum gain of 7%. Within Europe, the large countries Germany, France and the UK are the only ones losing some manufacturing. Interestingly, India and China also loses some manufacturing. The following discussion sheds light on the reasons.

The model we use has rather complex interactions between country characteristics, trade costs and geography, and every scenario provides a complete "synthetic world" with production, trade, wages and prices. Due to this complexity, it is not always straightforward to interpret results, and for individual countries there may be "idiosyncratic" effects due to the combination of location and other effects. It matters a lot whether you are surrounded by "Alaskas", "Shanghais" or "Lesothos". In order to see more clearly what drives these results, we regress the predicted changes for wages, welfare and manufacturing on country/region characteristics. Table 8.1 shows the results.

For nominal wages and welfare, adjusted R^2 is rather high, suggesting that these variables are largely driven by generic effects in the model. The impact on manufacturing is however much more "idiosyncratic", with much lower explained variation, and determined in a complex interaction of geography and country/region characteristics.

Table 8.1 Global trade liberalisation—determinants of effect on wages, welfare and manufacturing production

Independent variables	Dependent variable (change from base scenario)		
	Nominal wage	Welfare	Manufacturing firms
Intercept	−6.00*** (<0.0001)	−0.06 (0.7836)	−1.51* (0.0550)
Size (L)	−9.63E-07*** (<0.0001)	−4.43E-07*** (<0.0001)	−6.83E-07*** (0.0062)
K/L ratio	−0.03 (0.1212)	−0.02** (0.0298)	−0.03 (0.5560)
Natural resources (G/L)	0.10* (0.0863)	−0.00 (0.6481)	1.18*** (<0.0001)
Average import cost	1.40*** (0.0053)	3.77*** (<0.0001)	3.48*** (0.0034)
Average export cost	11.01*** (<0.0001)	1.25** (0.0143)	Not included
Observations	98	110	98
Adjusted R^2	0.842	0.916	0.416

Source: Own calculations, based on results from numerical simulation
Note: P values in brackets. Asterisks indicate whether estimates are significantly different from zero at the 1% level (***); 5% level (**) or 10% level (*)

Country size, measured by the labour stock L, is a key driver, with all three columns highly significant and negative, indicating that global trade liberalisation is relatively better for small countries. Perhaps this is an explanation why we find Chile, European Free Trade Association (EFTA) countries and Singapore on top of the FTA ranking in Chap. 3—these small countries benefit from global liberalisation and have a reason to be in the frontline of the FTA race, and to be stark defenders of the global trade system. It is also a main part of the explanation for why some large countries lose manufacturing in this scenario.

A second key driver is trade costs, especially import costs that are positive and significant for all three variables. Poor countries gain more from global integration because they have high trade costs. If trade costs are dropped from the regressions, the "richness" variable K/L becomes strongly significant and negative, suggesting that poor countries gain more from liberalisation. This is mainly a spurious result, due to the omitted trade cost variables. When the trade cost variables are included, the explained variation is much higher, and only a slight pro-poor effect of liberalisation survives for the welfare variable. This is a second indication that poor countries should not fear trade liberalisation. Hence income levels as such, to the extent they are driven by the K/L variable, do not strongly condition the effects of trade liberalisation, and to the extent they do, the impact is pro-poor according to our simulations. Since poor countries generally have higher trade barriers, they are likely to gain more from liberalisation.

This sunny story about poor countries and trade liberalisation is paradoxical in the context of the "Special and Differential Treatment" (SDT) of the WTO. As noted in Chap. 4, SDT allows positive tariff discrimination. SDT has also included longer transition periods for developing countries, and some other trade rules have SDT built in; for example, patent duration in the TRIPs (Trade-Related Intellectual Property Rights) Agreement. WTO also promotes aid-for-trade; for example, technical assistance to improve trade institutions such as customs. Some of the SDT is well motivated and some SDT measures aim to address gaps that our model does not capture at all—such as structural adjustment problems or the importance of tariffs as a source of revenue. It is still a paradox that if trade is as nice as everyone says, how can the best treatment be exemption from liberalisation? As seen in the discussion on tariffs, many poor countries put the credibility of the WTO into question by insisting on bound tariffs at very high levels. Such pro-poor politics rest on a misunderstanding, and the results here suggest that it would not be improper to request greater commitments from the poor countries.

Table 8.1 also shows that for countries with large natural resources, global liberalisation has a diversifying effect—promoting manufacturing production. For wages and welfare, the G/L ratio is not significant or just weakly so (for wages there is a weak positive effect). The positive impact on manufacturing in resource-rich countries is a surprise; in a Heckscher-Ohlin-type setting one expects that trade liberalisation promotes further specialisation—the opposite of what we observe here. In general, the complex interaction between all the model variables in a setting with many countries and regions can create non-standard results. The purpose of using a quasi-realistic global model is to capture these interactions.[1] Also in other results, we find this diversification impact for commodity exporting countries; for example, for Alaska in the context of US integration or Norway in the context of European FTAs.

For wages and welfare, Table 8.1 suggests that resource-rich countries are at least not worse off compared to other countries, and so their welfare gain is as large as for industrial countries. Here the mini-simulations with few countries (Appendix B, Appendix Table C.1) suggest an even more positive result—liberalisation is even more positive for welfare in resource-rich countries. In the model, trade in commodities is costless and so liberalisation is only for manufactures. But more manufacturing trade may generate more commodity trade and a terms-of-trade gain that add to the welfare gain for resource-rich countries, in addition to the direct gains from cheaper and more diversified manufacturing imports.

8.2 European Integration Options

Western Europe is a long-standing success story about regional integration, from the Rome Treaty of 1957 to the current deep integration. Combining deep integration with peace and stability, the value of trade integration has broad support. But the world has changed, with comparatively slower growth in the Organisation for Economic Co-operation and Development (OECD) countries and a massive expansion in Asia. It is plain intuition that trade policy has to take this change into account and reach out for stronger ties with Asia. Or is there something to fear from letting China even more into the European markets—will more manufacturing jobs get lost? And how much will Europe lose if the plans for TTIP (Transatlantic Trade and Investment Partnership) are eventually called off? The TTIP negotiations were put on halt when President Trump was elected in 2016, but by early 2018 they had not been formally and finally discontinued. At the time of writing, they are still in the freezer, although some discussion exists on new plans for the transatlantic trade partnership (Hamilton 2018).

In order to shed light on European trade options, using the world trade model in Appendix B, we simulate the following integration scenarios:

- Trade integration within Western Europe (including the EU and European Free Trade Association (EFTA)).
- Six scenarios where Western Europe integrates with the six other world regions (North America, South America, Africa, Middle East, Eastern Europe and Asia/Pacific).

- Two scenarios where trade barriers are lowered in relation to all other world regions; in both directions (World Integration) or non-reciprocal (Non-reciprocal World Integration). This is different from global liberalisation since all liberalisation is between Europe and the other regions, and not between the other regions; for example, between Asia and Africa, trade costs remain unchanged.

As explained in Appendix B, trade barriers in the numerical model include four components; tariffs, infrastructure, export-import costs and distance-related costs. In the simulations undertaken here, we assume that tariffs are eliminated; distance-related costs are reduced by one-fourth; export-import costs are cut by half; and infrastructure costs remain unchanged. Since reductions are in proportion to initial costs, trade agreements will realistically create more reciprocity by cutting higher trade costs more in absolute terms. With this methodology, trade cost reductions are in the range of 30–37% of initial trade costs for the inter-regional agreements and 27% for intra-European integration. The initial levels and reductions are shown in Appendix Table C.12. We are assuming a substantial reduction in trade costs. It is also ambitious to assume that all countries in each region engage in integration in the same way and at the same time. For the EU and EFTA, it would take many years to obtain FTAs with all countries in, for example, the Asia/Pacific. Our aim here is to shed light on the broad economic proportions rather than the details, and in the model we can do it all in one shot. What is feasible in the real world is another matter.

As earlier, we report, for each scenario, the changes from the base scenario for nominal wages, welfare (real income per capita) and the number of manufacturing firms. The results for the three variables are reported in Appendix Tables C.14–C-16. Results for price levels and nominal Gross Domestic Product (GDP) are not reported but these are highly correlated with results for the nominal wages. In the following, we show aggregated results for all of Western Europe. There is some variation across countries and this can be studied in Appendix C. Figure 8.1 shows the impact on Western Europe in the different scenarios. Figure 8.2 shows the impact for the integration partner or partners in each case/scenario; for example, for Western Europe-Asia integration, we show the results for Asia, and so on.

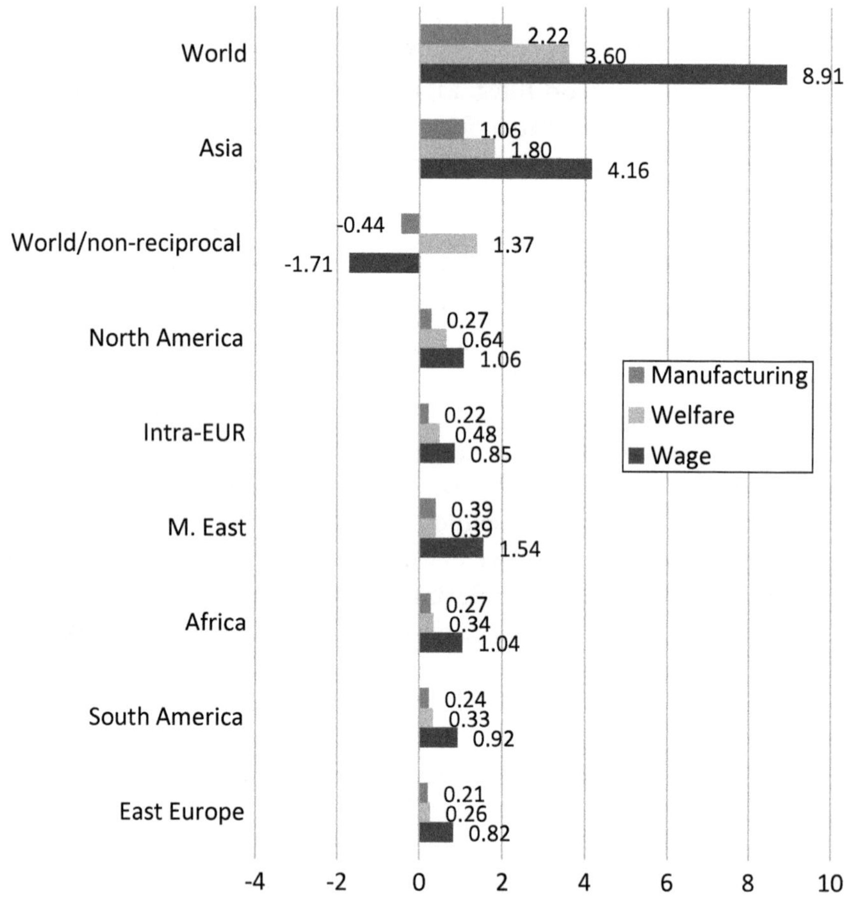

Fig. 8.1 The impact for Western Europe of trade integration with different world regions. Changes from the base scenario in percent. (Source: Own calculations. Results from numerical simulation)

The two figures only show results for countries participating in integration; results for third countries are presented in the Appendix C. For third countries, there is generally a slight negative impact of regional integration, due to the "production-shifting" effect of trade discrimination. From a closer look at Appendix Tables C.14–C.16, we find that the impact on third countries is zero or negative for all third countries with respect to wages or manufacturing production, and zero or negative in most cases for

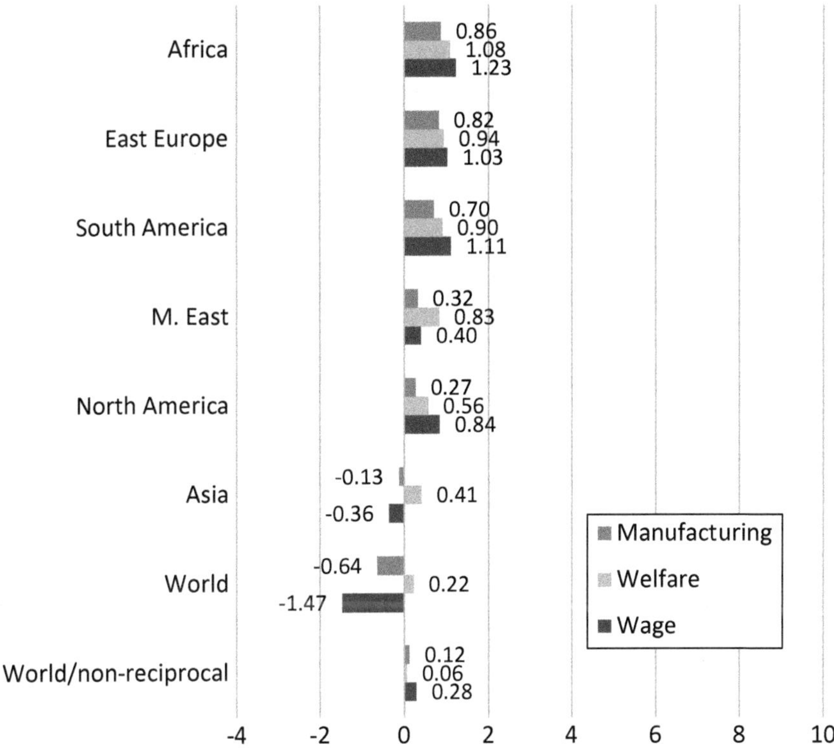

Fig. 8.2 The impact for the respective integration partners of trade integration between Western Europe and different world regions. Changes from the base scenario in percent. (Source: Own calculations. Results from numerical simulations)

welfare. For welfare, we also find third countries that gain, but the maximum gain is 0.01%. The negative effects are also mostly quite small. The maximum welfare loss for any outside country is the case of Moldova with Western Europe-Asia integration, at 0.38%. Moldova is situated closely to Western Europe and loses from the trade discrimination resulting from Western Europe-Asia integration. This stronger effect in the EU neighbourhood suggests that there is an "agglomeration shadow" resulting from trade integration, in the sense that geographically close outside countries have more to lose.[2]

Contrary to what is the case for outsiders, Figs. 8.1 and 8.2 show that there is always a welfare gain for the participating regions. A closer look at Appendix C confirms that it also holds for individual countries or regions: For Western Europe-Asia integration for example, every country or region gains welfare. In the multi-regional scenarios, this is no longer the case: Some countries lose. But also for multi-regional liberalisation, most countries gain and only a handful lose. Once more, the losers are found in Europe's vicinity, but the losses are small this time.

Considering the FTAs with other regions individually, Fig. 8.1 shows an interesting ranking: Western Europe can gain more from integrating with Asia and North America than with itself. As said, this is for a similar reduction in trade costs in all cases; if integration is ten times deeper in Europe, the ranking will be changed. But a key message remains, Asia's growth has moved the world's economic mass to the east, and economic integration with Asia can create large benefits. Trade integration with other regions is also of importance, and Fig. 8.1 shows the ranking.

In the analysis of US trade policy in Chap. 7, we found a size asymmetry in trade policy which is present also here. Africa, South America and Eastern Europe are at the bottom of the ranking for Western Europe, but at the top of Fig. 8.2: These are the regions that have most to gain from integrating with Europe.

In most of the region-to-region integration scenarios, there is production shifting from third countries so that manufacturing may increase in all participating countries. With Western Europe-Asia integration, however, this is no longer the case. The two regions comprise a large share of the world economy, and so there is less production outside to "shift", and there is some relocation of manufacturing inside the bloc. While all Western European countries increase their manufacturing production, the outcome is ambiguous for countries in Asia/Pacific and the majority of them face a falling number of manufacturing firms. Part of the explanation is also that trade integration creates more reciprocity; as seen from Appendix C.13, trade costs are higher for Europe's exports to Asia than in the other direction. Trade integration contributes to convergence, and the reduction in percentage points is the largest for Western Europe's exports to Asia.

The reciprocity and production-shifting issues are even more clearly illustrated by the multi-region scenarios. The World scenario involves the whole world, and so all partners get better market access in Europe and there is no gain from discrimination or production shifting for Europe's partners. On the other hand, Europe obtains new privileges in all other regions, and can increase its market share in each of the other regions, at the expense of other partner regions and third countries. The partner regions, on the other hand, have to "share the pie" in Western Europe in the multi-region "World" scenario. As a result of this hub-and-spoke pattern of integration, liberalisation leads to a manufacturing increase in Western Europe. The difference in inward and outward trade costs plays a similar role here. For Western Europe, integration gains are more or less additive, the more FTAs the more gains. The Western European gain in the World scenario is almost equal to the sum of gains from gains from FTAs with individual regions. For other world regions, there is manufacturing decline and wage reductions, in spite of a welfare gain from integration.

As for the US case in Chap. 7, Western Europe's gains from integration are considerably reduced if trade cost reduction is unilateral. If Western Europe unilaterally reduces her trade costs for imports, manufacturing and wages are reduced. There is still a welfare gain from cheaper imports, but a pain in the form of lower activity in manufacturing. As in Chap. 7, we find that reciprocity is a key issue in trade policy.

So we have to give President Trump a point for raising the issue of reciprocity in trade agreements. On the other hand, Mr. Trump has misunderstood the role of FTAs: These generally promote reciprocity rather than eliminating it. Reciprocity is a key issue for goods as well as services. For services, we have seen in Chap. 5 how OECD countries have promoted unilateral liberalisation. The same is the case for investment, although the model used here does not address it.

At the WTO, an issue is how much non-reciprocity should be allowed for developing countries. For rich countries, there is a cost of SDT and Fig. 8.2 suggests that this cost could be larger than the gain for the partner countries that benefit. The EU recently tightened its Generalised System of Preferences (GSP, see Chap. 3) system by eliminating upper-middle-income countries, and more or less nobody raised an eyebrow even if this was a breach of a 40 years tradition, including all middle-income countries in the group of developing countries that should benefit from GSP. With manufacturing decline in the West, it is perhaps the course of history that trade policy becomes more miserly. Poor countries have no reason to fear trade; so they may obtain larger benefits by more trade integration on their own, rather than relying on the mercy of the rich countries. For the world trade system, reciprocity may be more healthy than extensive SDT, with too many back-benchers at the WTO fighting to be exempted from the new trade rules.

8.3 Champions of Intra-regional Integration: A Chance for Africa?

As seen from Chap. 3, on the spread of FTAs, a large share of trade within world regions is already covered by FTAs, although some regions, especially Africa, are lagging behind. In Chap. 5, we have also seen that intra-regional FTAs are in some cases much deeper than the inter-regional ones. In this chapter, we examine how large gains that may be obtained from integration within the respective world regions. This depends on geography, income levels and country characteristics, and we will see that there is considerable variation across world regions. For these trade integration scenarios, we use the same method for trade cost reduction as in the preceding paragraph and obtain average trade cost reductions in the range of 25–40% within each region in the respective scenarios. The results for welfare are presented in Appendix Table C.18 for all countries and regions, and Appendix Table C.17 presents results aggregated by world region for wages, welfare, manufacturing production and prices.[3] Figure 8.3 shows results for the integrating regions, for intra-regional trade integration:

The regions are ranked by their welfare gains, and we find Asia on top, surprisingly followed by Africa. Asia is a large region with high economic density and manufacturing production, and so it is logical that gains from intra-regional integration are large. Africa is poorer and starts from a low level but trade costs are high and so trade cost reductions are larger. Along with earlier results, we find that the poor countries may also gain from trade. It is therefore good news that in March 2018, 44 African leaders signed the framework leading to the establishment of the African Continental Free Trade Area (AfCFTA).[4]

The commodity regions Middle East, South America and Eastern Europe have least to gain from intra-regional integration, mainly because liberalisation is for manufacturing, which has a lower share of gross

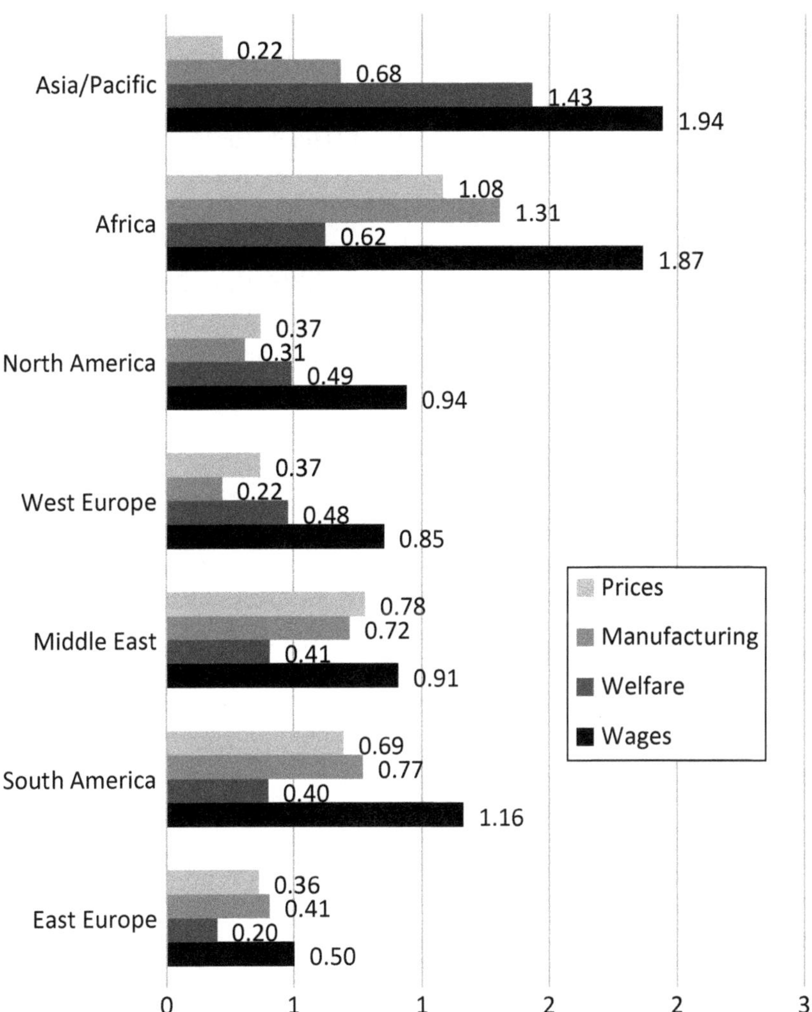

Fig. 8.3 The economic impact of intra-regional trade integration within world regions. (Source: Own calculations. Results from numerical simulation)

domestic product (GDP) in these regions. But also these regions gain from integration, and intra-regional FTAs will stimulate their manufacturing production. For Eastern Europe, low economic density is also an issue; with huge distances creating large trade costs within the region that limit trade and the trade potential from integration. The Eurasian

Economic Union (EAEU) is therefore no panacea, even if it will have a positive impact. We have already seen that for the USA and Europe, global integration is in principle more important than local integration. Although not included among the scenarios here, it is likely that for the commodity regions, the balance is even more strongly tilted towards global integration. For Eastern Europe, we see from Fig. 8.2 that the gains from integration with Western Europe are much larger than the gains from integration within the former Soviet area. The same will be the case for integration between Eastern Europe and Asia. Russia and Eastern Europe should therefore be a "globalist" more than any other world region.

Notes

1. In small-scale simulations with the model (with 10 countries) we also obtain a more standard result—the impact of liberalisation on manufacturing is inversely related to the natural resources endowment. The result found in Table 8.1 should therefore be interpreted with some caution.
2. Here we use the term agglomeration shadow in a bit more general sense than standard in the new economic geography; see, for example, Fujita and Krugman (1995) or an overview in Fujita and Mori (2005) or Fujita et al. (1999).
3. In these tables, world integration (flat trade cost reduction of 30%) is also included for reference.
4. "Africa's big new free trade agreement, explained". Washington Post 29 March 2018, by Landry Signé.

References

Fujita, M., & Krugman, P. (1995). When Is the Economy Monocentric? von Thünen and Chamberlin Unified. *Regional Science and Urban Economics, 25*, 505–528.

Fujita, M., & Mori, T. (2005). Frontiers of the New Economic Geography. *Papers in Regional Science, 84*(3), 377–405.

Fujita, M., Krugman, P. R., & Venables, A. J. (1999). *The Spatial Economy: Cities, Regions and International Trade*. Cambridge, MA: MIT Press.

Hamilton, D. S. (2018). *Creating the North Atlantic Marketplace for Jobs and Growth. Three Paths, One Detour, A U-Turn, and the Road to Nowhere.* Washington, DC: Center for Transatlantic Relations, John Hopkins School of Advanced International Studies.

9

Trade Policy Spillovers and Regulatory Cooperation

In the analysis of non-tariff issues in Chap. 5, a key finding was that beyond tariffs, Free Trade Agreements (FTAs) are often non-discriminatory. But in the economic analysis of FTAs, non-tariff measures are treated just like tariffs; we call this the "tariff equivalent syndrome": By this we mean that economists are brainwashed to "think like tariffs"—every regulation is represented by a "tariff equivalent" that can be scaled up or down. In trade policy some decades ago, tariffs were the heart of the matter and the economic theory of regional integration was developed in the window of "customs union theory"; for example, including the seminal book on "The Customs Union Issue" (Viner 1950; see Robson 1980 for discussion). Models of regional integration therefore routinely assume that FTAs are about discriminatory trade cost reduction.

This "tariff equivalent syndrome" is widespread and this book is no exception: In the analysis of Chaps. 7 and 8, FTAs are indeed represented as discriminatory trade cost reductions.[1] When CGE (Computable General Equilibrium) models are applied to predict the impact of FTAs, tariff equivalents are generally introduced in order to quantify non-tariff barriers. For example, non-tariff issues dominated the USA-EU TTIP (Transatlantic Trade and Investment Partnership) negotiations, but in the CGE economic analysis, tariff equivalents were used for their quantification (as an example,

A. Melchior, *Free Trade Agreements and Globalisation*,
https://doi.org/10.1007/978-3-319-92834-0_9

see CEPR 2013, see also Ecorys 2009, 2016). In the name of tractability and measurability, we are all guilty of this practice. But it needs to be asked: Is it really true that other forms of trade integration may me represented as if they were akin to tariffs? Are FTAs on services, investment, technical trade barriers and veterinary standards just like new layers of tariff discrimination? In this chapter, we discuss whether the tariff analogy is appropriate or misleading. If it is misleading, we have to think in new ways about FTAs and develop new models.

In Sect. 9.1 we review the "tariff equivalent syndrome" through the lens of so-called "trade policy spillovers": Some recent analysis of FTAs has predicted a more positive outcome for third countries because it was assumed that that trade barrier reductions in the FTA also benefited third countries in the form of "trade policy spillovers". Section 9.1 examines the conceptual and empirical foundation for such spillovers and concludes that they are real and a potentially important phenomenon, but need a stronger theoretical and empirical foundation. Spillovers take different forms and vary across sectors and trade policy measures, and they often reach only a subset of countries rather than the whole world. The fear of trade diversion from FTAs can also create "domino effects" whereby third countries initiate new agreements. We argue that some types of spillovers can be handled in standard trade models, but others require new approaches.

Our analysis of FTAs and globalisation also suggests that regulatory cooperation on a global scale is a not so easy to achieve. How can we avoid that world regions are "drifting apart" in the regulatory field, leading to segmentation of world markets into different regulatory clubs? In Sect. 9.2 we examine the hierarchy of regulatory cooperation, with special focus on European integration as an illustrative case. The extension of the EU internal market to EFTA (European Free Trade Association) countries under the EEA (European Economic Area) agreement illustrates that deep regulatory cooperation requires an extent of legal homogeneity that is impossible on a global scale. Global regulatory cooperation is therefore the "art of the possible", depending on coalitions and finding the right moment. The WTO found this moment in 1993–1995, and the WTO is a success in terms of global governance, with binding rules and jurisdiction in a complicated field. But the WTO may at least temporarily have hit the wall for major new reforms; and this will create a need for more plurilateral initiatives or international negotiations with systematic representativity. After Brexit, the UK will face a dilemma between accepting the legal homogeneity of the internal market, and negotiating FTAs with the USA or other countries having different practices and standards.

Section 9.3 discusses important issues not fully covered by the analysis of this book. The interaction between trade and international investment is a key issue that needs more attention in future research on FTAs. Another area is issue linkages: Trade is a generic activity and therefore linked to many other policy fields, from exchange rates to environmental standards. For better or worse, the TRIPS agreement on intellectual property was made possible by issue linkages at the WTO, with protests from developing countries, Nobel Laureate Joseph Stiglitz and others. Since the TRIPS agreement—pushed by the USA—is the key instrument available for handling the IPR conflict between the USA and China, the current US critique of the WTO is somewhat paradoxical in this light.

The book ends in Sect. 9.4 by referring to Jaques Delors famous statement that "you cannot fall in love with the internal market" (Delors 1989). There is some fatigue related to the quantification of gains from FTAs: The numbers do not convince people any more. We argue that research should aim to deliver qualitative knowledge and reason rather than "the right number". In the book, we have tried to contribute by using a numerical model but with an aim to shed light on options and proportions, and qualitative insight rather than the right numbers.

9.1 Trade Policy Spillovers

In some recent studies of FTAs, it was assumed that trade cost reductions "leaked out" to third countries in the form of "trade policy spillovers". With such spillovers, trade cost reduction within an FTA leads to some corresponding reduction in trade costs for third countries. In the case when the FTA trade cost reduction is fully MFN or non-discriminatory, the spillovers are complete and the FTA would have the same impact as unilateral liberalisation by the FTA parties. Trade policy spillovers reduce or eliminate the discriminatory impact of an FTA. Chapters 7 and 8 showed that discrimination and production shifting are important for the economic impact of an FTA (see e.g. Baldwin and Venables 1995), but trade policy spillovers will modify the outcome.

Trade policy spillovers have been taken into account in some recent analyses of FTAs. Some studies of TTIP made specific assumptions about such spillovers (CEPR 2013; Aichele et al. 2014), and a closer look reveals that the predicted impact of TTIP on third countries was strongly affected by these assumptions. These predictions varied across studies from substantial losses to significant gains, and the assumptions regarding trade policy spillovers were a main reason why the results differed so much. CEPR (2013, 28ff.) assumed that for non-tariff measures, some of the reductions obtained for EU-USA trade would also apply automatically to trade between EU/USA and third countries, and they called this "direct spillovers". "Indirect spillovers" could also occur if the other countries voluntarily adopt standards set in TTIP. The logic was that "the EU and the US act as a regulatory hegemon" and "there is scope for setting de facto common, global standards" (ibid., 29). In the case of indirect spillovers, the USA and the EU would also obtain better access in third country markets.[2] Trade policy spillovers were also included in studies of the Trans-Pacific Partnership (TPP) (Kawasaki 2014; Petri and Plummer 2016). The issue was raised earlier by Copenhagen Economics (2009) in a study on EU-Japan trade, maintaining that for non-tariff measures (NTMs) "many of the identified instruments available for reducing the NTMs are multilateral in nature" (p. 83) and "other countries may free-ride on the benefits of NTM reduction" (p. 13). As we have seen in Chap. 5, several studies on non-tariff issues in FTAs point in the same direction.

It is not a new idea that trade cost reductions between two countries also affect trade barriers for other countries. Smith and Venables (1991) analysed how common rules and regulations in the EU internal market could benefit third countries, and that some changes were non-discriminatory. For third countries, one standard is better than 28. We may call this a harmonisation effect. If there is a fixed cost of adapting to a standard, or a cost of learning, there will be a cost reduction for third country firms selling to more than one country within the FTA. A caveat is that even if harmonised standards represent a simplification, they may have a differential impact across suppliers. For example; strict food standards may be easier to comply with for trade partners that are similarly strict and have developed institutions for quality control. This is an emerging theme in the literature on food standards (see e.g. Medin and Melchior 2015). Hence institutional similarity may increase the extent of direct policy spillovers, so they may apply only to some countries and not be global in scope.

Trade policy spillovers dampen the discriminatory impact of trade integration for outsiders. This is however not the only channel by which the discriminatory impact of regional trade integration may be dampened or nullified. Another such channel is global value chain (GVC) effects. Due to globalisation, value chains have become increasingly international, with goods and services produced with inputs from many countries (see e.g. Timmer et al. 2014). Even if an FTA reduces the demand for final goods or services from third countries, there could be a compensating increase in the demand for parts or services used in production or distribution. We may call this GVC demand spillovers. For example, if an FTA stimulates the production of cars in the EU, it could increase the demand for car components also from third countries. Or if TTIP would lead to larger EU-USA trade in cars, it could increase the demand for transport services from third countries. General economic growth due to an FTA may also add to this demand effect, across the whole range of sectors. Fontagné et al. (2013) e.g. found that TTIP could lead to an increase in EU trade with third countries due to GVC demand spillovers. Hence in this case, trade diversion is eliminated and even reversed due to the GVC effects.

A third channel by which the discriminatory impact of PTAs may be reduced or eliminated, is via political-economy responses—if third countries adjust their own trade policies as a compensatory measure. Baldwin (1993) suggested a "domino theory of regionalism" whereby the discriminatory impact of PTAs would strengthen the motive for outside countries to join the FTAs or negotiate new ones. In Baldwin's model, the more countries that are members of the PTA, the greater is the gain from joining, and this creates the "domino effect". Baldwin and Jaimovicz (2016) provide some empirical support for the existence of such effects.

While the domino effect requires trade policy negotiation, a different type of political-economy spillover is the diffusion or multilateralisation of standards through unilateral adaptation by third countries. This is the "gold standard" effect of trade agreements suggested by some advocates for "megalaterals" such as TPP and TTIP. This is underlying the concept of "indirect spillovers" suggested by CEPR (2013). In this case, trade costs would be lowered due to an FTA not only for the trade between the FTA partners and third countries (in both directions), but also between third countries. According to this, e.g. TTIP would lead to lower trade costs even between e.g. Russia and China.

Chapter 5 showed that rules in the WTO and the OECD promote non-discriminatory implementation of trade and investment policies, and in some fields even forbid discrimination. This illustrates that trade policy spillovers may sometimes be due to legal provisions in trade agreements. In the European context, a particular type of such "legal spillovers" is due to the legal homogeneity of the EEA (European Economic Area) agreement involving Iceland, Liechtenstein and Norway. The EEA provides full access to the EU internal market in all sectors except agriculture and seafood, and full regulatory homogeneity in the sense that the EFTA countries adopt all new regulations (with a veto right that is rarely used). If the EU agrees with a third country on a new standard or regulation that is written into the internal market legislation, it may automatically apply also to the EEA. If FTAs only lead to looser forms of regulatory cooperation (e.g. mutual recognition agreements), this will not necessarily be the case.

The legal spillover in the EEA illustrates that trade policy spillovers could be limited to a subset of countries. For Baldwin's domino effects, Melchior (1997) shows there is a saturation affect; existing members of a trade bloc gain from enlargement up to a point only; and would not be interested in all outside countries joining.[3] In real trade policy, the incentive to form a compensating PTA would also differ across countries, depending on economic, institutional and geographical features. For example, the domino effects of TTIP would be stronger for the neighbours of the EU and the USA since a very large part of their trade is with TTIP, as illustrated by Pelkmans et al. (2014). The reach of spillovers is also an issue related to the global diffusion of standards. The extent of multilateral diffusion may depend on institutional aspects such as the prevalence of multilateral processes and standards; the institutional and legal similarity of trade partners; the patterns of economic interests; and the extent of conflict. For regulatory cooperation there are international organisations and active processes in a number of fields. In some cases, it is possible for major countries to become global hegemons and set a "gold standard". More often than not, however, it is difficult to achieve such hegemony. And if there is no "gold standard", it can hardly be diffused across the globe.

Hence trade policy spillovers are of different types so an important task is to distinguish between them and to examine to what extent non-tariff measures are discriminatory or not. It is also likely that spillovers are not global in scope so a second key issue is to find out whether they are local or global. With knowledge about these dimensions, trade policy spillovers may be modelled in a suitable way. Spillovers are real and existing phenomena that should be taken into account in future research on FTAs. For the case of trade facilitation, Park and Park (2016) verify the existence of trade policy spillovers and provide evidence about their magnitude. Econometric work we may provide similar knowledge in other fields.

To what extent do trade policy spillovers create a need for new models? If the FTA trade cost reduction is non-discriminatory and trade costs are proportional to sales, it can be studied with the same type of models and tariff equivalents, but with other assumptions about trade cost reduction; assuming complete or partial spillovers. For standards, there is often a fixed trade cost element, so models should take this into account, in the spirit of the early contribution by Smith and Venables (1991). In most trade theory applications, fixed costs are assumed to be exogenous, but they may also be endogenous; firms may have a choice regarding how much to invest in order to enter a particular market (Melchior 2002); also addressed in some of the literature on firm heterogeneity (see e.g. Arkolakis 2010). For standards related to quality or safety, models should take into account the value of quality or safety; standard utility functions will not capture the essence of this. For domino effects and the like, we need models that capture the political economy of FTAs, building on the extensive literature in the field (see, for example, Maggi 2014; or the discussion in Baldwin 2009). For the partial reach of trade policy spillovers across countries, gravity models could be relevant, or perhaps network models (see e.g. Rauch 1999; Chaney 2016). In conclusion, standard trade models with proportional trade costs may capture some forms of trade policy spillovers, but other approaches may be needed in many cases.

9.2 Trade Policy and Global Governance: Regulatory Cooperation

Trade policy is also about global governance. Could the FTA be "building blocks" for better global governance? Historically, there has been a continuous debate on whether FTAs would strengthen or undermine the global trade system. There is a considerable "building block or stumbling block" literature (see Baldwin 2009 for a discussion and overview). As noted in the introductory chapter, many nations opted for a two-pillar or even three-pillar approach to trade policy after the turn of the century; with bilateral, plurilateral and multilateral approaches as the three options but upgrading the FTA track. According to self-perception, FTAs are in harmony with the WTO, and do not preclude progress at the WTO. In one sense this seems true; it was not the prospects for FTAs that made the Doha Development Round at the WTO fail. The "champions of the FTA race", as we called them in Fig. 3.1 (those on top of the ranking) were not those who prevented a successful outcome of the Doha Round. A broader assessment of the Doha Round and the WTO is beyond the scope of this book; the perception of the author is that the Doha Round failed due to an unsettled North-South dilemma at the WTO, and partly because of the hesitation of the USA, and a growing USA-China friction.[4] We know that India will hesitate, but when the USA does, it is even more serious. A pack of 164 heterogeneous nations needs strong leaders, and with the USA abdicating from its 70-year role, it becomes difficult to make the final steps for an agreement. The conflict between the USA and the WTO about the functioning of the WTO Appellate Body, with the USA obstructing the appointment of new members, is also a signal.[5] This conflict started before Trump. According to the US view, the WTO dispute settlement system has tightened disciplines for the use of contingent protection (safeguards and measures against subsidies, anti-dumping) beyond what was agreed whet the WTO was established (see USTR 2018 for a more complete account of the US WTO critique).

Given the difficulty of obtaining global agreement on binding rules and jurisdiction in the economic area, the WTO is an exceptional success. Are FTAs an alternative track for global governance? On tariffs, we have seen in Chap. 4 that FTAs are successful, ambitious and discriminatory. Paradoxically, however, WTO rules are a main reason for this success: Article XXIV of the General Agreement on Tariffs and Trade (GATT) makes ambitious tariff cuts a prerogative in FTAs. A second paradox is that on jurisdiction, the majority of FTAs are in fact, according to Chap. 5, less ambitious than the WTO itself—with its quasi-legal system with permanent dispute settlement institutions. Third, on regulatory cooperation, the verdict was that beyond a minority of deep FTAs within the world regions, the FTAs have not delivered the "gold standards": The TTIP promised to do so, but could not make it. The FTAs can establish institutional cooperation and mutual recognition of standards or procedures, but if the rules as such are untouched, there are limits as to what the FTAs may accomplish.

Global governance in regulatory cooperation is the "art of the possible", with a hierarchy of methods ranging from legally binding rules with strong jurisdiction at one end, to information exchange or non-binding expressions of intent at the other. Regulatory cooperation takes a variety of forms, ranging from legally binding harmonisation of standards and procedures at one end, to ad hoc exchange of information at the other. OECD (2013) reviews the multitude of approaches, suggesting a hierarchy as shown in Table 9.1, from the most to the least legally binding.

Table 9.1 An illustrative hierarchy of international regulatory cooperation

Integration of the EU type
Treaties, conventions
Regulatory partnerships
MRAs (Mutual Recognition Agreements)
Transgovernmental networks
Soft law, Guidelines, Principles
Voluntary standards
Ad hoc exchange of information

Source: OECD (2013, 50)

The ranking is illustrative only since the content and impact of each form of cooperation may differ dramatically from case to case. Voluntary standards may sometimes be good intentions only, with little impact. In other cases, voluntary standards may become de facto international law and to a considerable extent binding. For example, IOSCO (International Organisation of Securities Commissions, see www.iosco.org) is an international network of national financial regulators that has succeeded in establishing (voluntary) standards that are nevertheless applied by more than 100 countries. Hence even if the success of IOSCO is partial and the organisation failed in areas where the conflicts of interest were too large (Verdier 2009), it shows that transnational regulatory networks and voluntary standards can be important channels for international regulatory cooperation. Similarly, the Basel Accords for banking supervision were decided by a small group of countries but nevertheless became standards widely applied worldwide (see e.g. Basel Committee for Banking Supervision 2016). In the light of Brexit, it may be observed that the Basel Accords were pushed especially by the USA and the UK, with strong opposition at times from Germany and France (Verdier 2009). Due to a mixture of economic interests, coercion and the importance of reputation in financial markets, it was possible to establish a global standard (ibid.).

An issue is how trade and regulation should be linked—in one agreement or separate? The reference to international standards in WTO's SPS (Sanitary and Phytosanitary) Agreement is an interesting example of creating a "constructive interaction" between trade agreements and regulation. The WTO did not set the standards, but the reference to the standards of, for example, Codex Alimentarius gave these standards a new legal significance. In the regulatory field, there are many plurilateral organisations (cf. examples above)—many of them less known—that that are important building blocks for global regulatory cooperation. It is beyond the scope here to analyse and draw firm conclusions on how this is to be done in each field; for example, trade agreements for financial services could be linked to international regulatory cooperation. In principle, such linkages should be explored in fields where regulatory issues are important. Rather than considering regulation as "necessary evil" in a setting where trade liberalisation is the only main objective, trade policy could seek for more harmony. In some areas, this could also facilitate trade negotiations that may "beat around the bush" unless regulatory issues are addressed. Also in the economic models, the value of regulation should be taken into account; free trade in toxic chemicals is not welfare-enhancing.

An obstacle to international regulatory cooperation is that institutional approaches differ across countries, for example, the scope of legislation versus voluntary standards where, for example, the EU and the USA are very different. For example, a regulation may set health-related requirements for a product or process, and a standard may be a way of fulfilling these requirements. In the EU, some standardisation bodies are officially recognised as European Standardisation Organisations and create EU-wide standards that replace national standards. Contrary to this centralised procedure, the USA has a more decentralised pattern of standardisation, with a large number of competing standard-setting bodies (Kommerskollegium 2013). In the centralised European system, standards have a semi-legal status, but in the USA this is not the case. Even for trade within the EEA, Nordås (2016) found that differences with respect to the origin of legal systems had a strong impact on cross-border services trade. The differences between EU and US legal systems and approaches to regulation therefore impede regulatory cooperation in a transatlantic FTA.

The European system of standardisation is an example of extensive harmonisation of regulation. When the EU internal market was formed in 1992, mutual recognition of standards was also an important approach in cases where standardisation was not possible and this is still an element of the EU system. According to Correia de Brito et al. (2016) it is only in the EU and the Trans-Tasman agreement between Australia and New Zealand that Mutual Recognition Agreements (MRAs) apply to standards as such. For analysis of various forms of "soft governance", see also Veggeland and Sørbye (2015), or Elliott and Pelkmans (2015). When neither standardisation nor MRAs on standards is possible, FTAs may go down the ladder towards less extensive forms regulatory cooperation. For example, MRAs on testing procedures and data exchange may be established. In some fields such as the approval of cars and chemicals, such trade-facilitating measure may be significant and lead to large cost savings.

While the EU internal market could be extended to EFTA through the EEA (see text box), this is not a realistic model for global governance, due to the far-reaching need for legal homogeneity. In order to obtain global coordination on regulation, one has to rely on "the art of the possible" as illustrated above for IOSCO and the Basel Code. In several areas, there are international organisations involved in regulatory cooperation. As seen in Chap. 5, many regulatory issues are multilateral by nature and not really fit for bilateral FTAs and discriminatory practices. This is an argument for more plurilateral initiatives in the future and a closer link between trade policy and the regulatory processes. Especially in the field of services trade, sector agreements covering trade as well as regulatory issues are an option that could be explored further. Sectors such as, for example, finance and air traffic have considerable regulatory complexity, and specific expertise is needed to handle the issues. This provides another argument for sector agreements, rather than leaving the issues to the all-round diplomats. It makes limited sense to exchange free trade in financial derivatives against vegetable tariffs, and so we can live with the loss of this issue linkage. In finance, universal liberalisation is not an objective as such—the aim is trade and market efficiency combined with the necessary regulation for prudential and stability purposes.

The idea that the "big boys" such as the EU and the USA should agree on the standards, and other countries follow later, seems often unrealistic and a bit undemocratic. It is unrealistic because there is no guaranty that the major actors will agree—as shown by the TTIP negotiations. It is undemocratic because other countries should also have a say. But if the decision is to be made jointly by whole world, it would be difficult to come to an agreement. One solution is the plurilateral track, forming clubs of the willing in one area after the other. Another option is to think of better models of representativity; could groups of countries speak with one voice? At the WTO, there is a long tradition of "green room" meetings where only a subset of countries participates, with some representativity although not formalised. The G-20 does not have systematic representativity, but invites non-participating countries to the meetings, with rotation over time. Institutions such as the Basel Committee, where the country composition was pretty ad hoc from the start, have added new members to become more representative. It would be good for the international system to have more representativity; this is not necessarily formalised since that would create very complicated negotiations.

In the context of Western Europe and Brexit, an interesting case of trade policy coordination between large and small countries is the Open

Skies Agreement on air transportation between EU and the USA, where Iceland and Norway participates with the EU as spokesperson. Alternative to a standard inter-governmental approach with equal partners in the legal sense, this agreement has an asymmetric setup where Europe speaks with one voice. The EU and the USA entered into an agreement first; and Norway and Iceland acceded to the agreement later and are to be treated "as though they were Member States" of the EU and "Iceland and Norway shall have all of the rights and obligations of Member States under that agreement". According to the agreement, the EU Commission shall represent Norway and Iceland in matters under EU jurisdiction; and in this case "take adequate measures to ensure full participation of Iceland and Norway in any coordination, consultation or decision shaping meetings with the Member States".[6]

Will the UK spend years and huge efforts to build a worldwide network of new FTAs or could they accept the Open Skies model and remain part of EUs FTA network? As shown in Chap. 3, small countries top the FTA ranking and so it is certainly possible also for the UK, which is larger than Chile, Singapore and the EFTA countries, to negotiate many FTAs. But it will take time and considerable effort. Furthermore, the smaller nations cannot set the rules alone, and so if there is an ambition to develop global traffic rules in the regulatory area, the model of "United Europe" in the Open skies Agreement is an interesting precedent. The precondition for this model is the EEA—Norway and Iceland are part of the intra-European agreements on air traffic and can therefore participate "as though they were members". As an alternative, the UK may gang up with the USA as they did in the Basel Accord negotiations, in order to influence global standard-setting. The USA and the UK are historically strong allies but their trade policies currently have the opposite signs, at least when it comes to global integration and liberalisation. This adds a question mark regarding the power of their alliance in the trade policy field. But this could change, and in the post-Trump world, the USA-UK alliance might develop without some of the current paradoxes. Perhaps they could both join TPP? A more permanent limitation is that the UK has and will likely continue to have European standards, and cannot become like the USA in the regulatory field. This limits the scope for USA-UK cooperation in the regulatory field.

EFTA and the EU Internal Market

The EU approach to regional integration has been extended to some EFTA countries through the EEA Agreement, whereby Norway, Iceland and Liechtenstein obtain full access to the EU internal market with its four freedoms, except for agriculture and fisheries that are partly exempted. In order to obtain such full access to the internal market, the EFTA countries have to guaranty the legal homogeneity of the EEA, by the quasi-automatic adoption of new EU legislation, and a legal system with a separate EFTA court and surveillance authority. EFTA countries have the right to veto new regulations, but the EU may then suspend relevant parts of the EEA. In practice, the veto right has been mostly asleep and so the EEA means legal homogeneity for the relevant parts of the EU internal market.[7] The current EEA is a comprehensive regulatory "machinery" with a flow of new legislation. In Norway, there is a Parliamentary subcommittee reviewing new legislation and publishing a quarterly list of new legislation. As an illustration, the list of new EEA legislation reviewed during 1 January–23 March 2018 was 35 pages long—including the titles only (EEA Committee of the Norwegian Parliament 2018)! The good thing about the EEA is the market access; a burden is the democratic deficit—EFTA is involved at the technical level but the EU makes the decisions, and EFTA generally has to abide. Technically, it might be possible to enhance EFTAs' influence at least a little without compromising the EU legal system, and one day perhaps the EFTA countries will stand up for their rights. But the EU is wary about its legal autonomy, and so this may not be easy. An issue is whether Brexit will make the EU even more wary. It might be better to go in the opposite direction and facilitate enhanced participation in decision-making by non-EU countries that participate fully in the internal market and accept the need for legal homogeneity.

The predecessor of EEA was *ad hoc* integration of internal market legislation through an inter-governmental process, based on the EU-EFTA Luxemburg declaration of 1984.[8] With the ever-increasing flow of new internal market legislation around 1990, this

"Luxemburg process" failed to deliver the hoped for "European Economic Space" and parallelism with the EU internal market (see e.g. Gstöhl 2002), and this was one of the drivers behind the formation of the EEA. Another matter is that the EEA at that time was seen by some as a stepping stone to EU membership. The rest is history: Three EFTA countries (Sweden, Finland and Austria) became EU members; Norway and Iceland remained in the EEA, whereas Switzerland did not accept the lack of legal autonomy and negotiated bilateral agreements with the EU.

9.3 Missing Pieces: Investment and Issue Linkages

This book kind of ends here, but let us add some remarks on important issues that we have not addressed.

A serious issue is that trade-based analysis of FTAs—including the model used in this book—often neglects the interaction between trade and foreign direct investment (FDI). With multinationals and globalisation around for a very long time (see e.g. UNCTAD 2016), sales from affiliates abroad are often larger than cross-border trade (see e.g. Hamilton and Quinlan 2016), and a big chunk of global trade is intra-firm trade. It is well-known from the literature that trade barriers affect investment motives; for example, some international investment is "tariff jumping" (investing to avoid trade costs) and some is "export platform" FDI (e.g. investment in the UK for sales to the EU) (see e.g. Navaretti and Venables 2006). Changes in barriers to trade may have other effects in the presence of FDI and changes in investment barriers may affect trade (World Bank 2010). Trade and investment may be complements or substitutes (see e.g. Wong 1995). International value chains have been a key issue in recent years (see e.g. Timmer et al. 2014) but the trade policy implications have not yet been fully resolved (for a discussion, see e.g. Elms and Low (Eds.) 2013). In future analysis of FTAs, analysis of investment should have priority.

A second non-addressed theme is about issue linkages between trade policy and other policy areas. Trade is a generic activity and therefore linked to a range of other issues and fields; investment, macroeconomics and exchange rates, environmental regulations, intellectual property rights, human rights, labour right and regulations, taxation, food and health standards, state-owned companies, public procurement, competition policies and more. In a number of areas, we can make valid "level playing field" arguments about how other aspects affect trade. Some fields are already integrated in trade agreements, and others are not. The trend over recent years has been that FTAs become more and more comprehensive, the negotiating delegations bigger and bigger, and the complexity is ever larger. This raises issues about what should be in trade agreements and not: Should we, for example, leave labour standards wholly to the ILO (International Labour Organisation), or should we incorporate it into trade agreements? If we include it, should it be lip talk or enforceable rules with strict jurisdiction?

When the WTO was established, there was an issue linkage between goods, services, intellectual property rights and the institutional setup, including dispute settlement. The TRIPS agreement on intellectual property rights (IPR), pushed by the USA, could hardly have succeeded without the issue linkage. This agreement makes IPR protection mandatory. It is a paradox of history that President Trump accuses China of unfair practices on intellectual property, and at the same accuses the WTO for being unable to handle China: The TRIPS Agreement, pushed by the USA, is exactly the tool needed to address IPR issues with China—in a civilised way. This is another example of the inconsistencies of US trade policies under President Trump, again with the wrong sign. Another example is TPP, which Trump should support in the light of his own priorities, but which was characterised by him in the election campaign as a "disaster" and a "rape of our country".[9] The TRIPS agreement was established against strong opposition from many developing countries and also some economists including Nobel Laureate Joseph Stiglitz (Stiglitz 2008) maintaining that strict IPR protection creates excessive rents and unduly slows down technology transfer from rich to poor countries.

The case of TRIPS illustrates that linking issues can facilitate agreements that would otherwise not have been possible (see e.g. Horstmann et al. 2001; or Harstad 2015). On the other hand, including contentious issues could also block agreements. If the WTO aims to solve all the world's problems, little imagination is required to see that negotiations would fail. Even the relatively standard "Singapore issues" (investment, competition policy, public procurement and trade facilitation) created considerable conflict at the WTO, and only trade facilitation eventually succeeded.[10] To a large extent, this is about politics and coalitions, and it is beyond the scope of this book to examine the prospect for issue linkages in the various areas. The flavour of our examination of non-tariff issues in FTAs (Chap. 5) is that, at the global level, FTAs are generally not able to set the standards and make the rules; here the WTO has been more important. Countries can add something here and there in bilateral FTAs, the USA can push for even more IPR protection in the FTAs, but the FTAs across world regions do not really set new standards.

The mother of all issue linkages is perhaps the one between trade and security: The post-war reconstruction led to the cold war, with a high wall between the Warsaw Pact and the West, economically and militarily. At the time of writing, there are signs of a new cold war, with the US-China conflict at the core and threats of a trade war. The USA has introduced tariffs for aluminium and steel that are legally based on US laws related to security.[11] Trump's key trade policy advisor has argued that trade policy should be used to contain China economically but also militarily, by reducing its economic capacity to build defence (Navarro 2015). Trump portrays the USA as a victim of the unfair practices of other nations, having naively entered into trade agreements that are abused by the others.

The analysis of this book tells that President Trump raises real issues, but the narrative is flawed: First, the USA has not been cheated in trade agreements; on the contrary, the USA forced developing countries to accept the TRIPS agreement at the WTO, and via FTAs, the USA obtained better market access for services and even more IPR protection. The TPP was not a rape of America but actually in line with US trade policy under Trump. The analysis in this book suggests that the USA lags behind in the formation of FTAs worldwide, and this may weaken the US economy.

Our analysis underpins the concern for reciprocity in trade agreements: Non-reciprocal trade liberalisation leads to the "cheap shirts, fewer manufacturing jobs" problem. So here we give Trump one point. But trade agreements are not the major cause of non-reciprocity; on the contrary, trade agreements are tools for obtaining more reciprocity. So trade agreements are not the problem but the solution.

The US trade deficit has become larger because of China's growth, but the deficit is generic and unlikely caused by the unfair practices abroad. Unfair practices exist, but trade agreements make it possible to address these problems without going to trade war. China's growth creates an industrial adjustment problem, but this is the course of history and cannot be solved by trade policy.

This book shows that the WTO is a considerable success in terms of jurisdiction and governance. In spite of the proliferation of FTAs, the WTO still rules many of the world's trade flows. The WTO has its flaws and limitations, but it covers almost the whole world, with binding jurisdiction and dispute settlement in difficult areas. The world trade system has promoted peace and prosperity during 70 years, and it should continue to do so.

In this book, we have also seen that many of the "new" trade policy issues are of a multilateral nature and should be addressed in plurilateral or multilateral settings. FTAs are an important supplement in the world trade system, promoting freer trade and cooperation across world regions. Within regions, some FTAs are deep and comprehensive and "set the standards" far beyond the WTO. But such agreements can hardly be replicated on a global scale. Plurilateral initiatives or discussions with better representativity are therefore important in order to create global traffic rules and avoid that the world economy is regionalised, with regulatory convergence within but not across world regions.

9.4 Epilogue: The Love for Free Trade, and Numbers Versus Reason

When the EU internal market was established around 1990, Jaques Delors became famous for (on top of his other accomplishments), the statement that "you cannot fall in love with the internal market". The full meaning of this is not exact but Delors hinted that "numbers are not enough" and that flanking policies are needed to give meaning and political support:

> But—as I have often said in recent months—you cannot fall in love with the single market. Fernand Braudel, a lucid observer of the moves towards integration in the early 1960s, was thinking of the same thing when he

said: 'It would be mistaking human nature to serve up nothing but clever sums; they look so pallid beside the heady, though not always mindless, enthusiasm which has mobilized Europe in the past. Can a European consciousness be built purely on figures? Or is that not precisely what figures may fail to capture, what may develop in ways that cannot be calculated?' That is why I am constantly stressing the need not only for a frontier-free area but also for the flanking policies which will open up new horizons for the men and women who make up this Community of ours. To put it succinctly, the Single Act but all the Single Act. (Delors 1989)

Delors' statement also hints to an existing fatigue when it comes to the appeal of the numbers in trade policy. The numbers often come from CGE (computable general equilibrium) models of international trade. Planned FTAs are frequently supported by ex-ante economic analysis of their impact, using CGE models. These are generally complex models with many countries and sectors, calibrated to data for a given year. The models may then be used for numerical simulation of trade agreements; for example, by changing the level of trade costs (tariff equivalents again!). An example is CEPR (2013), examining the potential effects of TTIP. For Brexit, there are, at the time of writing, a number of CGE estimates on the impact of leaving the EU. The CGE models have sometimes been criticised for being "black boxes" where the transparency of the underlying mechanisms driving the results is limited (see e.g. Ackerman and Gallagher 2008). As an alternative to CGE, there are the "new quantitative trade models", where the model is built on econometric analysis of trade effects, typically using a gravity model of trade; and the model including the estimated parameters is then used to predict effects of new trade agreements (see e.g. Felbermayr et al. 2018). While the CGE models are big constructions using data and inputs from often many sources, the new quantitative trade models are built on one data set and thereby more transparent and data-driven. As a third option tried in this book, we may use more "lean" models which are quasi-realistic and "theory with numbers", but provide qualitative insight on key issues. Recent contributions such as Caliendo and Parro (2014) or Felbermayr et al. (2018) bring models closer to empirics. On the other hand, every model has its limitations and no model can produce "the right number". Delors may have a point and it may be that people are not impressed: How much does it matter whether the gain or loss is 1% or

2%? Perhaps we should focus more on the qualitative insights and what the models can address and not. "More reason, less numbers" could be an aim. Numbers will remain important, but their interpretation should be upgraded relative to the absolute values.

Notes

1. Using tariff equivalents for non-tariff barriers, the revenue aspect of tariffs is often neglected and this also applies to Chaps. 6, 7 and 8 of this book. It would be technically possible to account for tariff revenue in Chaps. 6, 7 and 8 but it would likely not lead to a major change in the results. Tariffs represent below one-third of the trade cost reductions undertaken in the regional integration scenarios studied in these chapters.
2. For TTIP, CEPR (2013) assumed that one-fifth of the NTM trade cost reductions for trade between the EU and the USA also applied to trade between EU/USA and third countries. In addition to these "direct spillovers" they also assumed that one-tenth of the intra-TTIP NTM trade cost reductions applied to trade between third countries because of "indirect spillovers". Source: CEPR (2013), Appendix 5, Table A.1.
3. In the "domino" model of Baldwin (1993), the number of manufacturing firms is exogenous and the PTA is fully open and so all new members are welcome. As shown by Melchior (1997) in a model with many countries and endogenous number of firms, there may be a saturation level since for existing members, the gains from further enlargement reaches a maximum for a certain size of the PTA. Hence, while for outsiders the incentive to join increases with bloc size, the incumbent's incentive to enlarge reaches a maximum before all outsiders have joined. The logic is simple: In the new trade theory, some of the gains for insiders are obtained by discriminating against outsiders, but this advantage is eliminated if all countries join. The global welfare level would still be the highest if all countries join. In this model, trade policy is still exogenous; for a review and discussion of related political-economy models where FTA formation is endogenous, see Baldwin (2009).
4. The Financial Times 5 October 2017, "Tariffs and energetic protection of US trade is the American way", also supports this interpretation: "The decade-long so-called 'Doha round' of global trade talks had myriad problems, but what killed it was the US refusal to countenance a deal

that did not give its rice, wheat, soy and other farmers more access to markets such as India and China."

5. See, for example, Financial Times 16.10.2017; "EU's top trade official warns on Trump impact on WTO". For a presentation of current US policies, see USTR (2018, 22ff.).
6. The agreement text is available at http://www.state.gov/e/eb/rls/othr/ata/i/ic/170684.htm or Official Journal of the European Union (L 283, 29 October 2011, https://eur-lex.europa.eu/legal-content/EN/ALL/?uri=OJ:L:2011:283:TOC).
7. In 2011, the Norwegian Government signalled that it would veto EU's third postal directive. The decision was reversed by a new Norwegian Government in 2013.
8. The Luxemburg declaration of 1984, between the EU and EFTA, is available at http://www.efta.int/sites/default/files/documents/about-efta/EFTA-EC-joint-declaration-1984.pdf.
9. "Trump calls trade deal 'a rape of our country'"; Politico 28 June 2016, by Cristiano Lima, at www.politico.com. See also Noland et al. (2016) for documentation of Trump's colourful statements on trade policy.
10. These were four issues suggested at the WTO Ministerial Conference in Singapore in 1996, to be considered for further WTO negotiations. An agreement on trade facilitation was concluded at the WTO Ministerial Conference at Bali in 2013 and entered into force in 2017.
11. The tariffs on steel and aluminium products announced by the USA in March 2018 were based on Section 232 of the Trade Expansion Act of 1962. At the WTO, the USA has referred to the WTO "security exception" (Article XXI). Together with Russia, the USA maintains that the interpretation of Article XXI is self-judging and not subject to dispute settlement at the WTO. See inside US Trade/World Trade Online 17 April 2018: "U.S. agrees to enter into WTO consultations with China over 232, 301 tariffs". https://insidetrade.com/daily-news/us-agrees-enter-wto-consultations-china-over-232-301-tariffs. See also Alford (2011) for a discussion of WTO Article XXI.

References

Ackerman, F., & Gallagher, K. P. (2008). The Shrinking Gains from Global Trade Liberalization in Computable General Equilibrium Models. A Critical Assessment. *International Journal of Political Economy, 37*(1), 50–77. https://doi.org/10.2753/IJP0891-1916370103.

Aichele, R., Felbermayr, G., & Heiland, I. (2014). *Going Deep: The Trade and Welfare Effects of TTIP* (CESIFO Working Paper No. 5150). Munich: CESIFO.

Alford, R. P. (2011). The Self-Judging WTO Security Exception. *Utah Law Review, 3*, 697–759.

Arkolakis, C. (2010). Market Penetration Costs and the New Consumers Margin in International Trade. *Journal of Political Economy, 118*(6), 1151–1199.

Baldwin, R. (1993). A *Domino Theory of Regionalism* (CEPR Discussion Paper 857; NBER Working Paper 4465).

Baldwin, R. (2009). Big-Think Regionalism: A Critical Survey. In A. Estevadeordal, K. Suominen, & R. The (Eds.), *Regional Rules in the Global Trading System* (Chapter 2, pp. 17–95). Cambridge: Cambridge University Press, in cooperation with the Inter-American Development Bank (IDB) and the World Trade Organization (WTO).

Baldwin, R., & Jaimovicz, D. (2016). Are Free Trade Agreements Contagious? *Journal of International Economics, 88*(1), 1–16.

Baldwin, R. E., & Venables, A. J. (1995). Regional Economic Integration. In G. M. Grossmann & K. Rogoff (Eds.). *Handbook of International Economics* (Vol. 3, Chapter 31, pp. 1597–1644). Amsterdam: North-Holland.

Basel Committee on Banking Supervision. (2016). *Tenth Progress Report on Adoption of the Basel Regulatory Framework*. www.bis.org

Caliendo, L., & Parro, F. (2014). Estimates of the Trade and Welfare Effects of NAFTA. *The Review of Economic Studies, 82*(1), 1–44.

CEPR. (2013, March). [J. Francois, M. Manchin, H. Norberg, O. Pindyuk & P. Tomberger] *Reducing Transatlantic Barriers to Trade: An Economic Assessment Prepared for the European Commission*. Final Project Report. London: Centre for Economic Policy Research (CEPR).

Chaney, T. (2016). Networks in International Trade. In Y. Bramoullé, A. Galeotti, & B. Rogers (Eds.), *The Oxford Handbook of the Economics of Networks* (pp. 754–775). Oxford: Oxford University Press.

Copenhagen Economics. (2009, November). *Assessment of Barriers to Trade and Investment between the EU and Japan*. Final Report, at www.copenhageneconomics.com. Authors: E. R. Sunesen, J. F. Francois & M. H. Thelle.

Correia de Brito, A., Kauffmann, C., & Pelkmans, J. (2016). *The Contribution of Mutual Recognition to International Regulatory Co-operation* (OECD Regulatory Policy Working Papers No. 2). Paris: OECD Publishing. https://doi.org/10.1787/5jm56fqsfxmx-en

Delors, J. (1989, January 17). *Address Given by Jacques Delors to the European Parliament* (Bulletin of the European Communities, Supplement 1/89). Luxembourg: Office for official publications of the European Communities.

Ecorys. (2009, December 11). *Non-tariff Measures in EU-US Trade and Investment—An Economic Analysis.* Rotterdam: ECORYS Nederland BV (authors Dr. K. G. Berden, Prof. Dr. J. Francois, Mr. M. Thelle, Mr. P. Wymenga & Ms. S. Tamminen). Final Report for the European Commission, Directorate-General for Trade Reference: OJ 2007/S 180-219493.

Ecorys. (2016, May). *Trade SIA in the Transatlantic Trade and Investment Partnership (TTIP) between the EU and the USA.* Draft Interim Technical Report. Brussels: European Commission/Ecorys.

EEA Committee of the Norwegian Parliament. (2018). *Beslutninger vedtatt i EØS-komiteen 2018.* List of decisions made in 2018, as of 23 March 2018, at https://www.regjeringen.no/no/aktuelt/eos_beslutninger2018/id2589345/

Elliott, E. D., & Pelkmans, J. (2015). *Greater TTIP Ambition in Chemicals: Why and How* (Paper No. 10 in the CEPS-CTR project 'TTIP in the Balance' and CEPS Special Report No. 114 / July 2015). Brussels: CEPS (Centre for European Policy Studies).

Elms, D. K., & Low, P. (2013). *Global Value Chains in a Changing World.* Geneva: WTO Publications; Fung Global Institute (FGI), Nanyang Technological University (NTU), and World Trade Organization.

Felbermayr, G., Gröschl, J., & Heiland, I. (2018). *Undoing Europe in a New Quantitative Trade Model* (Ifo Working Paper No. 250). Munich: Ifo Institute, Leibniz Institute for Economic Research at the University of Munich.

Fontagne, L., Gourdon, J., & Jean, S. (2013). *Translatantic Trade: Whither Partnership, Which Economic Consequences?* (CEPII Policy Brief No. 12). Paris: CEPII. www.cepii.fr

Gstöhl, S. (2002). *Reluctant Europeans. Norway, Sweden and Switzerland in the Process of Integration.* London/Colorado: Lynne Rienner Publishers, Inc.

Hamilton, D. S., & Quinlan, J. P. (2016). *The Transatlantic Economy 2016: Annual Survey of Jobs, Trade and Investment Between the United States and Europe.* Washington, DC: Center for Transatlantic Relations.

Harstad, B. (2015). Issue Linkages and Negotiations—Basic Theory. In A. Melchior & U. Sverdrup (Eds.), *Conflicts of Interest in Norwegian Trade Policy* (Chapter 4, pp. 86–104). Oslo: Universitetsforlaget. In Norwegian.

Horstmann, I. J., Markusen, J. R., & Robles, J. (2001). *Multi-Issue Bargaining and Linked Agendas: Ricardo Revisited or No Pain No Gain* (NBER Working Papers 8347). National Bureau of Economic Research, Inc.

Kawasaki, K. (2014). *The Relative Significance of EPAs in Asia-Pacific* (RIETI Discussion Paper Series 14-E-009). Tokyo: Research Institute of Economy, Trade and Industry (RIETI).

Kommerskollegium (National Board of Trade). (2013). *Regulativt samarbete och tekniska handelshinder inom ramen för Transatlantic Trade and Investment Partnership (TTIP)*. Stockholm: Kommerskollegium.

Maggi, G. (2014). International Trade Agreements. Chapter 6. In G. Gopinath, E. Helpman, & K. Rogoff (Eds.), *International Economics* (Vol. 4, pp. 317–390). Amsterdam: North-Holland/Elsevier, Handbooks in Economics.

Medin, H. & Melchior, A. (2015). *Trade Barriers or Trade Facilitators? On the Heterogeneous Impact of Food Standards in International Trade* (NUPI Working Paper No. 855). Oslo: Norwegian Institute of International Affairs.

Melchior, A. (1997). *On the Economics of Market Access and International Economic Integration* (Economic Dissertations No. 36). Oslo: University of Oslo, Department of Economics.

Melchior, A. (2002). *Sunk Costs in the Exporting Activity: Implications for International Trade and Specialisation* (NUPI Paper No. 634). Oslo: Norwegian Institute of International Affairs.

Navaretti, G. B., & Venables, A. J. (2006). *Multinational Firms in the World Economy*. With Barry, F. G., Ekholm, K., Falzoni, A. M., Haaland, J. I., Midelfart, K. H. & Turrini, A. Princeton: Princeton University Press.

Navarro, P. (2015). *Crouching Tiger. What China's Militarism Means for the World*. Amherst: Prometheus Books.

Noland, M., Hufbauer, G. C., Robinson, S., & Moran, T. (2016, September). *Assessing Trade Agendas in the U.S. Presidential Campaign* (PIIE Briefing 16-6). Washington, DC: Peterson Institute of International Economics.

Nordås, H. K. (2016). *Services Trade Restrictiveness Index (STRI): The Trade Effect of Regulatory Differences* (OECD Trade Policy Papers No. 189). Paris: OECD Publishing. https://doi.org/10.1787/5jlz9z022plp-en

OECD. (2013). *International Regulatory Co-operation. Addressing Global Challenges*. Paris: OECD, www.oecd.org

Park, I., & Park, S. (2016). Trade Facilitation Provisions in Regional Trade Agreements: Discriminatory or Non-discriminatory? *East Asian Economic Review, 20*(4), 447–467.

Pelkmans, J., Lejour, A., Schrefler, L., Mustilli, F., & Timini, J. (2014). *The Impact of TTIP. The Underlying Economic Model and Comparisons* (CEPS Special Report No. 93 / October 2014 [TTIP Series No. 1]). Brussels: CEPS (Centre for European Policy Studies).

Petri, P. A., & Plummer, M. G. (2016). *The Economic Effects of the Trans-Pacific Partnership: New Estimates* (Working Paper Series, WP 16-2). Washington, DC: Peterson Institute for International Economics. www.piie.com

Rauch, J. E. (1999). Networks Versus Markets in International Trade. *Journal of International Economics, 48*(1), 7–35.

Robson, P. (1980). *The Economics of International Integration* (Studies in Economics 17). London: George Allen & Unwin.

Smith, A., & Venables, A. J. (1991). Economic Integration and Market Access. *European Economic Review, 35*, 388–395.

Stiglitz, J. (2008). Economic Foundations of Intellectual Property Rights. *Duke Law Journal, 57*, 1693–1724.

Timmer, M. P., Erumban, A. A., Los, B., Stehrer, R., & de Vries, G. J. (2014). Slicing Up Global Value Chains. *Journal of Economic Perspectives, 28*(2), 99–118.

UNCTAD. (2016). *World Investment Report 2016. Investor Nationality: Policy Challenges*. Geneva: UNCTAD. www.unctad.org

USTR. (2018). *2018 Trade Policy Agenda and 2017 Annual Report of the President of the United States ion the Trade Agreements Program*. Washington, DC: Office of the United States Trade Representative (USTR). ustr.gov.

Veggeland, F., & Sørbye, S. E. (2015). *Hard and Soft Governance in World Food Trade: Dispute Settlement and Equivalence as Trade-Facilitating Tools* (NUPI Working Paper No. 852). Oslo: Norwegian Institute of International Affairs.

Verdier, H. (2009). Transnational Regulatory Networks and Their Limits. *The Yale Journal of International Law, 34*, 113–172.

Viner, J. (1950). *The Customs Union Issue*. Washington, DC: Carnegie Endowment for International Peace.

Wong, K. (1995). *International Trade in Goods and Factor Mobility*. Cambridge, MA: MIT Press.

World Bank. (2010). *Investing across Borders 2010. Indicator of Foreign Direct Investment Regulations in 87 Countries*. Washington, DC: The World Bank.

Appendix A: Data Tables

A. Melchior, *Free Trade Agreements and Globalisation*,
https://doi.org/10.1007/978-3-319-92834-0

Appendix Table A.1 Trade in goods between major world regions, 1995 and 2015, and change during the period. Shares of total world trade (average of shares based on export and import data), and relative change (change in world trade = 100)

Shares of total world trade in goods, 2015:

		Importing region							
		Africa	Asia/Pacific	East Europe	Latin Am	M East	North Am	West Europe	World
Exporting region	**Africa**	0.40	0.77	0.01	0.08	0.16	0.17	0.91	2.50
	Asia/Pacific	1.07	19.31	0.55	1.12	2.26	6.96	5.20	36.47
	East Europe	0.05	0.67	0.48	0.04	0.28	0.11	1.32	2.94
	Latin Am	0.08	1.04	0.05	0.79	0.15	0.87	0.61	3.60
	M East	0.22	2.49	0.11	0.05	0.91	0.41	1.10	5.29
	North Am	0.17	3.06	0.09	1.05	0.56	6.66	2.25	13.84
	West Europe	0.97	4.38	0.76	0.65	2.05	3.51	23.03	35.37
	World	2.95	31.72	2.05	3.78	6.39	18.69	34.42	100

Shares of total world trade in goods, 1995:

		Importing region							
		Africa	Asia/Pacific	East Europe	Latin Am	M East	North Am	West Europe	World
Exporting region	**Africa**	0.18	0.29	0.01	0.05	0.06	0.33	1.06	1.98
	Asia/Pacific	0.40	14.64	0.18	0.55	0.83	6.63	4.57	27.79
	East Europe	0.02	0.36	0.14	0.01	0.10	0.11	0.92	1.67
	Latin Am	0.05	0.46	0.02	0.82	0.08	0.91	0.80	3.14
	M East	0.10	1.25	0.06	0.04	0.36	0.42	0.98	3.21
	North Am	0.18	4.66	0.08	1.13	0.52	7.77	3.23	17.57
	West Europe	1.15	4.49	0.76	0.95	1.78	3.52	31.99	44.63
	World	2.08	26.15	1.26	3.55	3.74	19.69	43.54	100

(*continued*)

Appendix Table A.1 (continued)

Change from 1995 to 2015 (change in total world trade in goods = 100):

		Importing region							
		Africa	**Asia/Pacific**	**East Europe**	**Latin Am**	**M East**	**North Am**	**West Europe**	**World**
Exporting region	**Africa**	216	269	188	167	253	51	86	126
	Asia/Pacific	270	132	306	204	273	105	114	131
	East Europe	280	183	331	280	276	106	143	176
	Latin Am	152	225	203	97	199	95	77	115
	M East	211	199	173	125	255	98	112	165
	North Am	94	66	116	92	107	86	70	79
	West Europe	84	98	100	69	115	100	72	79
	World	142	121	163	107	171	95	79	100

Source: Own calculations based on trade data from WITS/COMTRADE

Appendix Table A.2 Counting Free Trade Agreements (FTAs) between 40 countries plus the EU

	Number of bilateral flows affected by FTA categories:							
Country/unit	In force	Signed	Many	North-South	Negotiations	Suspended	Failed	Number in Fig. 3.1
Chile	21		5	5			12	21
Switzerland	20		1		6	3		20
Singapore	18	2	5		16		9	20
Korea, Rep.	19				8			19
Norway	17	1			7	3		18
EU	13	4			13	1		17
China	16	1	3		13			17
India	15	2	4		15			17
Malaysia	15	2	12	8	6		9	17
Peru	16		5	5			12	16
Indonesia	13	1	4	8	10			14

(*continued*)

Appendix Table A.2 (continued)

	Number of bilateral flows affected by FTA categories:							
Country/unit	In force	Signed	Many	North-South	Negotiations	Suspended	Failed	Number in Fig. 3.1
Vietnam	13	1	1		8		9	14
Japan	13		3		8	2	11	13
Thailand	13		3		8	4		13
Philippines	12	1	1		7			13
Mexico	12				3		12	12
Australia	12		3		11	1	9	12
Colombia	9	3	5	5			7	12
Turkey	11	1	6	9	3			12
Egypt, Arab Rep.	12		6	7	2	2		12
Myanmar	11							11
Canada	9	1			3		11	10
United States	8				2		13	8
Pakistan	8		5	9	7			8
Brazil	7		5	6	3	1	7	7
Argentina	7		5	6	3	1	7	7
Saudi Arabia	5	2	3	9	4	1		7
United Arab Emirates	5	2	3	8	4	2		7
Israel	6	1						7
Hong Kong SAR, China	4	1			7			5
Bangladesh	5		6	9	2			5
Nigeria	4	1		6				5
South Africa	5		1		2			5
Ukraine	4		1		1			4
Iran, Islamic Rep.	4		6	8	3			4
Kenya	4							4
Ethiopia	3							3

(continued)

Appendix Table A.2 (continued)

	Number of bilateral flows affected by FTA categories:							
Country/unit	In force	Signed	Many	North-South	Negotiations	Suspended	Failed	Number in Fig. 3.1
Congo, Dem. Rep.	3				1			3
Russian Federation	2		1		3	2		2
Algeria	1					2		1
Tanzania	1							1

Data sources:

The following are links to some important sources used to construct the FTA matrix between the 40 countries plus the EU. In addition, news was used as supplementary information in some cases

Americas: Organization of American States, http://www.sice.oas.org

Asia: Asian Development bank, https://aric.adb.org/fta-country

Canada: Government of Canada, https://www.international.gc.ca/trade-commerce/trade-agreements-accords-commerciaux/agr-acc/index.aspx?lang=eng

EFTA: http://www.efta.int/

EU: European Commission, http://trade.ec.europa.eu/doclib/docs/2006/december/tradoc_118238.pdf

Free Trade Area of the Americas: http://www.ftaa-alca.org/alca_e.asp

Hong Kong: https://www.tid.gov.hk/english/ita/fta/index.html

Non-Western FTAs: http://www.bilaterals.org

SACU: http://www.sacu.int/list.php?type=Agreements

USA: US Trade Representative; https://ustr.gov/trade-agreements/free-trade-agreements

Worldwide: WTO database, http://rtais.wto.org/UI/PublicMaintainRTAHome.aspx

Note: The table counts bilateral trade flows/links covered by an FTA as of August 2017, between the 41 countries/units included in the sample. For example, North American Free Trade Area (NAFTA) will be counted three times, since three bilateral trade flows are affected. The count does not include FTAs made between the 41 and countries outside the sample

Note: The TPP (Trans-Pacific Partnership) Agreement is classified as failed as of August 2017 since the USA withdrew and it could not be ratified in its original form

Explanation of table headings:

Appendix Table A.2 (continued)

In force = FTA in force
Signed = FTA signed but not in force
Negotiations = Negotiations on an FTA
North-South = Preferential Trade Agreement notified under the World Trade Organization (WTO) "Enabling Clause"
Suspended = Negotiations or agreements suspended
Failed = Failed negotiations on an FTA
Many = Cases with more than one agreement related to the same trade link

Appendix B: A World Trade Model with Commodities and Differentiated Goods

Model Overview

We refer to Chap. 6 for a general overview of the model; for example, Fig. 6.1 describes the production factors, sectors and trade flows. We build a model that captures intra-industry trade (IIT) in manufacturing as well as commodity trade. For the analysis of North-South trade we also need to reflect the large variation in skills and capital endowments. Markusen and Venables (2000) incorporated a manufacturing sector with monopolistic competition and differentiated goods into an otherwise standard HOS (Heckscher-Ohlin-Samuelson) model with factor endowment differences. Even with two countries, numerical simulation is necessary for deriving most results, and this is the case also for the model presented here. With 110 countries/regions in the model version used in this book, we have to solve an equation system with 110 unknowns. This is not straightforward and tractability is therefore important.

Key simplifications for the purpose of tractability are the following:

- Commodities are represented as a natural resource endowment G that cannot be consumed, but enters into the production of traded goods and services—for simplicity we call this manufacturing or

A. Melchior, *Free Trade Agreements and Globalisation*,
https://doi.org/10.1007/978-3-319-92834-0

tradables. Commodities can be used domestically or exported with zero trade costs; this guarantees one global commodity price *g*.[1] The tradability of *G* makes our model different from the so-called specific-factor models. Due to the assumption of zero trade costs for *G*, a country[2] does not need own endowments of *G*; the necessary quantity may be imported. The commodity price *g* is determined by global supply and demand, and the commodity income *gG* adds to the total income of the one representative consumer of each country. The *G* endowment affects the wage level and thereby also competitiveness for tradables; this drives the "deindustrialisation" effect we observe for resource-rich countries.

- In each country, capital (*K*) and labour (*L*) are fully utilised and combined in the production of services *S* that may either be consumed domestically or used as an input into the production of tradables. There is no international trade in *S* directly. Using Cobb-Douglas production functions that are the same for all countries, the *K*/*L* ratio determines the productivity level of a country. There is no other variable in the model representing total factor productivity; the *K*/*L* ratio may therefore be interpreted as an expression of a country's technology level.[3] The literature has shown there is a strong capital-skill complementarity and in the model both are reflected in *K*. The *K*/*L* ratio will reflect and endogenise productivity differences. With all *K* and *L* used in the production of *S*, the wage/capital price ratio *w*/*r* will be fixed and this increases the tractability of the model. With another sector included, the *w*/*r* ratio would depend on trade; in the model here the two vary in tandem. The model can be extended later to include more tradable sectors with varying factor intensities.
- The tradables sector *X* is the production of different product varieties combining *G* and *S* (again using Cobb-Douglas technology), with increasing returns to scale and monopolistic competition. This is a standard "Dixit-Stiglitz" sector where there are also real trade costs. As known from the recent trade literature, market access affects industrial location or wage levels, and such effects are fully incorporated in the model. For each country, total trade must be balanced and so a trade deficit for *X* across all trade partners has to be matched by a trade surplus in *G*, and vice versa.[4]

The simplifications we make for the sake of tractability have some cost in terms of realism:

- The assumption of zero trade costs for commodities could be defended in the light of trade policy: In trade policy and the WTO, barriers for commodity trade are mostly low. On the other hand, trade infrastructure is crucial for many commodities and sometimes costly, and in further work it may be of interest to extend the model to account for such costs.
- In the model, we treat commodities as a "gift from heaven"—it is used in manufacturing and traded but not processed in any way using capital and labour. Because of this we will miss the "resource movement effect" demonstrated by Corden and Neary (1982) which is certainly important in some cases.
- We assume that services are produced with the same factor proportions for consumption and for use in manufacturing production. By having only one tradable sector beyond *G*, the model does not capture the role of international specialisation in capital-intensive versus labour-intensive goods. Because of this we do not examine sector shifts due to different factor proportions; be it clothing versus machinery or information technology services versus floor cleaning. While such inter-sectoral differences certainly play a role we abstract from them here in order to analyse aggregate patterns across countries.

With the simplifications made, we obtain a model that can be solved numerically. In later work, new elements may be added. Adding commodities also adds complexity compared to earlier own work using numerical models (e.g. Melchior 2010), and we proceed step by step to be sure that the model is tractable.

Model Structure: Services[5]

Services are homogeneous and produced and sold under perfect competition. With the inputs K_i and L_i fixed for each country, the production volume S_i is also fixed, given the Cobb-Douglas production function:

$$S_i = K_i^{\alpha} L_i^{1-\alpha} \tag{1}$$

With perfect competition, the services price p_i must also be equal to marginal unit costs

$$p_i = Z_s r_i^{\alpha} w_i^{1-\alpha} \tag{2}$$

where $Z_s = \alpha^{-\alpha}(1-\alpha)^{(\alpha-1)}$ is a constant.

Here r_i and w_i are the prices for K and L respectively, and we have used standard properties of the Cobb-Douglas production functions; see, for example, Melchior (2004) for a more detailed explanation. With the Cobb-Douglas production function, α and $1-\alpha$ are the cost shares for K and L respectively, so we have

$$\frac{r_i K_i}{w_i L_i} = \frac{\alpha}{1-\alpha} \tag{3}$$

With K_i and L_i exogenous, the w/r ratio is given and we have effectively only one unknown parameter (w or r). Expressing r in terms of w, plugging into (2) and simplifying, we obtain:

$$p_i = \frac{1}{1-\alpha}\left(\frac{K_i}{L_i}\right)^{-\alpha} w_i \tag{4}$$

So the price of services is proportional to the wage rate, with the factor of proportionality defined by the capital-labour ratio K/L and the factor shares in production.

Manufactured Goods (Tradables)

We use the terms tradables and manufacturing interchangeably; both meaning traded goods and services. Manufacturing is a standard Dixit-Stiglitz setup with firms producing individual varieties of a differentiated good under increasing returns to scale at the firm level (see Fujita et al.

1999, Chap. 4 for an overview). For an individual firm, the total cost function is:

$$C_{xi} = \left[f + \sum_j x_{ij} t_{ij} \right] c_{xi} \tag{5}$$

Here f is a fixed cost, assumed to be the same for firms in all countries. x_{ij} is the quantity shipped by a firm in country i to country j, subject to real trade costs t_{ij} that are expressed as a mark-up on marginal costs, $t_{ij} \geq 1$.[6] c_{xi} are unit costs. Manufactured goods are made by combining services S_{xi} (from the production of S that we have described) and commodities G_{xi}, taken from the domestic natural resource endowment G_i or imported from other countries, G_{mi}. The manufacturing unit costs c_{xi} are defined by the implicit production function:

$$X_i = G_{xi}^{\beta} S_{xi}^{1-\beta} \tag{6}$$

where $G_{xi} = G_i + G_{mi}$ is the sum of domestically produced and net imports of commodities; G_{mi} can also be negative if raw materials are exported.

The "production services" S_{xi} are supplied under perfect competition and so the price equals the cost c_{xi}, and with the Cobb-Douglas technology unit costs in manufacturing must be:

$$c_{xi} = Z_x g_i^{\beta} p_i^{1-\beta} \tag{7}$$

where $Z_x = \beta^{-\beta}(1 - \beta)^{(\beta - 1)}$ is a constant.

The cost function (5) implies that the same factor mix is used for the production processes underlying fixed costs, marginal production costs and trade costs. This common assumption (see e.g. Markusen and Venables 2000) greatly simplifies the model. One might object that the factor composition underlying trade costs might not be similar to the one used for production of goods; however, international transport costs are not only services but also among the world's largest consumers of energy and so it is not implausible to assume that raw materials are also used for the international shipment of tradables.

The profits of an individual firm in country i are as follows:

$$\pi_{xi} = \sum_j x_{ij} p_{ij} - \left[f + \sum_j x_{ij} t_{ij} \right] c_{xi} \tag{8}$$

Differentiating with respect to sales x_{ij} in market j, we derive the equilibrium price under monopolistic competition:

$$p_{ij} = \frac{\sigma}{\sigma - 1} c_{xi} t_{ij} \tag{9}$$

Where σ is the elasticity of substitution between different varieties; see later section on demand. Plugging the price into (8) and assuming zero pure profits under monopolistic competition, the equilibrium size of the firm will be:

$$\sum_j x_{ij} t_{ij} = (\sigma - 1) f \text{ in volume, or } \sum_j x_{ij} p_{ij} = \sigma f c_{xi} \text{ in value.} \tag{10}$$

Substituting this into the total cost function (5) it is easily seen that total costs equal the value of firm output. Differentiating this with respect to factor prices p_i and g_i, we obtain the per-firm factor demands:

$$\frac{G_{xi}}{n_i} = \sigma f Z_x \beta \left(\frac{p_i}{g_i} \right)^{1-\beta} \tag{11}$$

$$\frac{S_{xi}}{n_i} = \sigma f Z_x (1 - \beta) \left(\frac{p_i}{g_i} \right)^{-\beta} \tag{12}$$

Where n_i is the number of manufacturing firms in country i.

Demand

We use a standard set-up with demand for varieties defined by a CES (constant elasticity of substitution function) sub-utility function, and a Cobb-Douglas utility function for the upper tier choice between services consumption S_{ci} and total manufacturing consumption defined by the CES aggregate X_{ci}. We have

$$U_i = X_{ci}^a S_{ci}^{1-a} \qquad (\text{utility}) \tag{13}$$

$$S_{ci} = (1-a) p_i^{-1} Y_i \qquad (\text{consumer demand for services}) \tag{14}$$

$$X_{ci} = a P_{xi}^{-1} Y_i \qquad \begin{pmatrix} \text{consumer demand for the} \\ \text{manufacturing aggregate} \end{pmatrix} \tag{15}$$

$$x_{ij} = p_{ij}^{-\sigma} P_{xj}^{\sigma-1} a Y_j \qquad \begin{pmatrix} \text{demand for a firm / variety} \\ \text{from country } i \text{ in market } j \end{pmatrix} \tag{16}$$

P_{xi} is the aggregate CES price index, see, for example, Fujita et al. (1999, Chap. 4) for its derivation.

Y_i is the total income, which must equal:

$$Y_i = K_i r_i + L_i w_i + G_i g_i \tag{17}$$

since we assume that all factors are fully utilised. Using Eq. (3) to substitute for $K_i r_i$, we obtain:

$$Y_i = \frac{w_i L_i}{1-\alpha} + G_i g_i \tag{18}$$

If commodities are costlessly traded across countries, g_i must be the same in all countries and so we can drop the subscript i. In the numerical simulations, we will use the commodity price g as the numeraire, equal to one. Hence in this case, total country income is a simple function of the wage only, since all the other parameters are constants or given.

In later calculations, we will sometimes use the notation $v_{ij} = x_{ij}p_{ij}$ for the value of sales from a single firm from country i to market j. It is then useful to observe that if we multiply by p_{ij} on both sides of (16) and then the same for home market sales v_{jj} from firms in market j, we can divide the two expressions and obtain (also using (10) and (12)):

$$\frac{v_{ij}}{v_{jj}} = \left(\frac{p_{ij}}{p_{jj}}\right)^{1-\sigma} = \left(\frac{c_{xi}t_{ij}}{c_{xj}t_{jj}}\right)^{1-\sigma} \tag{19}$$

We mostly assume that there are no trade costs in the home market and so $t_{jj} = 1$. Sometimes, however, we would like to aggregate many countries into larger regions and it may then be plausible to assume that $t_{jj} > 1$. We therefore maintain this possibility by keeping t_{jj} and allowing it to differ from one when appropriate. Using (4) and the property that the raw material price g is the same in both countries, the expression can be transformed into:

$$\frac{v_{ij}}{v_{jj}} = \left(\frac{w_i}{w_j}\right)^{(1-\beta)(1-\sigma)} \left[\frac{\frac{K_i}{L_i}}{\frac{K_j}{L_j}}\right]^{\alpha(\beta-1)(1-\sigma)} \left(\frac{t_{ij}}{t_{jj}}\right)^{1-\sigma} \tag{20}$$

This will be used in the further calculations.

Deriving the Model Structure

When solving the model, we use, without loss of generality, the raw material price g as the numeraire, equal to one. In the following, we simplify notation by using $R_i = K_i/L_i$ for the capital-labour ratio of countries.

Using $g = 1$ and (10), total sales across all markets can be rewritten as:

$$\sum_j v_{ij} = \sigma f Z_x (1-\alpha)^{\beta-1} (R_i)^{\alpha(\beta-1)} w_i^{1-\beta} \tag{21}$$

We assume there are N countries or regions. Using (20) and expressing sales across all markets, we obtain for firms in country 1:

$$v_{11} + v_{22}\left(\frac{w_1}{w_2}\right)^{(1-\beta)(1-\sigma)}\left[\frac{R_1}{R_2}\right]^{\alpha(\beta-1)(1-\sigma)}\left(\frac{t_{12}}{t_{22}}\right)^{1-\sigma} + \dots$$

$$\dots + v_{NN}\left(\frac{w_1}{w_N}\right)^{(1-\beta)(1-\sigma)}\left[\frac{R_1}{R_N}\right]^{\alpha(\beta-1)(1-\sigma)}\left(\frac{t_{1N}}{t_{NN}}\right)^{1-\sigma}$$

$$= \sigma f Z_x (1-\alpha)^{\beta-1}(R_1)^{\alpha(\beta-1)} w_1^{1-\beta} \tag{22}$$

Multiplying through with the inverse of the numerators involving w_1 and R_1, we obtain a "symmetrical" equation system with all left-hand-side terms similar:

$$v_{11}(w_1)^{(\beta-1)(1-\sigma)}\left[R_1\right]^{\alpha(1-\beta)(1-\sigma)} + v_{22}(w_2)^{(\beta-1)(1-\sigma)}\left[R_2\right]^{\alpha(1-\beta)(1-\sigma)}\left(\frac{t_{12}}{t_{22}}\right)^{1-\sigma}$$

$$\dots + v_{NN}(w_N)^{(\beta-1)(1-\sigma)}\left[R_N\right]^{\alpha(1-\beta)(1-\sigma)}\left(\frac{t_{1N}}{t_{NN}}\right)^{1-\sigma}$$

$$= \sigma f Z_x (1-\alpha)^{\beta-1}(R_1)^{\sigma\alpha(\beta-1)} w_1^{\sigma(1-\beta)} \tag{23}$$

This can be expressed in matrix form. We define the vectors and matrixes as follows:

- V, W and R are column vectors with home market sales $v_{ii,}$ wages w_i and capital-labour ratios R_i as elements, respectively.
- $W^{(\beta-1)(1-\sigma)}$, for example, means that each individual element of W is raised to this power.
- Diag(..) is a diagonal matrix with the variable .. (V, R, L, etc.) as elements.
- Q is the constant expression (scalar) $\sigma f Z_x(1-\alpha)^{\beta-1}$.
- T is the N × N matrix of trade costs with elements $(t_{ij}/t_{jj})^{1-\sigma}$ where elements in the first column are divided by t_{11}, and so on.

The N equations of type (23) may then be expressed as follows:

$$\mathrm{T}_{\mathrm{N}\times\mathrm{N}}{}^{*}\, diag\left(\mathrm{W}^{(\beta-1)(1-\sigma)}\right)_{,\mathrm{N}\times\mathrm{N}}{}^{*}\, diag\left(\mathrm{R}^{\alpha(1-\beta)(1-\sigma)}\right)_{,\mathrm{N}\times\mathrm{N}}{}^{*}\, \mathrm{V}_{\mathrm{N}\times 1}$$
$$= \mathrm{Q}^{*}\, diag\left(\mathrm{R}^{\sigma\alpha(\beta-1)}\right)_{,\mathrm{N}\times\mathrm{N}}{}^{*}\, \mathrm{W}^{\sigma(1-\beta)}{}_{,\mathrm{N}\times 1} \tag{24}$$

Here the unknowns are wages and home market sales v_{ii} and so we have 2N unknowns and N equations. This equation can be rearranged as follows:

$$\mathrm{V}_{\mathrm{N}\times 1} = \mathrm{Q}^{*} diag\left(\mathrm{R}^{\alpha(\beta-1)(1-\sigma)}\right)_{,\mathrm{N}\times\mathrm{N}}{}^{*}\, diag\left(\mathrm{W}^{(1-\beta)(1-\sigma)}\right)_{,\mathrm{N}\times\mathrm{N}}{}^{*}\, \mathrm{T}^{-1}{}_{\mathrm{N}\times\mathrm{N}}$$
$${}^{*} diag\left(\mathrm{R}^{\sigma\alpha(\beta-1)}\right)_{,\mathrm{N}\times\mathrm{N}}{}^{*}\, \mathrm{W}^{\sigma(1-\beta)}{}_{,\mathrm{N}\times 1} \tag{25}$$

where W is the only unknown on the right hand side.

As the next step, total manufacturing sales by all firms in all markets have to add up to local manufacturing demand, and from (15) we see that the total value must be aY_i in market *i*. For sales in market *j* we must have:

$$\sum_i n_i v_{ij} = aY_j \tag{26}$$

We now also define the column vectors $\mathrm{F}_{\mathrm{N}\times 1}$ for the number of firms, and $\mathrm{Y}_{\mathrm{N}\times 1}$ for total income. Using (25) and (26) and rearranging, with similar techniques and terminology as above, we obtain the equation system:

$$\mathrm{T'}_{\mathrm{N}\times\mathrm{N}}{}^{*} diag\left(\mathrm{W}^{(1-\beta)(1-\sigma)}\right)_{,\mathrm{N}\times\mathrm{N}}{}^{*}\, diag\left(\mathrm{R}^{\alpha(\beta-1)(1-\sigma)}\right)_{,\mathrm{N}\times\mathrm{N}}{}^{*}\, \mathrm{F}_{\mathrm{N}\times 1}$$
$$= \mathrm{a}^{*} diag\left(\mathrm{R}^{\alpha(\beta-1)(1-\sigma)}\right)_{,\mathrm{N}\times\mathrm{N}}{}^{*}\, diag\left(\mathrm{W}^{(1-\beta)(1-\sigma)}\right)_{,\mathrm{N}\times\mathrm{N}}$$
$${}^{*}\mathrm{Diag}\left(\mathrm{V}^{-1}\right)_{,\mathrm{N}\times\mathrm{N}}{}^{*}\, \mathrm{Y}_{\mathrm{N}\times 1} \tag{27}$$

Hence we have added N new equations but also 2N unknowns, the number of firms F and income levels Y. Country income is from (18) a function of wages and so we can add the matrix form equations:

$$Y_{\mathrm{N}\times 1} = \frac{1}{1-\alpha}\mathrm{Diag}\left(L\right)_{\mathrm{N}\times\mathrm{N}} W_{\mathrm{N}\times 1} + G_{\mathrm{N}\times 1} \tag{28}$$

where W and G are wages and natural resource endowments, respectively; both N×1 column vectors.

We thereby have 3N equations but 4N unknowns. In order to find the missing piece, we use the condition that the combined demand for services for consumption and as input into manufacturing production has to equal total services production, given by Eq. (1).

Using (1), (12) and (14) we obtain:

$$S_i = K_i^{\alpha} L_i^{1-\alpha} = S_{ci} + S_{xi} = \left(1-a\right) Y_i p_i^{-1} + n_i \sigma f Z_x \left(1-\beta\right) p_i^{-\beta} \tag{29}$$

Substituting for Y_i and p_i and rearranging, we obtain:

$$\sigma f Z_x \left(1-\beta\right)\left(1-\alpha\right)^{\beta} n_i R_i^{\alpha(\beta-1)} w_i^{-\beta} = aL_i - \left(1-a\right)\left(1-\alpha\right) w_i^{-1} G_i \tag{30}$$

Moving all except n_i on the right hand side and expressing in matrix form we have equivalently:

$$\begin{aligned} \mathrm{F}_{\mathrm{N}\times 1} &= \mathrm{a} / \mathrm{Q}_2{}^{*} diag\left(\mathrm{L}\right)_{\mathrm{N}\times\mathrm{N}}{}^{*}\, diag\left(\mathrm{W}^{\beta}\right)_{\mathrm{N}\times\mathrm{N}}{}^{*}\, \mathrm{R}^{\alpha(1-\beta)}{}_{\mathrm{N}\times 1} \\ &\quad - \left(1-\mathrm{a}\right)\left(1-\alpha\right) / \mathrm{Q}_2{}^{*} diag\left(\mathrm{W}^{\beta-1}\right)_{\mathrm{N}\times 1}{}^{*}\, \mathrm{diag}\mathrm{R}^{\alpha(1-\beta)})_{\mathrm{N}\times\mathrm{N}}{}^{*}\, \mathrm{G}_{\mathrm{N}\times\mathrm{N}} \end{aligned} \tag{31}$$

where Q_2 is the constant expression $\sigma f Z_x(1 - \beta)(1 - \alpha)^{\beta}$.

Here n_i and w_i are the only unknowns, and we have obtained a fourth set of N equations with 4N unknowns and the system is determined.

Complete Specialisation and Autarky

An issue is whether regions may become fully specialised in their trade, with commodities in exchange for manufactured goods and no two-way trade in manufactured goods. This is indeed the case. In the later simulation of the model, we will see that relatively large endowments of natural resources drive up the wage and this reduces manufacturing production. This also reduces domestic absorption of commodities and so a rising share of commodities is exported. At some point, a country may become fully deindustrialised, exporting all its commodities in exchange for imports of manufactured goods. If income and expenditures are to be equal, it is evident that in this case we must for a specialised country s have (from the demand Eq. (15), using that $G_s = X_{cs}P_{xs}$):

$$G_s = aY_s \quad \text{or equivalently} \quad Y_s = {G_s}/{a} \tag{32}$$

From Eq. (28) we have an alternative expression for Y_s. Inserting (31) in (28) we obtain:

$$w_s = \frac{(1-a)(1-\alpha)}{a} \times \frac{G_s}{L_s} \tag{33}$$

For the specialised country, national income as well as the wage are proportional to the raw material stock. For the specialised country, nominal wages are not affected by international competition. Welfare is however affected by international competition and trade policies, since it depends on the price index for manufactured goods.

Equations (32) and (33) are derived under the assumption that specialisation occurs, but they do not determine the "point of complete specialisation". It is evident that this must occur when the share of manufacturing in GDP, or the number of firms, is equal to zero, and imports of manufactures exceed a share of a in GDP. As we shall see, the location of the "break point" is mainly determined by the commodity endowment, but other aspects that affect the manufacturing share also play a role. Hence the location of this point also depends on country size, the capital-labour ratio and trade costs/geographical location, in addition to G.

For the case with specialised countries, it may appear from (32) and (33) as if wages and income are set by domestic relationships and unaffected by the international economy; this is however a false impression since g is the numeraire and so all nominal figures are reflecting world demand and supply conditions. Contrary to this, autarky is a case where indeed all matters are determined within each region or country. In autarky, all the factors endowments of a region are used in the production of services and manufacturing for domestic use. It is then easily derived that

$$w_{\text{autarky}} = (1-\alpha)\left(\frac{1}{a\beta}-1\right)\frac{G}{L} \tag{34}$$

Also in this case, the nominal wage is positively and linearly related to the G/L ratio, and this time the factor intensity in manufacturing (β) also plays a role. If natural resources become more abundant, the relative price of labour increases. The same applies to the price of capital, since the w/r ratio is fixed. Equation (34) also demonstrates how the wage depends on all the technology parameters of the model. In the autarky case, the wage is inversely related to α, β, and a. For the first two, the intuition is clear—lowering the labour cost share reduces the wage. For the share of manufacturing in demand (a), the reason is that switching from services to manufacturing also switches demand towards commodity-using activity and therefore reduces the wage.

Numerical Simulation of the Model

Equations (25), (27), (28) and (31) cannot be solved explicitly and so we must use numerical simulation. From these equations we have the pattern shown in Table B.1.

If we find the solution for wages W, this can be plugged into (25), (28) and (31) and the solutions for V, Y and F then follow. Hence in the

Table B.1 Unknowns in the equation system

Equation	Relationship	Unknowns
(25)	Allocation of firm sales	W, V
(27)	Manufacturing sales = demand	W, F, V, Y
(28)	Total factor income	Y, W
(31)	Supply = demand for services	F, W

Note: The vectors are W = wages, V = home market sales of tradables sector firms, F = number of tradables sector firms, and Y = total (factor) income for a country/region

numerical simulations, we do not have to solve for 4N unknowns but only the N unknown wage levels. This simplifies the task considerably.

For the simplest simulations with all regions diversified, we therefore create an objective function based on (27) that is to be minimised, with the three other equations as side conditions. Using *lhs* and *rhs* for the left and right hand side of (27), respectively, the aim is *lhs* = *rhs* for all the N equations. The objective function could be formed in different ways, and the following form performed best (of the alternatives attempted):

$$M_1 = \sum_i \left(\frac{lhs}{rhs} - 1 \right)^2 \tag{35}$$

This case applies only if all regions are diversified. If some regions become specialised, Eqs. (25) no longer apply (since the "home market sales" of their firms make no sense) whereas the other three sets of equations are still valid. In this case, simulations have to be undertaken in a different way. In this case, we start by calculating the N×N matrix with elements $F_i v_{ij}$; that is, the matrix of manufacturing sales across all markets. Let us call this the sales matrix. The number of firms vector F is a function of wages according to (31), and v_{ij} follows from (16). Now with row 1 containing $F_1 v_{11}$, $F_1 v_{12}$,...,$F_1 v_{1N}$, row 1 will be the total sales of tradables from country 1. This must be equal to firm size (10) multiplied by the number of firms in region 1. Using all these horizontal sums of the sales matrix, we form an expression such as (35). Second, the vertical sums of the sales matrix must be equal to total demand for manufactured goods in each region; that is aY_i for country i. Taking all these horizontal sums, we obtain a second expression similar to (35). In the simulations, we minimise the sums of these two partial objective functions simultaneously. Using h for the horizontal and v for the vertical relationships, the objective function is then:

$$M_2 = \sum_i \left(\frac{lhs_h}{rhs_h} - 1 \right)^2 + \sum_i \left(\frac{lhs_v}{rhs_v} - 1 \right)^2 \tag{36}$$

Contrary to Table B.1/ function (35), this form also works if manufacturing production is zero. In this case, we first simulate the model assuming that all countries have non-zero manufacturing production and obtain negative manufacturing production (and number of firms) for to-be specialised countries. Based on this preliminary simulation, we re-run the simulation setting the manufacturing number of firms equal to zero and using wage levels (33) for the specialised countries. If all countries have non-negative manufacturing production in the new results, we have found the solution. It may however also be the case that new countries have negative manufacturing production in the second set of results; in that case, the procedure has to be repeated (this rarely happens, and so the solution is mostly found in two steps).

The model was solved using MATrix LABoratory (MATLAB) version 2012a, using the Global Optimization Toolbox. While some small-scale simulations could be handled by the "genetic algorithm" of MATLAB, the most powerful tool was the constrained non-linear minimisation FMINCON algorithm (shorthand for Find Minimum of Constrained Nonlinear Multivariable Function); using either the "Interior Point" or "SQP—Sequential Quadratic Programming" sub-algorithms.[7] The challenge, especially for the larger-scale world economy simulation, is to find the global minimum in the presence of many local minima and maxima, and a powerful algorithm is needed for this purpose.

An issue is how small M_1 or M_2 should be for the model solution to be sufficiently accurate. In order to evaluate this, we check trade balances and the *lhs* and *rhs* above. In order to obtain this with accuracy in the simulations, the value of M has to be close to zero. In the small-scale simulations results we present here, M always had a value of less than 5E-07. In the large-scale world economy simulations, M_2 was always smaller than 5E-11. Hence we were always able to obtain convergence with great accuracy, with the data sets applied. For the world economy model, it was tried with 195 regions and countries but then it was difficult to obtain convergence in some cases. The number of countries/regions was therefore reduced to 110. The ability to solve the model (find the global minimum) therefore depends on the number of regions as well as the algorithms at hand. Potentially, techniques can be improved in the future so that the model is easily solved with a larger number of regions.

In all simulations, W was bounded to be non-negative. While we were always able to find unique global solutions in the simulations we present, it is possible with such a complex non-linear model that there could be negative or even complex roots. For a discussion on the existence of solutions in similar models, see Shoven and Whalley (1992).

Commodities and Intra-industry Trade: Some Model Features

Before proceeding to the world economy model, it is useful to illustrate some of the general properties of the model. Given that the equation system in Table B.1 is impossible to solve analytically, we run some stylised small-scale simulations to illustrate the model properties. With set values for the model parameters, we let factor endowments (G, K, L) or trade costs (T) vary. If countries are similar in all respects and there is no core-periphery pattern, there will be no reason to trade commodities, and so in this case there will only be intra-industry trade in manufacturing. In the following we examine how the outcome is affected by various changes in the exogenous variables. Details are presented in Appendix Table C.1. As a point of departure, recall that commodities are the numeraire and so all prices are relative to commodities. We can however also calculate the physical quantities produced and consumed so we are still able to compare across scenarios.

First, we assume that all countries are equal except for their commodity endowment G. The simulations (Appendix Table C1, case 1) then show that the countries with larger natural resource endowments have higher wages and utility and GDP (total income, Y) per labour unit. The higher cost level generated by this "spending effect" (Corden and Neary 1982) however also leads to deindustrialisation, and so the resource-abundant country is a net exporter of commodities and a net importer of manufacturing, with a relatively low manufacturing share of GDP.

Result 1 Natural resource abundance relative to other countries raises wages, costs, income and welfare but leads to deindustrialisation in the sense that the manufacturing share of GDP declines, with net exports of commodities and net imports of manufacturing.

As a second experiment, we assume that all countries have equal factor proportions and face the same trade barriers but that their size varies (Appendix Table C1, case 2). The model exhibits a "home market effect" whereby large countries tend to have a larger share of manufacturing production, due to their larger home market (Krugman 1980). The largest countries have higher wages, a higher share of manufacturing in GDP, higher utility and are net importers of commodities.

Result 2 Other things equal, large countries tend to have higher wages and utility, and be net importers of commodities and net exporters of manufactured goods.[8]

A similar effect of market access could be obtained in the case of regional trade integration, where some countries lower trade costs between them and thereby create an extended home market, or by geography—where some countries are more peripheral. As a third experiment (Appendix Table C1, case 3), we assume that all countries have equal factor endowments and size but that their location varies with a core-periphery pattern, In this case, we put the ten countries along a line so that between countries 1 and 10 there are nine "distance units", and so on. In this case, countries 5 and 6 are at the core whereas countries 1 and 10 are the most peripheral, with higher average trade costs for manufacturing. The central countries have better market access and we therefore obtain:

Result 3 Other things equal, peripheral countries tend to have lower wages and utility, and be net exporters of commodities and net importers of manufactured goods.

Result 3 illustrates the "gravity" characteristics of the model, producing monocentric concentration rather than a "duocentric" pattern with two agglomerations somewhere between the centre and the ends of the line. The issue of monocentric, duocentric or policentric equilibria is examined, for example, by Fujita and Krugman (1995), Fujita and Mori (1997) and Fujita et al. (1999). In the "New Economic Geography", models with "cumulative causation" are usually applied (e.g. with labour migration or vertical input-output linkages. The model used here has no cumulative causation, and this is a deliberate choice for the sake of tractability. The issue of single versus multiple agglomerations is however still relevant. Melchior (1997) shows that with ten regions along a line, the standard model of Krugman (1980) (with a numeraire sector) generates a duocentric equilibrium. An issue is whether locational advantages show up in the form of trade effects (net export of manufactures) of wage effects (higher wages). The "numeraire" model of Krugman (1980) is driven by trade effects; if we drop the numeraire sector there will be only wage effects (since there is only intra-industry trade and aggregate manufacturing trade must be balanced). Melchior (2009) shows that models with wage effects tend to be more monocentric than models with trade effects. The model user here has both wage and trade effects, but the wage effects dominate and support a monocentric outcome in our 10-country illustration. In the real world with 110 countries, the patterns can be more complex.

As a final case (Appendix Table C1, case 4), we assume that countries are similar except for their capital endowments K. As noted in the introduction and Chap. 6, the K/L ratio reflects productivity. This variation in capital endowments creates gaps in productivity, wages, utility, and manufacturing production (Appendix Table C.1, case 4). The countries with more capital have much larger manufacturing production and therefore use more commodities; for this reason, they are net importers of commodities from countries at the other end of the K/L scale.[9]

Result 4 Countries with higher productivity (driven by a larger capital stock) tend to be commodity importers and manufacturing exporters, and have higher wages, utility per capita and income per capita.

On the whole, the results replicate characteristics of new trade theory models but place them in a new setting where the standard "numeraire sector" of some models has been replaced by the more realistic feature of commodity trade. Commodity trade allows imbalances in the tradables sector. Other things equal, countries with better market access or higher productivity tend to have higher tradables production and exports, and therefore also be commodity importers. But higher productivity and better location also show up in higher wages, and so the model combines trade and wage effects in a useful way.

Cases 1 through 4 above illustrate the various mechanisms in isolation, but they may also interact, and be reinforcing or counteracting each other. For example; capital stock growth in (for other reasons) commodity-importing countries may lead to increased commodity trade, further deindustrialisation of commodity-exporting countries, and a rising wage gap between commodity-exporting and commodity-importing countries. Combining the various features, the model provides a useful tool for examining the complex interactions of the world economy.

World Economy Model: Data and Simulation

For simulating the model, the inputs needed are (i) the factor stocks of each region; (ii) the matrix of bilateral trade costs between all regions, including transport costs; and (iii) the technical coefficients of the model, that is factor and consumption shares and the elasticity of substitution for tradables. We construct a data set based 2014 data and simulate a corresponding base scenario. We thereafter simulate scenarios or counterfactual experiments where some of the model inputs are changed.

Countries and Regions

In order to capture geography in a better way, we disaggregate seven large countries counties (Brazil, Canada, China, India, Kazakhstan, Russia and USA) into 47 regions. The regional sub-division is presented in Appendix Table C.2.

Having the necessary country data for 152 countries, we obtain a data set of 152 + 47–7 = 192 countries and regions. Simulations were undertaken with this data set; this was however too much for the available algorithms and it was often difficult to obtain convergence and find the solution. The data set was therefore reduced by aggregating 101 countries into 19 country groups; thereby cutting the data set to 110. The 19 country groups are shown in Appendix Table C.3.[10]

In the final data set we have 44 individual countries, 19 country groups and 47 sub-regions of large countries. In the following, we describe the data requirements and inputs.

Factor Endowments

In the model, factor stocks are G, K and L, with corresponding prices g, r and w. Assuming g as the numeraire, we have Gg and L directly observed:

- From the World Bank's "Changing Wealth of Nations" project (World Bank 2006, 2011) we obtain data by country on total natural resources rents (% of Gross Domestic Product (GDP)). This includes oil, gas, coal, minerals and forestry but not agriculture. Multiplied by GDP, this provides a proxy for Gg in the model, which is the income from natural resources.
- We use data on the labour force from ILO (International Labour Organization) and the World Bank as a measure of the labour stock L. Observe that L is "raw labour" that does not reflect skills; however, skills or human capital will be reflected in our measure of K.

Definition and data sources for these and other variables are found in Appendix C.4. In general, country data are downloaded from the WDI (World Development Indicators) database.

Regarding the capital stock K; it should include physical as well as human capital. In order to derive this, we draw on results from the growth accounting literature (see e.g. Caselli 2005; Hsieh and Klenow 2010 for overviews). Zuleta and Sturgill (2015) derived estimates of per worker endowments of natural, physical, and human capital per worker for many countries. For 2005, they provide results for 56 countries. For these 56 countries, we use their estimates to derive factor stocks, multiplying our labour stock L with their estimates we obtain estimates for the stocks of natural, physical, and human capital. With the resulting hypothetical data, we calculate the share of physical and human capital in total factor endowments except natural resources ($K/(K + L)$ in terms of our model). Figure B.1 plots this hypothetical factor share against the log of non-natural resource income per worker ($(Y - Gg)/L$). For GDP we use PPP (Purchasing Power Parity) estimates, since that gives a slightly better fit.

There is a strong correlation; with $R^2 = 0.88$ for the fitted (logarithmic) line. We use this relationship (the equation in the chart) to derive estimates for the capital stock in our whole sample of 110 regions.[11]

According to the results of Zuleta and Sturgill (2015), the average factor shares across the 56 countries in their sample for 2005 were 49% for physical capital, 12% for human capital, 11% for natural capital, and 28% for "raw" labour.[12] Hence in terms of our model, the K/L ratio will be on average (49 + 12)/28 = 2.2. This is also the weighted average we obtain for our

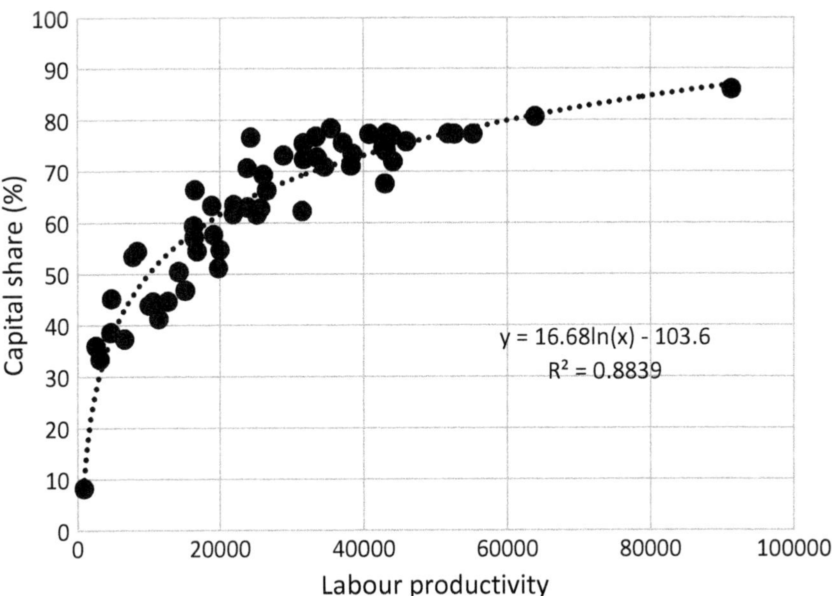

Fig. B.1 Capital share of factor stock except natural resources, versus non-resource income per labour unit. (Source: Own calculations. Data sources: See text)

data set with 110 regions, using the constructed K estimates. Sturgill (2009) finds a considerably higher share for human capital; for example, close to 50% for USA, Canada and Japan. Hence there is some uncertainty about the magnitudes. Zuleta and Sturgill (2015) find, along with some other contributions in the literature (see references therein), that the shares of raw labour and natural resources are inversely related to income per capita, while physical and human capital shares are rising with income (as shown in Fig. B.1). Caselli (2005) similarly concludes there is a strong correlation between per capita income and the K/L ratio.

Having data for *Gg* and *L*, and estimates on *K*, we also need to determine the cost share parameters. These technological parameters are set to be common across countries, even if actual factor use will vary, depending on endowments. Figure B.1 suggests that productivity increases up to a capital share of 70–80% of non-resource factor stocks. Based on this, we set the parameter α, the capital cost share in the production of our universal "services" sector equal to 0.75.

We also need to determine the parameter β; that is the cost share of natural resources in manufacturing. In our data, the share of total natural resource income in GDP is 5% on average (weighted), while the estimate of Zuleta and Sturgill is 11%. The gap may partly be due to raw material prices and we prefer to stick to our own data since these are up-to-date and available for all the 110 regions. For *Gg*, we therefore use our own data rather than the estimate based on Zuleta and Sturgill. There is also an issue about scaling and units; if we measure labour in numbers and *Gg* in dollars, the G/K and G/L ratios will be very large. Since it is the physical quantities that enter into production function, this matters, and we scale *gG* so that the world average corresponds to the parameter β.

In order to set the parameter β in the manufacturing production function, use data on the manufacturing share of GDP for 146 countries. Added up for the world this share is equal to 18%. Natural resources are inputs into this production and we therefore set the parameter β equal to 5/(5 + 18) or 0.23.[13] Our tradables sector could also include services but we do not have appropriate data to include tradable services.

For the simulations, we also need to set the parameters a (the share of manufacturing in demand) and ε (the elasticity of substitution between manufacturing product varieties). For the latter, we use a value of 5, based on the summary of the empirical literature in Head and Mayer (2014, pp. 163–165), where the median estimate across several studies based on data for tariffs and transport costs is 5.03. Regarding the share of manufacturing in demand, global production is equal to global consumption in the model. The gross value of manufactured goods includes the natural resource cost, and since all income is consumed the share should be 5 + 18% or 0.23 also in this case.[14]

Trade and Infrastructure Costs

A key feature of the model is that some trade costs depend on geographical location and distance, while others do not. For example, a tariff may be the same for countries across the globe, and all suppliers may face the same costs of red tape and local infrastructure. The interaction between these two types of costs is driving the spatial patterns observed in the model. The mix of the two gives effects that are qualitatively different from those obtained by each of them separately. For example, changing a non-spatial trade cost (e.g. a tariff) will have an impact that differs across space, due to the presence of geography.

For the non-spatial trade costs, we construct two different indicators based on World Bank/World Development Indicators data; shown in Table B.2.

The expcost/impcost variables are specifically related to the foreign trade of countries. We scale these variables to 0–100 and then use weighted averages (with 50% for cost to export/import). A similar procedure is used for the three infrastructure variables that are also scaled to 0–100 and averaged. For merged country groups, we use averages across countries weighted by GDP. For countries split into regions, we assume that the values are the same for all sub-regions of a country.

For tariffs, we depart from the simple mean of MFN (Most Favoured Nations) applied tariffs for all products. Then we use the corresponding figure for preferential tariffs and calculate the percentage tariff reduction due to preferences. The calculation thereby includes all trade preferences recorded in the UNCTAD/TRAINS (United Nations Conference on Trade and Development/Trade Analysis Information Systems) tariff data base. The majority of cases are FTAs, but tariff preferences for developing countries also matter. In the trade costs matrix there are 100 × 110 = 12,100 cells, and for the

Table B.2 Trade cost data

Variable name	Variable from WDI	Transformation
Expcost	Cost to export (US$ per container) Documents to export (number) Time to export (days)	Average of variable scaled to 0–100, with 50% weight for cost and 25% for the other two
Impcost	Cost to import (US$ per container) Documents to import (number) Time to import (days)	
Infrastr	Internet users (per 100 people) Logistics performance index: Overall (1=low to 5=high) Costs of business start-up (% of per capita GNI)	Average of variables, all scaled to 0–100
Tariff	Tariff rate, most favoured nation, simple mean, all products (%); adjusted for tariff reductions for all free trade agreements and other preferences recorded in the UNCTAD/TRAINS data base	Tariff multiplied by tariff cuts due to preferences
Geography	Distance in kilometres, raised to the power 0.4	

Note: Variables for expcost, impcost and infrastr are taken from World Development Indicators (WDI). See Appendix C.4 for more detail. Tariff data are taken from WDI (MFN tariffs) and from UNCTAD/TRAINS (using WITS—World Integrated Trade Solution) (preferential tariffs)

domestic trade within large nations (367 cells) there are no tariffs. For the remaining 11,733 cells, we have data for non-zero tariff reductions in 4193 cases or 36%.[15]

For geography, the point of departure is air distance in kilometres, ranging from a few hundred to sixteen thousand kilometres. Following Melchior (2010), we raise distance to the power of 0.4 so that the increase in trade cost from 1000 to 10,000 km is not 10 times but 2.51 times. We consider this more plausible in the light of available evidence on transport costs, which suggests that transport costs do not increase exponentially at large distances (mainly due to cheap sea freight). In future work, the intention is to take into account transport modes and shipping routes explicitly; the simple scaling of distance used here is a first approach.

While tariff rates are given in exact magnitudes, the trade cost and infrastructure variables are on a 0–100 scale and geography in yet another scale and so we do not know the magnitudes measured in tariff equivalents. The scaling of the three non-tariff components is indeed a difficult issue. A useful point of departure for the assessment is Anderson and Wincoop (2004) who estimated total trade costs excluding retail/distribution costs at 70% for industrial countries; with transport costs at 21% and other costs at 44% (8% policy barriers including tariffs, 7% language, 6% information costs, 3% security, and 14% currency), and 1.21*1.44 = 1.70 giving the resulting 70% overall. Looking at the sub-components, there is however great uncertainty about the appropriate magnitudes, and some recent work on FTAs provides estimates that differ considerably from the above (e.g. Francois et al. 2013; Felbermayr et al. 2016). While the average tariff in our data is 6% and thereby in the range of Anderson and Wincoop, the tariff equivalents of other trade costs remain uncertain. Furthermore, it is likely that many of the non-tariff components are increasing depend on geography (information costs, borders, currencies, etc.). It is beyond the scope of this paper to eliminate this uncertainty, and in this first application of the model we make ad hoc choices on the scaling of various components that may be updated later in the light of better data. We use the data on infrastructure and export/import costs directly with no scaling; this gives averages of 7% for infrastructure, and 7% and 10% for export and import costs combined, respectively. We scale distance so that the average distance-related cost is 33% (unweighted average, the trade-weighted average is 29%). With the chosen scaling, for example, Germany faces a "distance cost" within Europe at 10–15%, while this cost related to the Far East, South America and Oceania is above 30%. Adding the various components, including average tariffs at 6%, total trade costs in our data are 56%. That is lower than the Anderson and Wincoop (2004) estimate, but this is plausible since we use more recent data. The weighting choices made here is a first approach that may be improved upon later based on better data.[16]

Regional Data for Large Countries

Sources of regional data for the seven large countries are presented in Appendix Table C.5. We have satisfactory data on population, GDP, geodata (coordinates) and land area for the regions. We scale up or down the regional data as appropriate to secure that they add up to the country-level WDI data that are comparable across countries. On natural resources, we mostly use regional shares of mining and quarrying in GDP as a tool to allocate the nationwide gG value (the income from natural resources) across regions. Labour force statistics were missing in many cases and the national labour force was then allocated across regions using population shares. Regarding trade costs, tariffs do not apply within countries and we assume that the same is the case for expcost/impcost. More detail on regional data is provided in Appendix Table C.5.

Baseline Scenario

As noted earlier, we are generally able to solve the model (i.e. find the global minimum of the objective function) with great precision. In the baseline scenario, there are 12 countries/regions that are fully specialised in commodities, with no manufacturing production. We must therefore solve the model in two steps; first to trace the specialised regions and second to find the global solution with manufacturing production set at zero for the 12 specialised regions. The objective function converges to a value close to zero (4.28E-12). This means that the solution is very consistent; for example, net exports of commodities and manufacturing are equal (with opposite signs) with minimal deviation. If we sum the absolute values of these deviations from zero and express this sum as a percentage of total trade, the fraction is zero with six digits.

Among the 12 regions specialised in manufacturing, we find seven Russian regions, of which six are from Ural and eastward, and the seventh is the Murmansk-Arkhangelsk north-western region. The five remaining specialised regions are West Kazakhstan, Azerbaijan, the Arabian country group, Iran and Inner Mongolia in China. More detail is presented in Appendix Table C.6, which shows some key data and results for the baseline scenario. Figure B.2 plots predicted real income levels per capita against empirically observed levels in 2014. The empirical fit is good, with a correlation coefficient at 0.96 and R^2=0.93 for the simple linear regression shown in the diagram.

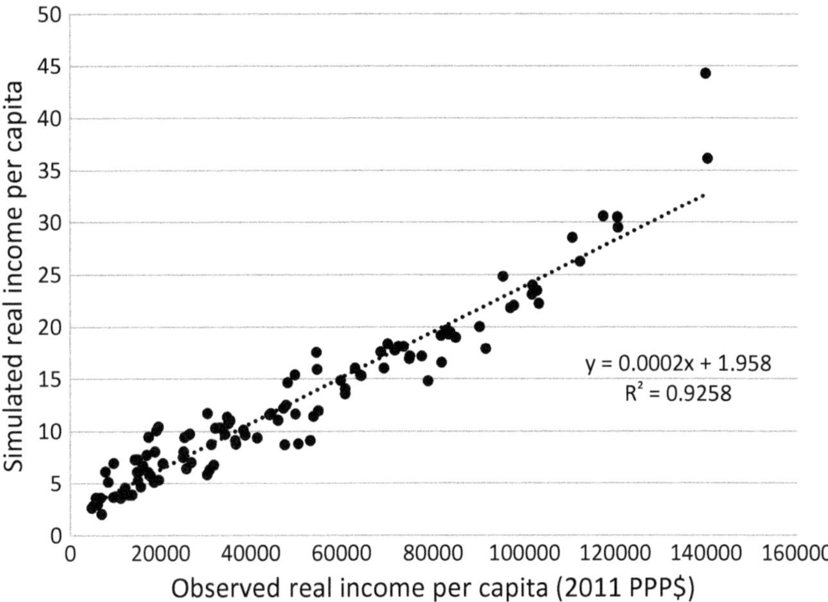

Fig. B.2 Simulated versus observed real income per capita. (Source: Own calculations. Observed income from World Development Indicators, see Appendix C.4 for details)

We also examine the correspondence between predicted bilateral manufacturing trade flows and the empirically observed levels for the 44 individual countries in the data set. The correlation in this case is at 0.65, which we consider as a good fit in the light of all the idiosyncratic features that affect bilateral trade flows.

Given that we have only one tradable sector, the percentage of intra-industry trade in trade flows will be higher as compared to if we had more sectors. It corresponds to our real-world aggregated measure of IIT in Chap. 2 (two-way trade in manufactured goods). Figure B.3 plots the percentage of intra-industry trade in the total trade of each country (with IIT measured at the bilateral level and summed across all trade partners for every country) against the share of natural resource rents in GDP.

As we might expect, there is a very strong correspondence; commodity-reliant regions have a low share of intra-industry trade (observe that the lowest point contains all the 12 specialised regions). The maximum is reached for a positive share of natural resource rents in GDP; regions with

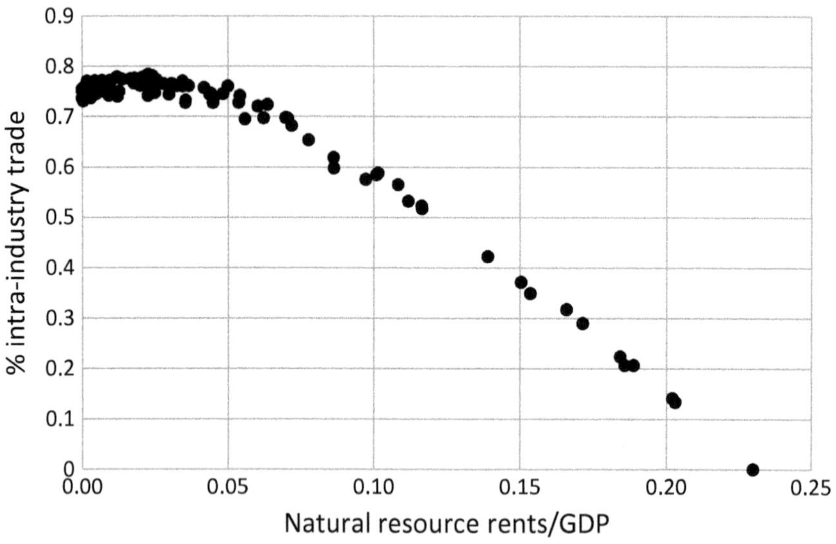

Fig. B.3 Natural resource rents and intra-industry trade (simulated). (Source: Own calculations. Results from numerical simulation)

lower shares must import more commodities and this reduces the IIT share. The pattern in Fig. B.3 replicates the patterns shown for the real world in Chap. 2; with the commodity regions exchanging commodities for manufacturing, and the industrial regions exporting and importing manufactured goods at about 60–80% of their total trade.

A virtue of a general equilibrium model like this is that all international interactions are accounted for, as well as the complex interaction between different drivers of specialisation and income levels. In the small-scale simulations shown in Appendix Table C.1, we could change one variable at the time, and study the effect. In the full-fledged world trade model, it is more complex, with all forces present at the same time.

Notes

1. Except for the case of autarky, where g will (implicitly) differ across regions.
2. In this introductory section, we drop country subscripts, for simplicity. In the theoretical sections later, we use the term country; in the world economy

model simulations this may be countries, country groups, or regions within countries, and we then use the terms country and region interchangeably.

3. In the numerical application of the model, productivity is increasing in K/L for most of the actual range; but productivity stagnates for very high levels of K/L.
4. Since raw materials G is a homogeneous product with zero trade costs, bilateral trade flows are not determined by the model, only the aggregate trade balance. For X, however, bilateral trade balances are determined and for practical purposes in the simulations, we may if necessary assume that bilateral trade is also balanced; with this assumption the bilateral raw material trade is also determined.
5. Sections B.2, B.3, B.4, B.5 and B.6 contains the technical description of the model and the more generally interested reader may proceed to Sect. B.7 without losing the thread.
6. We assume that real trade costs are added, not that some goods melt away in transports as in the standard iceberg approach. The two definitions are however in practice equivalent.
7. See https://se.mathworks.com/help/optim/ug/constrained-nonlinear-optimization-algorithms.html for explanation and references. For the small-scale simulations in Sect. B.8, many algorithms will do, but for the world economy model the SQP or "Interior Point" algorithms have the best performance.
8. Result 2 depends on the presence of trade costs, since it is the trade costs that create a wedge between markets, and with scale economies and imperfect competition we obtain the home market effect. Contrary to Krugman (1980), however, additional simulations not shown here (details may be provided upon request) indicate that the home market effect is not reinforced by trade liberalisation; on the contrary, general trade liberalisation reduces the deindustrialisation impact of commodity abundance.
9. The impact in this case is quantitatively much larger than the former cases. While the scale is affected by model parameters that are chosen arbitrarily, they are in plausible ranges and so it is of some interest to observe that all the effects related to natural resource abundance (case 1) or trade costs (cases 2 and 3) are very small compared to the impact of capital stock differences. This will also be the case in the more realistic simulations later.
10. The country aggregation was influenced by plans to use the model in studies related to Europe, Russia, and Asia; Africa and to some extent South America were therefore to a larger extent aggregated into groups.

Data are however assembled at the country level so the country groups may be changed if the model is to be used in studies focusing on other world regions.

11. This method has some shortcomings since 2005 data were used by Zuleta and Sturgill, but it is the best estimate we can find for physical and human capital combined. For physical capital, more recent estimates are available but human capital is very important and should be taken into account.
12. Based on the authors' Appendix 4 and our calculations.
13. In terms of the model, we need to use gross manufacturing value of production in order to calculate the cost share, not GDP/value added where inputs have been deducted.
14. The parameters a and $^{\beta}$ are similar in magnitude but this is by chance only.
15. For domestic regions in large countries, tariffs are the same for all regions in a country. For country groups, we calculate GDP-weighted averages of the country-by-country tariffs.
16. For the "calibration" of trade costs, the decomposition of large countries into regions implies that a "new quantitative trade theory" approach is not directly applicable for data reasons; one has to work on country data and then extrapolate to the 110-region setting.

References

Anderson, J. E. & van Wincoop, E. (2004). Trade Costs. *Journal of Economic Literature, 42*(3), 691–751.

Caselli, F. (2005). Accounting for Cross-Country Income Differences. In P. Aghion P. & Durlauf, S. N. (Eds.), *Handbook of Economic Growth, Volume 1A* (Chapter 9, pp. 679–741). Amsterdam/New York: North-Holland. https://doi.org/10.1016/B978-0-444-53538-2.00012-5.

Corden, M. & P. Neary. (1982). Booming Sector and De-Industrialisation in a Small Open Economy. *The Economic Journal, 92*(368), 825–848.

Felbermayr, G., Aichele, R., Heiland, I, Melchior, A., & Steininger, M. (2016). *TTIP: Potential Effects on Norway*. Munich: Ifo Working Paper 228/2016.

Francois, J., Manchin, M., Norberg, O., Pindyuk, O., & Tomberger, P. (2013). *Reducing Transatlantic Barriers to Trade. An Economic Assessment.* London: Centre for Economic Policy Research (CEPR), Final Project Report, March 2013, Prepared for the European Commission.

Fujita, M. & Krugman, P. (1995). When is the Economy Monocentric?: von Thünen and Chamberlin Unified. *Regional Science and Urban Economics, 25*, 505–528.

Fujita, M. & Mori. T. (1997). Structural Stability and Evolution of Urban Systems. *Regional Science and Urban Economics, 27*, 399–442.

Fujita, M., Krugman, P., & Venables, A. J. (1999). *The Spatial Economy. Cities, Regions and International Trade*. Cambridge, MA/London: The MIT Press.

Head, K. & Mayer, T. (2014). Gravity Equations: Workhorse, Toolkit, and Cookbook. In G. Gopinath, Helpman, E. & Rogoff, K. (Eds.). *International Economics Volume 4* (Chapter 3, pp. 131–195). Amsterdam: North-Holland/ Elsevier, Handbooks in Economics.

Hsieh, C. & Klenow, P. J. (2010). Development Accounting. *American Economic Journal: Macroeconomics*, *2*(1), 207–223.

Krugman, P. (1980). Scale Economies, Product Differentiation, and the Pattern of Trade. *American Economic Review*, *70*(5), 950–959.

Markusen, J. & Venables, A. J. (2000). The Theory of Endowment, Intra-industry and Multi-national Trade. *Journal of International Economics*, *52*, 209–234.

Melchior, A. (1997). *On the Economics of Market Access and International Economic Integration*. Oslo: University of Oslo, Department of Economics, Economic Dissertations No. 36.

Melchior, A. (2004). *North-South Trade and Wages with Complete Specialisation: Modifying the Stolper-Samuelson Relationship*. Oslo: NUPI Working Paper No. 666, www.nupi.no.

Melchior, A. (2009). *European Integration and Domestic Regions. A Numerical Simulation Analysis*. Warsaw: CASE Studies and Analyses No. 378/ 2009.

Melchior, A. (2010). Globalisation and the Provinces of China: The Role of Domestic Versus International Trade Integration. *Journal of Chinese Economic and Business Studies*, *8*(3), 227–252.

Shoven, J. B. & Whalley, J. (1992). *Applying General Equilibrium* (Cambridge Surveys of Economic Literature). Cambridge: Cambridge University Press.

Sturgill, B. (2009). *Cross-country Variation in Factor Shares and its Implications for Development Accounting*. Mimeo: Appalachian State University.

World Bank. (2006). *Where is the Wealth of Nations? Measuring Capital for the 21st Century*. Washington, DC: The World Bank.

World Bank. (2011). *The Changing Wealth of Nations. Measuring Sustainable Development in the New Millennium*. Washington, DC: The World Bank.

Zuleta, H. & Sturgill, B. (2015). *Getting Growth Accounting Right*. Bogota: Universidad de los Andes, CEDE (Centro de Estudios sobre Desarrollo Economico, Documentos CEDE No. 29, September 2015, ISSN 1657-7191.

Appendix C: Tables Related to Numerical Model Simulations

Appendix Table C.1: Small-scale Simulations to Illustrate Model Properties

We run these simulations with ten countries and the following model parameters: α = 0.5 (capital factor share in services production); β = 0.3 (commodities factor share in manufacturing); σ = 5 (elasticity of substitution between manufacturing varieties); a = 0.5 (services share in consumption); and f = 10 (the sunk cost of manufacturing firms). In cases 1, 2 and 4 below, the factor endowment variables (K, L and G) vary across scenarios and trade costs are set at 1.25 in all international trade flows. Case 3 is explained below. Since results follow regular patterns, we report only the results for countries 1, 5 and 10.

Case 1: Countries similar except for natural resource endowment G									
	Endowments			**Share in GDP of:**		**Wage**	**Utility per L unit**	**GDP/L**	**G trade**
	G	**L**	**K**	**X**	**gG**				
Low G	1000	5000	5000	0.670	0.03	3.100	0.897	6.40	−5428
	5000	5000	5000	0.517	0.14	3.115	1.008	7.23	−603
High G	10,000	5000	5000	0.369	0.24	3.134	1.146	8.27	5428

A. Melchior, *Free Trade Agreements and Globalisation*,
https://doi.org/10.1007/978-3-319-92834-0

Case 2: Countries similar except for country size									
	Endowments			Share in GDP of:		Wage	Utility per L unit	GDP/L	G trade
	G	L	K	X	gG				
Small	800	1000	1000	0.49	0.16	2.162	0.934	5.12	45
	2503	3129	3129	0.49	0.16	2.200	0.947	5.20	89
Large	10,417	13,022	13,022	0.51	0.15	2.333	0.992	5.47	−371

Case 3, core-periphery scenario: Ten countries are located along a line and indexed 1–10; trade costs between countries *i* and *j* are based on the difference $d = |i-j|$ and so $t_{ij} = 1 + b^*d$; we use $b = 0.1$ so that the largest trade cost (between countries 1 and 10) is equal to 1.9.

Case 3: Countries similar but core-periphery pattern of trade costs									
	Endowments			Share in GDP of:		Wage	Utility per L unit	GDP/L	G trade
	G	L	K	X	gG				
Periphery	4000	5000	5000	0.49	0.16	2.153	0.912	5.11	244
Core	4000	5000	5000	0.50	0.15	2.326	0.970	5.45	−127
Periphery	4000	5000	5000	0.49	0.16	2.153	0.912	5.11	244

Case 4: Countries similar except for capital endowment K									
	Endowments			Share in GDP of:		Wage	Utility per L unit	GDP/L	G trade
	G	L	K	X	gG				
Low K	4000	5000	1000	0.30	0.29	0.974	0.463	2.75	2770
	4000	5000	5000	0.50	0.15	2.247	0.901	5.29	41
High K	4000	5000	10,000	0.56	0.11	3.234	1.244	7.27	−2073

Further details may be provided upon request.

Appendix Table C.2: Regional Disaggregation of Large Countries

Seven countries are sub-divided into 47 regions.

Country	Region	Description	Sub-regions included
Brazil (5)	Brazn	Brazil norte	These are the standard regions used by Instituto Brasileiro de Geografia e Estatistica; see http://www.ibge.gov.br/home/estatistica/economia/contasregionais/2014/default_xls.shtm for more information.
	Brazne	Brazil nordeste	
	Brazse	Brazil sudeste	
	Brazse	Brazil sul	
	Brazco	Brazil centro-oeste	
Canada (5)	Caeast	Canada east	New Brunswick, Newfoundland and Labrador, Nova Scotia, Prince Edward Island, and Quebec
	Caont	Ontario	Ontario
	Camid	Mid-Canada	Alberta, Manitoba, and Saskatchewan
	Cabco	British Columbia	British Columbia
	Canor	Canada—north	Northwest Territories, Nunavut, Yukon
China (8)	Chicm	China coast intermediate	Jiangsu, Shanghai, and Zhejiang
	Chicn	China coast north	Beijing, Hebei, Liaoning, Shandong, and Tianjin
	Chics	China coast south	Fujian, Guangdong, and Hainan
	Chiin	China interior north	Anhui, Henan, Hubei, Ningxia, Shaanxi, Shanxi
	Chiis	China interior south	Chongqing, Guangsi, Guizhou, Hunan, Jiangxi, Sichuan, and Yunnan
	Chimo	China—Mongolia	Nei Mongol
	Chine	China north east	Heilongjiang and Jilin
	Chiwe	China west	Gansu, Qinghai, Xinjiang, and Xizang (Tibet)
India (6)	Indcen	India central	Madhya Pradesh, Maharashtra, Uttar Pradesh
	Indne2	India north east 2	Arunachal Pradesh, Assam, Manipur, Meghalaya, Mizoram, Nagaland, Sikkim, and Tripura
	Indne1	India north east 1	Bihar, Chhattisgarh, Jharkhand, Odisha, and West Bengal
	Indnor	India north	Himachal Pradesh, Jammu and Kashmir, and Uttarakhand
	Indsou	India south	Andhra Pradesh, Goa, Karnataka, Kerala, Tamil Nadu, Telangana, Puducherry
	Indwes	India north west	Gujarat, Haryana, Punjab, Rajasthan, Chandigarh, Delhi

Country	Region	Description	Sub-regions included
Kazakhstan (3)	Kaznor	Kazakhstan north	Akmolinskaya, Karagandinskaya, Kostanaiskaya, Pavlodarskaya, Severo-Kazakhstanskaya, and Astana city
	Kazsou	Kazakhstan south	Almatinskaya, Zhambylskaya, Yuzhno-Kazakhstanskaya, Vostochno-Kazakhstanskaya, and Almaty city
	Kazwes	Kazakhstan west	Aktubinskaya, Atyrauskaya, Zapadno-Kazakhstanskaya, Kyzylordinskaya, and Mangistauskaya
Russia (12)	Rucentr	Russia central incl. Moscow	Central Federal District
	Rufenor	Russia Far East—northern	Kamchatka, Magadan, and Chukotka
	Rufesou	Russia Far East—southern part	Primorsky Krai, Khabarovsk, Amur, Sakhalin, and Jewish Autonomous Region
Russia cont.	Runwest1	North West Russia—part 1 with St. Petersburg	Vologda, Kaliningrad, Leningrad, Novgorod, Pskov, and Saint Petersburg
	Runwest2	North West Russia—part 2 with Murmansk	Karelia, Komi Rep., Nenets, Arhangelsk, and Murmansk
	Rusakha	Russia Far East—Sakha	Sakha (Yakutia)
	Rusibea	Siberia—eastern part towards China	Buryatia, Tyva Rep., Transbaikal, and Irkutsk
	Rusibno	Siberia—northern part (Krasnoyarsk)	Krasnoyarsk
	Rusibwe	Siberia—western part with Novosibirsk	Altai Rep., Khakassia, Altai region, Kemerovo, Novosibirsk, Omsk, and Tomsk
	Rusouth	Russia South and North Caucasia	Southern Federal District and North Caucasian Federal District
	Ruural	Ural	Ural Federal District
	Ruvolga	Volga region	Volga Federal District

Country	Region	Description	Sub-regions included
USA (8)	Usalas	Alaska	Note: The regional subdivision for the USA follows the BEA (Bureau of Economic Analysis) regions, except that Alaska is separate from the Far West Region, and New England + Mideast Regions are merged. See https://www.census.gov/econ/census/help/geography/regions_and_divisions.html for more information
	Usnoea	New England Region and Mideast Region	
	Uslake	Great Lakes Region	
	Usplain	Plains Region	
	Ussoea	Southeast Region	
	Ussowe	Southwest Region	
	Usrock	Rocky Mountain Region	
	Uswest	Far West Region except Alaska	

Appendix Table C.3: Aggregated Country Groups

In order to reduce the number of countries/regions in simulations, the following 19 country groups were formed:

World region	Group	N	Description	Includes
Africa	Afrcen	7	Africa central	Burundi, Cameroon, Central African Republic, Chad, Congo, Rep., Gabon, and Rwanda
	Afreast	7	Africa east	Comoros, Djibouti, Ethiopia, Kenya, Sudan, Tanzania, and Uganda
	Afrnor	3	Africa north west	Algeria, Morocco, and Tunisia
	Afrsacu	5	Africa SACU (South African Customs Union)	Botswana, Lesotho, Namibia, South Africa, and Swaziland (South African Customs Union)
	Afrsadc	8	Africa SADC (Southern African Development Community)	Angola, Congo, Dem. Rep., Mozambique, Madagascar, Malawi, Mauritius, Zambia, and Zimbabwe (Southern African Development Community)
	Afrwest	16	Africa west	Benin, Burkina Faso, Cabo Verde, Cote d'Ivoire, Gambia, Ghana, Guinea, Guinea-Bissau, Liberia, Mali, Mauritania, Niger, Nigeria, Senegal, Sierra Leone, and Togo
America	Amecen	9	America central	Costa Rica, Dominican Republic, El Salvador, Guatemala, Haiti, Honduras, Jamaica, Nicaragua, Panama
	Amecen2	3	America central—2	Guyana, Suriname, Trinidad and Tobago
	Andean	5	Andean countries	Bolivia, Colombia, Ecuador, Peru, and Venezuela
West Asia	Arabia	7	Arab countries	Bahrain, Kuwait, Oman, Qatar, Saudi Arabia, United Arab Emirates, and Yemen
	Medeas	3	East Mediterranean	Israel, Jordan, and Lebanon
Asia	Asean1	4	ASEAN (Association of South East Asian Nations) subgroup	Cambodia, Lao PDR, Myanmar, and Vietnam (part of Association of South East Asian Nations)
	Asiasou	3	South Asia subgroup	Bangladesh, Bhutan, and Nepal

World region	Group	N	Description	Includes
Europe	Balkan	5	Balkan countries	Albania, Bosnia and Herzegovina, Macedonia, FYR, Montenegro, and Serbia
EU	Baltic	3	Baltic countries	Estonia, Latvia, and Lithuania
	Benelux	3	Be-Ne-Lux	Belgium, Luxembourg, and Netherlands
	Bulgrom	2	Bulgaria, Romania	Bulgaria and Romania
	Eucentr	6	EU central Europe	Austria, Croatia, Czech Republic, Hungary, Slovak Republic, and Slovenia
	Iberia	2	Iberian peninsula	Spain and Portugal
Total		101		

For these country groups, GDP-weighted averages were used for geo-data (longitude and latitude) and variables related to trade and infrastructure costs. Other variables were aggregated (GDP, population, labour force and land area).

Appendix Table C.4: Country Data

Category	Description	Source
Geography	Land area (sq. km)	WDI (FAO)
	Latitude	Global cities database
	Longitude	Global cities database
Macro-variables	GDP (current US$)	WDI (WB, OECD)
	GDP, PPP (constant 2011 international $)	WDI (WB-ICP)
	Labour force, total	WDI (ILO, WB)
	Population, total	WDI (UN)
	Total natural resources rents (% of GDP)	WDI (WB)
	Manufacturing, value added (% of GDP)	WDI (WB, OECD)

Category	Description	Source
Business cost	Cost of business start-up procedures (% of GNI per capita)	WDI (WB—doing business)
	Internet users (per 100 people)	WDI (WB, ITU)
	Logistics performance index: Overall (1=low to 5=high)	WDI (WB, Turku School of Economics)
Export cost	Cost to export (US$ per container)	WDI (WB—doing business)
	Documents to export (number)	WDI (WB—doing business)
	Time to export (days)	WDI (WB—WITS, TRAINS, CTS)
Import cost	Cost to import (US$ per container)	WDI (WB—doing business)
	Documents to import (number)	WDI (WB—doing business)
	Time to import (days)	WDI (WB—WITS, TRAINS, CTS)
Tariffs	Tariff rate, most favoured nation, simple mean, all products (%)	WDI (WB—WITS, TRAINS, CTS)
Trade	Exports of goods and services (% of GDP)	WDI (WB, OECD)
	Imports of goods and services (% of GDP)	WDI (WB, OECD)
	Trade (% of GDP)	WDI (WB, OECD)

Notes: WDI—World Development Indicators Database, see http://data.worldbank.org/data-catalog/world-development-indicators where more detailed information on variables is available. FAO—Food and Agriculture Organization. WB—World Bank. ICP—International Comparison Program. ILO—International Labour Organisation. ITU—International Telecommunication Union. WITS—World Integrated Trade Solution. TRAINS—Trade Analysis Information System (UNCTAD). CTS—Consolidated Tariff Schedules (WTO)

For business cost, export cost and import cost, the data was converted into 0–100 indexes with 0 as the minimum and 100 as the maximum. The three sub-components were thereafter averaged with the following weights:

- For business cost the three subcomponents were given equal weights (one-third) and aggregated into the variable INFRASTR.
- For export and import cost, the first sub-item (US$ per container) was given 50% weight and the other two (documents and time) were each given 25% weights, giving the variables EXPCOST and IMPCOST.

The variables INFRASTR, EXPCOST and IMPCOST are all indexes within the 0–100 range.

Appendix Table C.5: Regional Data for Large Countries

Data sources Country	Data sources for regional data
Brazil	Instituto Brasileiro de Geografia e Estatistica; see http://www.ibge.gov.br/home/estatistica/economia/contasregionais/2014/default_xls.shtm
Canada	Statistics Canada, CANSIM database; http://www.statcan.gc.ca/eng/start
China	National Bureau of Statistics of China: China Statistical Yearbook, various issues; http://www.stats.gov.cn/english/Statisticaldata/AnnualData/
India	Government of India, Ministry of Statistics and Programme Implementation; http://www.mospi.gov.in/data, and NITI Aayog (National Institution for Transforming India); nito.gov.in
Kazakhstan	Ministry of National Economic of the Republic of Kazakhstan, Committee on Statistics; http://www.stat.gov.kz. Land area from Regions of Kazakhstan. Brochure 2005–2009, Agency on Statistics of the Republic of Kazakhstan. Astana 2010.
Russia	Russian Federation. Federal State Statistics Service; http://www.gks.ru/free_doc/new_site/region_stat/sep_region.html
USA	BEA (Bureau of Economic Analysis); www.bea.gov. Land area from United States Census Bureau; https://www.census.gov/geo/reference/state-area.html

For all countries and regions, geographical data (latitudes and longitudes) are taken from the Global Cities Database. We use data for administrative centres/capitals for regions and countries, except for Russian regions where we also calculate the average coordinates across all cities within each region, and use an average between this and the capital/administrative centre coordinates in the calculations. The reason is for some Russian regions, the location of administrative capitals, and the economic mass may differ. This may be the case also for other countries, but it is more important for Russia due to the large space.

Notes on selected variables

Variable	Notes on regional data
Natural resources	The point of departure is country data on natural resource rents as a percentage of GDP. The total value of these rents is allocated across regions as follows: For Canada, India, Kazakhstan, and Russia, it is allocated proportional to the value added in mining and quarrying. For the USA, value added in "Natural resources and mining" (industry code 86) was used for the same purpose. For Brazil, there was a discrepancy between the World Bank estimate (5.01% of GDP) and Extractive industries (3.72%), and so a share of agriculture was added to construct a "hybrid" sector representing 5.01% of GDP. For China, regional stocks of petroleum, natural gas, coal, iron ore, manganese ore, copper, lead, zinc, and bauxite in 2015 (Tables 8.5 and 8.6 of China National Statistics Yearbook) were converted into value and aggregated using world prices and used to allocate the natural resource rent across regions.
Labour force	Regional labour force data were available only for Russia. For other countries, regional population shares were used to allocate the World Bank national labour force figure across regions.
GDP, population	Regional data were available for all countries and used to allocate the country-level World Bank figure across regions.

Appendix Table C.6: The Base Scenario—Key Variables and Results

Country/region	L	K/L ratio	Wage	Real inc. per cap.	X firms	Price level	G/GDP	G trade/GDP	Manuf./GDP	% IIT
Runwest1	55,195	3.24	1.91	12.45	579	1.93	1.3	−0.05	28.2	75
Runwest2	18,535	2.29	3.13	14.60	0	3.47	23.0	0.23	0.0	0
Rucentr	207,395	4.09	2.28	14.83	2596	1.94	1.2	−0.05	28.3	74
Rusouth	125,837	1.94	1.30	8.69	825	1.94	3.6	−0.02	25.2	73
Ruvolga	158,880	2.12	1.39	10.99	300	1.94	18.6	0.17	5.8	21
Ruural	65,361	2.42	6.89	18.07	0	6.16	23.0	0.23	0.0	0
Rusibwe	62,217	2.05	1.35	10.29	190	1.93	15.4	0.13	9.9	35
Rusibno	15,241	2.89	2.49	15.87	0	2.53	23.0	0.23	0.0	0
Rusibea	25,614	1.90	1.28	10.69	0	1.93	23.0	0.23	0.0	0
Rufesou	25,383	2.36	3.60	15.36	0	3.79	23.0	0.23	0.0	0
Rufenor	2782	3.36	2.66	17.50	0	2.46	23.0	0.23	0.0	0
Rusakha	5101	1.93	9.07	16.88	0	8.69	23.0	0.23	0.0	0
Belarus	44,890	2.49	1.57	9.07	373	1.95	2.2	−0.04	27.0	76
Kaznor	27,673	2.86	1.65	11.55	219	1.90	5.6	0.00	22.6	69
Kazsou	47,126	2.36	1.43	9.68	372	1.90	2.3	−0.04	26.9	74
Kazwes	18,049	2.68	4.91	17.55	0	4.55	23.0	0.23	0.0	0
Armen	15,600	1.28	0.95	6.09	78	1.95	2.5	−0.04	26.6	75
Kyrgyz	27,280	0.73	0.60	3.56	82	1.92	4.5	−0.01	24.0	73
Georgia	20,179	1.37	1.02	6.68	113	1.94	1.0	−0.06	28.6	75
Azerb	49,510	1.77	1.55	10.27	0	2.37	23.0	0.23	0.0	0
Tajik	36,763	0.68	0.55	3.05	120	1.89	0.9	−0.06	28.7	74
Uzbek	136,063	1.03	0.78	4.54	401	1.95	9.7	0.06	17.2	58

Country/region	L	K/L ratio	Wage	Real inc. per cap.	X firms	Price level	G/GDP	G trade/GDP	Manuf./GDP	% IIT
Ukraine	230,895	1.26	0.94	6.13	970	1.94	6.2	0.01	21.8	70
Moldova	12,369	1.23	0.92	3.86	65	1.95	0.3	−0.06	29.5	74
Benelux	142,607	6.49	3.29	19.97	2606	1.92	0.5	−0.06	29.3	77
France	301,838	5.71	3.00	16.54	5059	1.92	0.2	−0.07	29.6	76
Germany	422,135	5.88	3.07	19.45	7240	1.93	0.2	−0.07	29.6	75
Italy	257,852	5.44	2.87	14.77	4153	1.93	0.2	−0.07	29.6	76
Greece	49,372	3.57	2.08	11.38	579	1.94	0.2	−0.07	29.6	76
Unitedk	330,217	5.07	2.73	17.15	4924	1.92	1.0	−0.06	28.6	77
Ireland	21,851	8.04	3.84	22.19	473	1.91	0.2	−0.07	29.6	77
Denmark	29,205	5.75	3.00	19.26	464	1.92	1.8	−0.05	27.5	78
Spaport	287,243	4.03	2.27	14.00	3682	1.91	0.3	−0.07	29.5	76
Sweden	51,466	5.75	3.00	19.66	831	1.92	1.4	−0.05	28.1	77
Finland	27,146	5.23	2.79	17.15	398	1.92	2.1	−0.04	27.2	77
Eucentr	197,886	4.01	2.29	13.53	2499	1.93	0.7	−0.06	29.0	77
Baltic	32,615	3.10	1.88	12.16	319	1.93	2.3	−0.04	26.8	77
Poland	182,802	3.27	1.96	11.61	1904	1.93	1.8	−0.05	27.5	77
Bulgrom	128,483	2.62	1.65	9.61	1123	1.94	2.0	−0.04	27.3	76
Norway	27,272	8.96	4.15	30.48	359	1.91	11.6	0.08	14.7	52
Iceland	1925	4.72	2.55	18.31	28	1.91	0.0	−0.07	29.9	75
Switzer	47,532	7.08	3.51	24.78	939	1.92	0.1	−0.07	29.8	76
Turkey	283,607	3.34	1.98	8.75	3112	1.95	0.7	−0.06	28.9	75
Balkan	71,262	1.94	1.30	6.97	477	1.94	3.0	−0.03	26.0	74
Cabco	25,780	4.71	2.48	17.71	330	1.87	3.3	−0.03	25.6	76
Caeast	58,755	4.09	2.25	15.98	683	1.88	3.1	−0.03	25.8	76
Camid	36,132	7.22	3.43	28.52	221	1.88	17.1	0.15	7.6	29
Canor	648	8.00	3.70	30.57	5	1.88	16.6	0.15	8.3	32

Country/region	L	K/L ratio	Wage	Real inc. per cap.	X firms	Price level	G/GDP	G trade/GDP	Manuf./GDP	% IIT
Caont	75,950	4.95	2.61	18.07	1103	1.89	1.0	–0.06	28.6	77
Usalas	3723	12.38	5.16	36.11	66	1.89	10.8	0.07	15.8	56
Uslake	236,142	7.31	3.54	22.03	4666	1.91	0.7	–0.06	29.0	77
Usnoea	321,951	10.80	4.76	29.48	8631	1.91	0.3	–0.06	29.4	75
Usplai	106,114	7.66	3.65	23.08	2063	1.90	2.1	–0.04	27.2	78
Usrock	58,298	6.99	3.38	21.79	1000	1.89	3.5	–0.02	25.4	77
Ussoea	410,963	5.95	3.03	18.94	6887	1.91	1.0	–0.06	28.6	77
Ussowe	200,382	7.48	3.57	23.44	3325	1.90	5.4	0.00	22.8	74
Uswest	273,172	9.27	4.18	26.24	6387	1.89	0.9	–0.06	28.7	76
Mexico	555,615	2.41	1.52	8.75	3632	1.93	7.1	0.02	20.7	70
Amecen	303,733	1.46	1.02	5.66	1657	1.91	2.6	–0.04	26.5	77
Amecen2	12,292	2.61	1.58	11.02	17	1.94	20.2	0.19	3.6	14
Andean	684,347	1.69	1.12	8.03	2093	1.91	13.9	0.11	11.8	42
Brazn	94,384	1.41	0.99	6.92	412	1.91	7.0	0.02	20.8	70
Brazne	303,366	1.27	0.91	6.09	1489	1.91	2.5	–0.04	26.6	76
Brazse	460,289	2.41	1.48	10.38	2976	1.92	7.2	0.02	20.5	68
Brazse	156,916	2.26	1.41	9.42	1177	1.91	2.8	–0.03	26.2	76
Brazco	83,474	2.43	1.49	10.05	639	1.91	3.7	–0.02	25.1	76
Argenti	195,405	2.73	1.60	9.33	1572	1.90	4.4	–0.01	24.1	75
Paragua	32,028	1.40	0.96	6.03	156	1.90	4.4	–0.01	24.2	74
Uruguay	17,637	2.55	1.52	10.07	134	1.90	4.5	–0.01	24.0	74
Chile	87,450	2.57	1.55	11.63	177	1.89	18.9	0.18	5.3	21
Egypt	295,968	2.04	1.37	5.83	1572	1.98	8.6	0.04	18.6	60
Medeas	77,642	3.51	2.07	9.09	893	1.95	0.5	–0.06	29.2	74
Arabia	326,184	3.93	5.40	17.87	0	3.84	23.0	0.23	0.0	0
Iran	271,335	2.35	2.37	8.68	0	2.87	23.0	0.23	0.0	0

Country/region	L	K/L ratio	Wage	Real inc. per cap.	X firms	Price level	G/GDP	G trade/GDP	Manuf./GDP	% IIT
Afghan	83,344	0.78	0.63	2.02	302	1.94	0.9	−0.06	28.7	75
Pakista	653,614	1.16	0.91	3.87	3076	1.99	2.4	−0.04	26.8	75
Indcen	1,617,170	1.09	0.89	4.06	7082	2.02	3.1	−0.03	25.9	76
Indne1	1,188,372	0.90	0.77	3.64	3902	2.02	6.4	0.01	21.6	72
Indne2	188,786	0.94	0.79	3.71	683	2.01	5.0	0.00	23.4	76
Indnor	118,580	1.34	1.03	4.64	638	2.02	1.7	−0.05	27.7	77
Indsou	1,020,374	1.50	1.12	5.09	5848	2.01	2.2	−0.04	27.0	77
Indwes	836,320	1.53	1.14	5.28	4505	2.02	4.2	−0.01	24.4	76
Asiasou	949,657	0.67	0.60	3.59	3013	2.00	1.8	−0.05	27.6	77
Srilank	85,763	1.92	1.29	6.38	618	1.96	0.7	−0.06	28.9	75
Asean1	964,251	0.84	0.72	5.12	3220	2.00	4.8	−0.01	23.6	75
Thailan	400,558	1.85	1.29	9.39	2555	1.97	3.5	−0.02	25.4	76
Singapo	31,103	15.77	6.42	44.24	1124	1.92	0.0	−0.07	29.9	74
Philipp	438,072	1.29	0.98	5.25	2243	1.97	2.2	−0.04	27.1	78
Malaysi	133,000	3.35	2.00	11.91	935	1.94	10.2	0.06	16.7	59
Indones	124,0611	1.56	1.13	6.88	6407	1.98	5.4	0.00	22.9	73
Chicn	1,493,650	1.95	1.38	9.63	11,210	1.98	0.3	−0.06	29.4	75
Chics	913,545	1.95	1.37	9.69	6644	1.98	1.2	−0.05	28.3	78
Chiin	1,741,496	1.40	1.08	7.69	9464	1.99	2.4	−0.04	26.7	78
Chiis	2,094,649	1.24	0.98	7.26	8876	1.99	6.0	0.01	22.0	72
Chimo	148,282	1.67	1.56	11.68	0	2.40	23.0	0.23	0.0	0
Chine	389,794	1.51	1.12	8.02	2238	1.96	2.3	−0.04	26.9	78
Chiwe	342,735	1.04	0.85	7.26	394	1.97	18.4	0.17	6.0	22
Chicm	940,834	2.43	1.62	11.32	8359	1.98	0.2	−0.07	29.6	76
Mongol	13,281	1.57	1.08	7.47	12	1.93	20.3	0.20	3.5	13

Country/region	L	K/L ratio	Wage	Real inc. per cap.	X firms	Price level	G/GDP	G trade/GDP	Manuf./GDP	% IIT
Korea	263,562	4.29	2.43	15.26	3583	1.94	0.0	−0.07	29.8	75
Japan	653,023	4.65	2.54	15.98	9407	1.91	0.0	−0.07	29.8	73
Honkong	37,454	7.88	3.77	23.96	802	1.90	0.0	−0.07	29.9	75
Austral	124,169	5.19	2.59	19.13	1197	1.86	10.1	0.06	16.8	58
Newzeal	24,335	4.20	2.20	15.29	295	1.86	2.3	−0.04	26.9	76
Afrnor	288,766	1.95	1.32	6.29	885	1.98	15.0	0.13	10.3	37
Afrwest	1,219,385	0.98	0.77	3.55	3726	1.96	8.6	0.04	18.7	62
Afreast	1,179,543	0.61	0.53	2.83	3213	1.97	3.6	−0.02	25.2	73
Afrcen	296,484	0.60	0.52	2.97	506	1.96	11.7	0.08	14.7	52
Afrsadc	85,0217	0.50	0.45	2.61	1313	1.95	11.2	0.08	15.3	53
Afrsacu	234,050	2.14	1.34	6.74	1336	1.90	7.8	0.03	19.8	65

Appendix Table C.7: Counterfactual Scenario Inputs: Changes in Factor Endowments in "Commodity" and "Productivity" Scenarios (Chap. 6)

	Commodity scenario (G)			Productivity scenario (K/L)		
	Initial	Revised	% change	Initial	Revised	% change
Runwest1	5447	17,911	228.8	3.24	2.23	−31.2
Runwest2	69,311	6015	−91.3	2.29	2.23	−2.4
Rucentr	23,515	67,300	186.2	4.09	2.23	−45.4
Rusouth	24,229	40,834	68.5	1.94	2.23	14.7
Ruvolga	201,980	51,557	−74.5	2.12	2.23	5.0
Ruural	537,719	21,210	−96.1	2.42	2.23	−7.7
Rusibwe	61,012	20,189	−66.9	2.05	2.23	8.6
Rusibno	45,276	4946	−89.1	2.89	2.23	−22.9
Rusibea	39,078	8312	−78.7	1.90	2.23	17.2
Rufesou	109,108	8237	−92.5	2.36	2.23	−5.7
Rufenor	8858	903	−89.8	3.36	2.23	−33.6
Rusakha	55,297	1655	−97.0	1.93	2.23	15.6
Belarus	6389	14,567	128.0	2.49	2.23	−10.5
Kaznor	10,820	8980	−17.0	2.86	2.23	−21.9
Kazsou	6260	15,292	144.3	2.36	2.23	−5.5
Kazwes	105,901	5857	−94.5	2.68	2.23	−16.9
Armen	1527	5062	231.6	1.28	2.23	74.8
Kyrgyz	3083	8852	187.1	0.73	2.23	206.0
Georgia	820	6548	698.1	1.37	2.23	62.7
Azerb	91,407	16,066	−82.4	1.77	2.23	26.1
Tajik	761	11,930	1468.6	0.68	2.23	226.1
Uzbek	45,440	44,152	−2.8	1.03	2.23	115.6
Ukraine	57,635	74,925	30.0	1.26	2.23	76.9
Moldova	143	4014	2708.0	1.23	2.23	81.0
Benelux	8516	46,276	443.4	6.49	2.23	−65.6
France	6535	97,946	1398.8	5.71	2.23	−60.9
Germany	9448	136,983	1349.8	5.88	2.23	−62.1
Italy	7081	83,673	1081.6	5.44	2.23	−59.0
Greece	943	16,021	1599.7	3.57	2.23	−37.5
Unitedk	35,321	107,155	203.4	5.07	2.23	−56.0
Ireland	591	7091	1099.5	8.04	2.23	−72.3
Denmark	6450	9477	46.9	5.75	2.23	−61.2
Spaport	7237	93,210	1187.9	4.03	2.23	−44.6
Sweden	8639	16,701	93.3	5.75	2.23	−61.2
Finland	6389	8809	37.9	5.23	2.23	−57.4
Eucentr	12,517	64,214	413.0	4.01	2.23	−44.4
Baltic	5904	10,584	79.3	3.10	2.23	−28.0

	Commodity scenario (G)			Productivity scenario (K/L)		
	Initial	Revised	% change	Initial	Revised	% change
Poland	26,186	59,319	126.5	3.27	2.23	−31.9
Bulgrom	17,340	41,693	140.4	2.62	2.23	−14.9
Norway	59,730	8850	−85.2	8.96	2.23	−75.1
Iceland	0	625	216,116.7	4.72	2.23	−52.8
Switzer	360	15,424	4182.2	7.08	2.23	−68.5
Turkey	16,814	92,030	447.3	3.34	2.23	−33.2
Balkan	11,446	23,125	102.0	1.94	2.23	14.9
Cabco	8645	8366	−3.2	4.71	2.23	−52.7
Caeast	17,092	19,066	11.5	4.09	2.23	−45.5
Camid	102,496	11,725	−88.6	7.22	2.23	−69.1
Canor	1906	210	−89.0	8.00	2.23	−72.1
Caont	8072	24,646	205.3	4.95	2.23	−54.9
Usalas	9342	1208	−87.1	12.38	2.23	−82.0
Uslake	22,187	76,628	245.4	7.31	2.23	−69.5
Usnoea	20,383	104,473	412.5	10.80	2.23	−79.3
Usplai	32,515	34,434	5.9	7.66	2.23	−70.9
Usrock	28,219	18,918	−33.0	6.99	2.23	−68.1
Ussoea	48,543	133,357	174.7	5.95	2.23	−62.5
Ussowe	163,859	65,024	−60.3	7.48	2.23	−70.2
Uswest	40,205	88,644	120.5	9.27	2.23	−75.9
Mexico	255,728	180,297	−29.5	2.41	2.23	−7.5
Amecen	32,520	98,561	203.1	1.46	2.23	53.2
Amecen2	19,692	3989	−79.7	2.61	2.23	−14.6
Andean	497,551	222,070	−55.4	1.69	2.23	32.1
Brazn	28,019	30,628	9.3	1.41	2.23	57.9
Brazne	28,999	98,442	239.5	1.27	2.23	76.1
Brazse	211,557	149,364	−29.4	2.41	2.23	−7.5
Brazse	25,588	50,919	99.0	2.26	2.23	−1.4
Brazco	18,926	27,087	43.1	2.43	2.23	−8.4
Argenti	57,932	63,409	9.5	2.73	2.23	−18.2
Paragua	5677	10,393	83.1	1.40	2.23	59.0
Uruguay	5067	5723	13.0	2.55	2.23	−12.6
Chile	126,301	28,378	−77.5	2.57	2.23	−13.2
Egypt	153,421	96,042	−37.4	2.04	2.23	9.4
Medeas	3191	25,195	689.5	3.51	2.23	−36.5
Arabia	2,103,177	105,847	−95.0	3.93	2.23	−43.2
Iran	767,788	88,048	−88.5	2.35	2.23	−5.0
Afghan	1975	27,045	1269.4	0.78	2.23	186.3
Pakista	58,461	212,098	262.8	1.16	2.23	91.5
Indcen	182,030	524,771	188.3	1.09	2.23	105.0
Indne1	248,459	385,626	55.2	0.90	2.23	147.5
Indne2	31,600	61,261	93.9	0.94	2.23	136.2
Indnor	8287	38,479	364.3	1.34	2.23	67.0

	Commodity scenario (G)			Productivity scenario (K/L)		
	Initial	Revised	% change	Initial	Revised	% change
Indsou	104,820	331,111	215.9	1.50	2.23	49.0
Indwes	167,714	271,386	61.8	1.53	2.23	46.1
Asiasou	41,309	308,164	646.0	0.67	2.23	233.4
Srilank	3235	27,830	760.3	1.92	2.23	16.5
Asean1	141,468	312,899	121.2	0.84	2.23	164.6
Thailan	74,222	129,981	75.1	1.85	2.23	20.6
Singapo	6	10,093	159,476.3	15.77	2.23	−85.9
Philipp	37,939	142,154	274.7	1.29	2.23	72.6
Malaysi	120,363	43,158	−64.1	3.35	2.23	−33.5
Indones	319,390	402,578	26.0	1.56	2.23	42.7
Chicn	27,703	484,689	1649.6	1.95	2.23	14.4
Chics	60,923	296,445	386.6	1.95	2.23	14.4
Chiin	186,367	565,115	203.2	1.40	2.23	59.3
Chiis	528,947	679,713	28.5	1.24	2.23	80.4
Chimo	276,941	48,117	−82.6	1.67	2.23	33.7
Chine	40,576	126,488	211.7	1.51	2.23	48.0
Chiwe	261,996	111,217	−57.5	1.04	2.23	115.3
Chicm	10,721	305,300	2747.8	2.43	2.23	−8.1
Mongol	14,645	4310	−70.6	1.57	2.23	41.8
Korea	1205	85,526	6998.7	4.29	2.23	−47.9
Japan	3092	211,906	6753.7	4.65	2.23	−52.1
Honkong	17	12,154	70,511.5	7.88	2.23	−71.7
Austral	144,520	40,293	−72.1	5.19	2.23	−57.0
Newzeal	5092	7897	55.1	4.20	2.23	−46.9
Afrnor	269,560	93,705	−65.2	1.95	2.23	14.1
Afrwest	354,114	395,690	11.7	0.98	2.23	126.6
Afreast	92,610	382,761	313.3	0.61	2.23	266.8
Afrcen	80,756	96,209	19.1	0.60	2.23	272.9
Afrsadc	193,799	275,895	42.4	0.50	2.23	347.7
Afrsacu	105,697	75,949	−28.1	2.14	2.23	4.3

Appendix Table C.8: Counterfactual Scenarios: Changes in Real Income Per Capita and the Share of Tradables in GDP

	Real income per capita (% change from baseline)			Tradables/GDP (baseline % share)	Tradables/GDP: Percentage point change from baseline		
	Commodity	Productivity	Autarky		Commodity	Productivity	Autarky
Runwest1	2.8	−24.4	−27.5	28.2	−3.5	−0.7	−5.2
Runwest2	−31.9	−0.1	−43.1	0.0	23.2	0.0	23.0
Rucentr	2.2	−36.2	−21.3	28.3	−2.7	−1.1	−5.3
Rusouth	2.2	10.5	−22.2	25.2	−2.8	0.1	−2.2
Ruvolga	−14.0	4.2	−24.6	5.8	17.2	−0.7	17.2
Ruural	−42.7	−3.1	−45.7	0.0	23.5	0.0	23.0
Rusibwe	−10.5	6.5	−26.8	9.9	12.8	−0.1	13.1
Rusibno	−25.9	−12.6	−39.2	0.0	24.3	0.0	23.0
Rusibea	−18.3	11.3	−34.9	0.0	22.3	1.1	23.0
Rufesou	−33.9	−1.9	−43.0	0.0	23.4	0.0	23.0
Rufenor	−25.8	−20.0	−43.9	0.0	24.7	0.0	23.0
Rusakha	−48.0	10.3	−56.7	0.0	22.3	0.0	23.0
Belarus	2.7	−8.1	−26.7	27.0	−3.3	−0.5	−4.0
Kaznor	−1.1	−15.6	−24.7	22.6	1.4	−1.9	0.4
Kazsou	3.0	−3.8	−25.1	26.9	−3.8	−0.3	−3.9
Kazwes	−37.8	−8.8	−44.8	0.0	23.7	0.0	23.0
Armen	5.5	50.6	−33.3	26.6	−6.6	0.9	−3.6
Kyrgyz	7.9	126.0	−29.9	24.0	−9.2	3.1	−1.0
Georgia	6.6	43.3	−36.1	28.6	−8.0	0.3	−5.6
Azerb	−22.7	15.9	−34.3	0.0	21.8	0.0	23.0
Tajik	13.1	141.7	−32.7	28.7	−14.9	0.7	−5.7

	Real income per capita (% change from baseline)			Tradables/GDP (baseline % share)	Tradables/GDP: Percentage point change from baseline		
	Commodity	Productivity	Autarky		Commodity	Productivity	Autarky
Uzbek	−0.6	71.2	−20.3	17.2	0.7	4.8	5.8
Ukraine	1.6	49.8	−19.9	21.8	−1.9	2.3	1.2
Moldova	8.1	54.8	−41.2	29.5	−9.7	0.1	−6.5
Benelux	1.9	−55.3	−27.0	29.3	−2.4	−0.8	−6.3
France	2.5	−51.0	−28.7	29.6	−3.1	−0.3	−6.6
Germany	2.4	−52.1	−27.1	29.6	−3.0	−0.3	−6.6
Italy	2.5	−49.1	−28.0	29.6	−3.1	−0.3	−6.6
Greece	3.5	−29.9	−35.4	29.6	−4.4	−0.2	−6.6
Unitedk	1.9	−46.0	−20.6	28.6	−2.4	−1.3	−5.6
Ireland	1.9	−62.0	−37.6	29.6	−2.4	−0.4	−6.6
Denmark	0.8	−50.2	−28.3	27.5	−1.0	−2.7	−4.5
Spaport	3.2	−36.3	−27.6	29.5	−4.0	−0.2	−6.5
Sweden	1.2	−50.4	−26.8	28.1	−1.5	−2.1	−5.1
Finland	0.7	−46.5	−28.1	27.2	−0.9	−2.7	−4.2
Eucentr	2.7	−35.9	−25.3	29.0	−3.4	−0.6	−6.0
Baltic	1.7	−21.7	−28.8	26.8	−2.1	−1.1	−3.8
Poland	2.1	−25.0	−22.1	27.5	−2.7	−1.0	−4.5
Bulgrom	2.6	−11.5	−24.0	27.3	−3.3	−0.6	−4.3
Norway	−9.9	−57.0	−24.9	14.7	12.7	−14.7	8.3
Iceland	3.1	−43.5	−61.0	29.9	−3.9	0.0	−6.9
Switzer	2.2	−58.3	−40.1	29.8	−2.8	−0.1	−6.8
Turkey	3.2	−26.2	−23.1	28.9	−4.0	−0.4	−5.9
Balkan	2.9	10.1	−25.4	26.0	−3.5	0.1	−3.0
Cabco	−0.1	−41.9	−26.4	25.6	0.3	−3.6	−2.6
Caeast	0.3	−36.0	−23.8	25.8	−0.3	−2.8	−2.8

	Real income per capita (% change from baseline)			Tradables/GDP (baseline % share)	Tradables/GDP: Percentage point change from baseline		
	Commodity	Productivity	Autarky		Commodity	Productivity	Autarky
Camid	–15.2	–49.4	–26.4	7.6	19.4	–7.6	15.4
Canor	–14.8	–52.4	–41.0	8.3	18.9	–8.3	14.7
Caont	2.1	–45.3	–26.3	28.6	–2.5	–1.3	–5.6
Usalas	–9.4	–64.7	–31.3	15.8	12.1	–15.8	7.2
Uslake	1.6	–59.2	–22.3	29.0	–1.9	–1.4	–6.0
Usnoea	1.4	–69.7	–23.1	29.4	–1.7	–1.1	–6.4
Usplai	0.2	–59.6	–20.7	27.2	0.0	–4.5	–4.2
Usrock	–1.1	–55.9	–21.8	25.4	1.6	–6.5	–2.4
Ussoea	1.7	–52.4	–18.7	28.6	–2.0	–1.6	–5.6
Ussowe	–3.2	–56.6	–15.0	22.8	4.3	–10.5	0.2
Uswest	1.1	–65.6	–19.2	28.7	–1.2	–2.4	–5.7
Mexico	–2.1	–5.7	–13.3	20.7	2.8	–1.3	2.3
Amecen	5.0	35.7	–20.6	26.5	–5.9	0.7	–3.5
Amecen2	–16.2	–7.9	–35.2	3.6	20.1	–3.6	19.4
Andean	–7.7	20.4	–15.8	11.8	9.6	2.0	11.2
Brazn	0.5	37.9	–22.1	20.8	–0.4	2.0	2.2
Brazne	5.9	51.4	–19.1	26.6	–6.9	1.0	–3.6
Brazse	–2.2	–5.1	–12.9	20.5	2.8	–1.2	2.5
Brazse	2.7	–1.2	–19.7	26.2	–3.2	–0.3	–3.2
Brazco	1.5	–6.2	–21.7	25.1	–1.7	–0.7	–2.1
Argenti	0.4	–13.4	–16.2	24.1	–0.3	–1.4	–1.1
Paragua	3.5	39.4	–26.5	24.2	–4.0	1.3	–1.2
Uruguay	0.5	–9.2	–27.4	24.0	–0.5	–1.0	–1.0
Chile	–14.7	–7.4	–25.9	5.3	18.3	–3.8	17.7
Egypt	–3.4	6.7	–17.0	18.6	4.2	0.0	4.4
Medeas	3.3	–29.0	–31.0	29.2	–4.1	–0.3	–6.2

	Real income per capita (% change from baseline)			Tradables/GDP (baseline % share)	Tradables/GDP: Percentage point change from baseline		
	Commodity	Productivity	Autarky		Commodity	Productivity	Autarky
Arabia	−34.9	−26.8	−33.6	0.0	25.4	0.0	23.0
Iran	−26.7	−1.6	−27.7	0.0	23.5	0.0	23.0
Afghan	11.3	119.5	−30.2	28.7	−13.1	0.6	−5.7
Pakista	5.9	62.2	−18.2	26.8	−7.1	1.1	−3.8
Indcen	5.4	70.9	−13.6	25.9	−6.5	1.5	−2.9
Indne1	3.1	93.4	−14.3	21.6	−3.7	3.7	1.4
Indne2	4.3	87.8	−22.8	23.4	−5.1	2.8	−0.4
Indnor	5.8	47.2	−26.7	27.7	−7.0	0.6	−4.7
Indsou	4.5	35.3	−15.5	27.0	−5.5	0.6	−4.0
Indwes	2.3	32.7	−14.7	24.4	−2.8	1.1	−1.4
Asiasou	10.9	146.2	−20.2	27.6	−12.6	1.3	−4.6
Srilank	5.3	12.4	−29.5	28.9	−6.5	0.1	−5.9
Asean1	5.4	103.6	−17.0	23.6	−6.4	3.0	−0.6
Thailan	2.3	15.4	−18.1	25.4	−2.9	0.3	−2.4
Singapo	1.2	−76.9	−54.2	29.9	−1.6	0.0	−6.9
Philipp	5.6	50.0	−20.1	27.1	−6.7	0.8	−4.1
Malaysi	−6.6	−22.9	−20.7	16.7	8.3	−5.0	6.3
Indones	1.2	29.7	−11.9	22.9	−1.4	1.3	0.1
Chicn	5.2	10.9	−22.8	29.4	−6.5	0.0	−6.4
Chics	4.4	11.0	−18.9	28.3	−5.4	0.1	−5.3
Chiin	4.6	41.7	−14.4	26.7	−5.6	0.8	−3.7
Chiis	1.4	53.7	−11.6	22.0	−1.7	2.4	1.0
Chimo	−22.7	20.3	−32.7	0.0	22.1	0.0	23.0
Chine	4.5	33.8	−20.6	26.9	−5.5	0.6	−3.9
Chiwe	−10.9	65.3	−24.8	6.0	13.0	8.5	17.0
Chicm	4.6	−5.8	−27.2	29.6	−5.7	0.0	−6.6

	Real income per capita (% change from baseline)			Tradables/GDP (baseline % share)	Tradables/GDP: Percentage point change from baseline		
	Commodity	Productivity	Autarky		Commodity	Productivity	Autarky
Mongol	−14.5	24.7	−35.5	3.5	17.6	3.7	19.5
Korea	3.1	−38.8	−35.7	29.8	−4.0	0.0	−6.8
Japan	3.0	−42.7	−32.1	29.8	−3.8	−0.1	−6.8
Honkong	2.0	−61.1	−51.0	29.9	−2.6	0.0	−6.9
Austral	−7.3	−41.7	−17.2	16.8	9.3	−10.9	6.2
Newzeal	1.2	−36.9	−26.7	26.9	−1.4	−2.1	−3.9
Afrnor	−9.9	9.2	−20.6	10.3	12.2	0.4	12.7
Afrwest	0.7	78.3	−13.8	18.7	−0.8	4.5	4.3
Afreast	10.6	161.0	−16.4	25.2	−12.0	2.7	−2.2
Afrcen	1.8	149.8	−22.7	14.7	−2.0	8.7	8.3
Afrsadc	4.2	186.8	−18.1	15.3	−4.6	9.2	7.7
Afrsacu	−2.4	3.6	−17.6	19.8	2.9	−0.3	3.2

Appendix Table C.9: The impact of reducing China to its 1990 size. Changes from base scenario (%). Results from numerical simulations

Note: The values used for China 1990 are reported at the bottom of the table.

Region	Wage	Welfare	Manufacturing firms
Runwest1	6.68	−0.41	1.79
Runwest2	0.00	−1.85	
Rucentr	6.70	−0.40	1.78
Rusouth	6.65	−0.57	2.38
Ruvolga	6.54	−1.54	21.58
Ruural	0.00	−1.91	
Rusibwe	6.04	−1.51	10.29
Rusibno	0.00	−2.02	
Rusibea	5.20	−2.07	Gets diversified
Rufesou	0.00	−2.12	
Rufenor	0.00	−2.00	
Rusakha	0.00	−2.03	
Relarus	6.65	−0.39	2.01
Raznor	6.14	−0.80	2.83
Kazsou	6.03	−0.66	1.84
Kazwes	0.00	−1.78	
Armen	6.54	−0.46	2.05
Kyrgyz	6.04	−0.78	2.44
Georgia	6.56	−0.36	1.69
Azerb	0.00	−1.77	
Tajik	6.19	−0.51	1.58
Uzbek	6.22	−1.00	4.74
Ukraine	6.72	−0.61	3.34
Moldova	6.73	−0.21	1.58
Benelux	6.90	−0.11	1.65
France	6.94	−0.07	1.60
Germany	6.92	−0.08	1.59
Italy	6.90	−0.10	1.60
Greece	6.77	−0.17	1.57
Unitedk	6.93	−0.13	1.78
Ireland	6.84	−0.12	1.57
Denmark	6.80	−0.24	1.95
Spaport	6.92	−0.09	1.61
Sweden	6.72	−0.25	1.82
Finland	6.66	−0.33	1.98
Eucentr	6.86	−0.15	1.69
Baltic	6.70	−0.33	2.06

Region	Wage	Welfare	Manufacturing firms
Poland	6.80	−0.25	1.95
Bulgrom	6.78	−0.28	1.99
Norway	6.75	−0.93	6.58
Iceland	5.97	−0.41	1.34
Switzer	6.65	−0.18	1.50
Turkey	6.77	−0.28	1.68
Balkan	6.73	−0.36	2.25
Cabco	6.56	−0.46	2.27
Caeast	6.84	−0.33	2.32
Camid	6.64	−1.29	15.73
Canor	6.54	−1.29	13.87
Caont	6.89	−0.17	1.78
Usalas	6.44	−0.97	5.66
Uslake	6.98	−0.10	1.71
Usnoea	7.02	−0.05	1.65
Usplai	6.90	−0.22	2.04
Usrock	6.78	−0.37	2.40
Ussoea	7.03	−0.09	1.80
Ussowe	6.92	−0.43	3.11
Uswest	6.75	−0.22	1.71
Mexico	7.01	−0.55	3.84
Amecen	6.87	−0.29	2.17
Amecen2	6.94	−1.45	38.46
Andean	6.91	−1.00	9.28
Brazn	6.99	−0.50	3.80
Brazne	7.01	−0.20	2.21
Brazse	7.09	−0.47	3.94
Brazse	7.05	−0.20	2.30
Brazco	7.03	−0.27	2.55
Argenti	6.99	−0.34	2.79
Paragua	6.98	−0.38	2.77
Uruguay	6.94	−0.40	2.80
Chile	6.41	−1.40	23.01
Egypt	6.80	−0.62	4.53
Medeas	6.70	−0.26	1.61
Arabia	0.00	−1.77	
Iran	0.00	−1.78	
Afghan	5.46	−0.67	1.40
Pakista	5.80	−0.80	1.80
Indcen	6.49	−0.48	2.19
Indne1	6.23	−0.78	3.15
Indne2	5.88	−0.83	2.53
Indnor	6.31	−0.47	1.78
Indsou	6.46	−0.44	1.96
Indwes	6.46	−0.56	2.51

Region	Wage	Welfare	Manufacturing firms
Asiasou	5.04	−0.90	1.45
Srilank	5.94	−0.58	1.48
Asean1	4.43	−1.23	1.88
Thailan	4.70	−1.21	1.68
Singapo	4.93	−0.85	1.11
Philipp	4.38	−1.27	1.33
Malaysi	4.94	−1.38	4.01
Indones	5.33	−1.01	2.41
Chicn	−64.74	−67.79	−72.29
Chics	−63.98	−67.12	−77.73
Chiin	−68.34	−71.19	−72.04
Chiis	−71.34	−73.92	−76.77
Chimo	−76.05	−81.58	
Chine	−59.96	−63.94	−63.63
Chiwe	−72.36	−74.96	−78.69
Chicm	−67.01	−69.83	−75.16
Mongol	6.76	−1.49	38.95
Korea	4.93	−1.02	1.12
Japan	5.60	−0.74	1.27
Honkong	4.55	−1.23	1.03
Austral	6.18	−1.05	4.94
Newzeal	5.27	−0.81	1.63
Afrnor	6.96	−1.06	11.18
Afrwest	6.86	−0.71	4.55
Afreast	6.45	−0.51	2.32
Afrcen	6.48	−0.99	6.35
Afrsadc	6.27	−0.98	5.78
Afrsacu	6.65	−0.73	3.98

Note to Appendix Table C.9: Values used for Chinese regions in China 1990 scenario

	Region No.	L	G	K	R=K/L
Coast-North	91	1,189,017	5670	562,179	0.473
Coast-South	92	572,161	12,469	277,769	0.485
Interior-North	93	1,523,344	38,142	449,438	0.295
Interior-South	94	1,673,634	108,255	381,457	0.228
Inner Mongolia	95	126,735	56,679	22,597	0.178
North East	96	349,775	8304	149,282	0.427
West	97	258,020	53,620	46,005	0.178
Coast-Middle	98	718,459	2194	387,099	0.539

Appendix Table C.10: US Trade Integration Scenarios. Impact on Real Income Per Capita. Changes from the Base Scenario. Results from Numerical Model Simulations

Region	NAFTA	EU	EFTA	South Am	Asia/Pacific	All_5	All_5_uni
Runwest1	−0.020	−0.063	−0.003	−0.027	−0.108	−0.211	−0.094
Runwest2	0.002	−0.005	0.000	0.003	0.004	0.006	0.003
Rucentr	−0.019	−0.059	−0.003	−0.025	−0.105	−0.202	−0.089
Rusouth	−0.016	−0.051	−0.002	−0.022	−0.093	−0.176	−0.077
Ruvolga	−0.002	−0.014	0.000	−0.002	−0.018	−0.033	−0.017
Ruural	0.002	−0.002	0.000	0.004	0.003	0.008	0.001
Rusibwe	−0.005	−0.018	−0.001	−0.006	−0.040	−0.065	−0.032
Rusibno	0.003	0.000	0.000	0.004	0.001	0.009	−0.001
Rusibea	0.003	0.001	0.000	0.005	0.000	0.009	−0.002
Rufesou	0.002	0.002	0.000	0.004	−0.003	0.006	−0.002
Rufenor	0.001	−0.002	0.000	0.002	−0.005	−0.002	0.002
Rusakha	0.001	−0.001	0.000	0.003	−0.003	0.002	0.001
Belarus	−0.019	−0.067	−0.003	−0.026	−0.106	−0.211	−0.089
Kaznor	−0.015	−0.044	−0.002	−0.020	−0.094	−0.167	−0.070
Kazsou	−0.017	−0.049	−0.002	−0.024	−0.113	−0.196	−0.081
Kazwes	0.002	−0.005	0.000	0.004	0.003	0.006	0.002
Armen	−0.018	−0.059	−0.003	−0.024	−0.104	−0.198	−0.081
Kyrgyz	−0.015	−0.046	−0.002	−0.021	−0.102	−0.178	−0.073
Georgia	−0.019	−0.065	−0.003	−0.026	−0.111	−0.213	−0.088
Azerb	0.002	−0.006	0.000	0.004	0.003	0.005	0.003
Tajik	−0.019	−0.054	−0.002	−0.026	−0.120	−0.212	−0.085
Uzbek	−0.010	−0.034	−0.001	−0.014	−0.070	−0.123	−0.049
Ukraine	−0.015	−0.056	−0.003	−0.020	−0.082	−0.167	−0.068
Moldova	−0.021	−0.078	−0.003	−0.029	−0.115	−0.235	−0.093
Benelux	−0.021	0.355	−0.004	−0.028	−0.107	0.177	0.073
France	−0.021	0.355	−0.004	−0.029	−0.107	0.177	0.073
Germany	−0.020	0.331	−0.004	−0.027	−0.104	0.160	0.068
Italy	−0.020	0.332	−0.004	−0.028	−0.106	0.158	0.067
Greece	−0.020	0.328	−0.003	−0.028	−0.110	0.151	0.066
Unitedk	−0.021	0.357	−0.004	−0.028	−0.104	0.183	0.072
Ireland	−0.024	0.408	−0.004	−0.031	−0.118	0.212	0.085
Denmark	−0.020	0.356	−0.004	−0.026	−0.103	0.186	0.069
Spaport	−0.023	0.375	−0.004	−0.031	−0.112	0.187	0.077
Sweden	−0.021	0.367	−0.004	−0.027	−0.108	0.191	0.072

Region	NAFTA	EU	EFTA	South Am	Asia/Pacific	All_5	All_5_uni
Finland	−0.020	0.357	−0.003	−0.026	−0.106	0.185	0.069
Eucentr	−0.020	0.328	−0.004	−0.027	−0.105	0.157	0.066
Baltic	−0.019	0.339	−0.003	−0.025	−0.102	0.174	0.065
Poland	−0.019	0.326	−0.003	−0.025	−0.101	0.163	0.063
Bulgrom	−0.018	0.314	−0.003	−0.026	−0.099	0.152	0.060
Norway	−0.011	−0.049	0.378	−0.013	−0.056	0.226	0.040
Iceland	−0.028	−0.083	0.564	−0.034	−0.135	0.252	0.097
Switzer	−0.022	−0.087	0.468	−0.029	−0.113	0.190	0.073
Turkey	−0.018	−0.066	−0.003	−0.025	−0.101	−0.202	−0.091
Balkan	−0.018	−0.073	−0.003	−0.025	−0.097	−0.205	−0.087
Cabco	0.825	−0.076	−0.003	−0.041	−0.164	0.495	0.165
Caeast	0.880	−0.083	−0.004	−0.044	−0.161	0.540	0.182
Camid	0.600	−0.034	−0.002	−0.017	−0.066	0.449	0.064
Canor	0.555	−0.034	−0.002	−0.016	−0.064	0.409	0.060
Caont	1.027	−0.093	−0.004	−0.051	−0.188	0.636	0.230
Usalas	0.091	0.352	0.015	0.132	0.929	1.483	1.030
Uslake	0.130	0.376	0.016	0.178	0.840	1.517	0.763
Usnoea	0.125	0.394	0.017	0.178	0.824	1.516	0.754
Usplai	0.128	0.372	0.016	0.174	0.863	1.528	0.809
Usrock	0.125	0.362	0.015	0.169	0.898	1.540	0.857
Ussoea	0.126	0.363	0.016	0.189	0.806	1.479	0.749
Ussowe	0.132	0.334	0.014	0.174	0.803	1.432	0.844
Uswest	0.117	0.351	0.015	0.163	0.946	1.568	0.801
Mexico	0.629	−0.059	−0.003	−0.037	−0.119	0.375	0.124
Amecen	−0.038	−0.076	−0.003	0.682	−0.150	0.379	0.147
Amecen2	−0.006	−0.019	−0.001	0.316	−0.023	0.249	0.022
Andean	−0.016	−0.034	−0.001	0.397	−0.062	0.261	0.051
Brazn	−0.022	−0.049	−0.002	0.422	−0.095	0.231	0.074
Brazne	−0.023	−0.055	−0.003	0.391	−0.109	0.180	0.074
Brazse	−0.017	−0.041	−0.002	0.337	−0.080	0.178	0.054
Brazse	−0.023	−0.052	−0.002	0.380	−0.106	0.174	0.071
Brazco	−0.023	−0.053	−0.002	0.394	−0.105	0.189	0.073
Argenti	−0.023	−0.050	−0.002	0.378	−0.102	0.181	0.067
Paragua	−0.024	−0.056	−0.002	0.406	−0.108	0.194	0.072
Uruguay	−0.024	−0.052	−0.002	0.403	−0.106	0.196	0.069
Chile	−0.009	−0.021	−0.001	0.367	−0.033	0.284	0.026
Egypt	−0.010	−0.045	−0.002	−0.015	−0.058	−0.124	−0.059
Medeas	−0.021	−0.068	−0.003	−0.029	−0.116	−0.227	−0.094
Arabia	0.003	−0.005	0.000	0.004	0.003	0.005	0.002
Iran	0.002	−0.005	0.000	0.003	0.001	0.002	0.002
Afghan	−0.018	−0.053	−0.002	−0.025	−0.122	−0.212	−0.081
Pakista	−0.015	−0.044	−0.002	−0.021	−0.109	−0.182	−0.074

Region	NAFTA	EU	EFTA	South Am	Asia/Pacific	All_5	All_5_uni
Indcen	−0.012	−0.037	−0.002	−0.018	0.152	0.081	0.037
Indne1	−0.010	−0.030	−0.001	−0.014	0.154	0.096	0.030
Indne2	−0.012	−0.034	−0.001	−0.016	0.162	0.095	0.035
Indnor	−0.015	−0.043	−0.002	−0.021	0.174	0.090	0.045
Indsou	−0.013	−0.039	−0.002	−0.020	0.154	0.078	0.039
Indwes	−0.012	−0.036	−0.002	−0.017	0.162	0.092	0.036
Asiasou	−0.015	−0.042	−0.002	−0.020	0.160	0.079	0.043
Srilank	−0.018	−0.049	−0.002	−0.026	0.199	0.101	0.049
Asean1	−0.013	−0.035	−0.002	−0.018	0.174	0.104	0.037
Thailan	−0.012	−0.033	−0.002	−0.018	0.154	0.086	0.036
Singapo	−0.019	−0.046	−0.002	−0.026	0.226	0.129	0.058
Philipp	−0.015	−0.040	−0.002	−0.021	0.178	0.096	0.044
Malaysi	−0.008	−0.023	−0.001	−0.011	0.184	0.137	0.024
Indones	−0.012	−0.031	−0.001	−0.017	0.164	0.099	0.034
Chicn	−0.015	−0.037	−0.002	−0.020	0.157	0.080	0.045
Chics	−0.014	−0.035	−0.002	−0.018	0.146	0.075	0.040
Chiin	−0.012	−0.032	−0.002	−0.016	0.144	0.078	0.037
Chiis	−0.009	−0.025	−0.001	−0.012	0.143	0.093	0.028
Chimo	0.005	0.005	0.000	0.007	0.165	0.178	−0.009
Chine	−0.015	−0.039	−0.002	−0.020	0.192	0.112	0.048
Chiwe	0.000	−0.005	0.000	0.001	0.171	0.162	0.004
Chicm	−0.015	−0.037	−0.002	−0.020	0.150	0.074	0.044
Mongol	−0.001	−0.020	−0.001	−0.001	0.217	0.190	0.010
Korea	−0.020	−0.051	−0.002	−0.026	0.248	0.145	0.064
Japan	−0.020	−0.047	−0.002	−0.026	0.240	0.140	0.063
Honkong	−0.018	−0.046	−0.002	−0.024	0.222	0.127	0.055
Austral	−0.014	−0.032	−0.001	−0.019	0.278	0.205	0.043
Newzeal	−0.024	−0.051	−0.002	−0.034	0.306	0.191	0.067
Afrnor	−0.006	−0.041	−0.001	−0.009	−0.034	−0.087	−0.035
Afrwest	−0.014	−0.043	−0.002	−0.022	−0.073	−0.146	−0.060
Afreast	−0.017	−0.050	−0.002	−0.025	−0.099	−0.184	−0.073
Afrcen	−0.011	−0.035	−0.001	−0.017	−0.060	−0.118	−0.046
Afrsadc	−0.010	−0.033	−0.001	−0.017	−0.062	−0.117	−0.046
Afrsacu	−0.014	−0.043	−0.002	−0.022	−0.080	−0.153	−0.065

Appendix Table C.11: US Trade Integration Scenarios. Impact on the Number of Manufacturing Firms. Changes from the Base Scenario. Results from Numerical Model Simulations

Note: Blanks rows are for countries/regions with no manufacturing in both scenarios.

Region	NAFTA	EU	EFTA	South Am	Asia/Pacific	All_5	All_5_uni
Runwest1	−0.028	−0.072	−0.004	−0.038	−0.145	−0.277	−0.122
Runwest2							
Rucentr	−0.027	−0.069	−0.004	−0.037	−0.142	−0.268	−0.116
Rusouth	−0.036	−0.091	−0.005	−0.050	−0.192	−0.360	−0.153
Ruvolga	−0.339	−0.840	−0.044	−0.467	−1.819	−3.383	−1.452
Ruural							
Rusibwe	−0.175	−0.411	−0.021	−0.239	−0.978	−1.759	−0.737
Rusibno							
Rusibea							
Rufesou							
Rufenor							
Rusakha							
Belarus	−0.032	−0.086	−0.005	−0.044	−0.167	−0.321	−0.139
Kaznor	−0.047	−0.112	−0.006	−0.065	−0.263	−0.475	−0.197
Kazsou	−0.030	−0.071	−0.004	−0.042	−0.174	−0.310	−0.125
Kazwes							
Armen	−0.031	−0.084	−0.004	−0.044	−0.170	−0.321	−0.132
Kyrgyz	−0.041	−0.098	−0.005	−0.056	−0.232	−0.416	−0.165
Georgia	−0.026	−0.069	−0.003	−0.036	−0.139	−0.262	−0.107
Azerb							
Tajik	−0.025	−0.061	−0.003	−0.035	−0.144	−0.258	−0.102
Uzbek	−0.076	−0.184	−0.009	−0.106	−0.431	−0.778	−0.310
Ukraine	−0.051	−0.144	−0.007	−0.071	−0.270	−0.523	−0.219
Moldova	−0.024	−0.068	−0.003	−0.033	−0.126	−0.245	−0.102
Benelux	−0.026	0.141	−0.004	−0.035	−0.129	−0.057	0.081
France	−0.024	0.135	−0.004	−0.034	−0.123	−0.055	0.078
Germany	−0.024	0.124	−0.004	−0.033	−0.122	−0.062	0.074
Italy	−0.024	0.128	−0.004	−0.034	−0.123	−0.061	0.072
Greece	−0.024	0.128	−0.003	−0.034	−0.124	−0.061	0.068
Unitedk	−0.028	0.154	−0.004	−0.038	−0.139	−0.060	0.089
Ireland	−0.026	0.159	−0.004	−0.035	−0.129	−0.040	0.087
Denmark	−0.031	0.174	−0.005	−0.042	−0.157	−0.067	0.097
Spaport	−0.026	0.148	−0.003	−0.036	−0.128	−0.049	0.081
Sweden	−0.029	0.169	−0.004	−0.040	−0.150	−0.060	0.093
Finland	−0.032	0.185	−0.005	−0.044	−0.165	−0.067	0.100

Region	NAFTA	EU	EFTA	South Am	Asia/Pacific	All_5	All_5_uni
Eucentr	−0.026	0.136	−0.004	−0.036	−0.132	−0.066	0.077
Baltic	−0.033	0.184	−0.005	−0.045	−0.169	−0.074	0.100
Poland	−0.030	0.160	−0.004	−0.041	−0.155	−0.075	0.090
Bulgrom	−0.030	0.159	−0.004	−0.044	−0.158	−0.081	0.086
Norway	−0.110	−0.310	0.950	−0.148	−0.552	−0.211	0.345
Iceland	−0.027	−0.068	0.249	−0.035	−0.134	−0.027	0.092
Switzer	−0.024	−0.072	0.203	−0.033	−0.122	−0.058	0.073
Turkey	−0.025	−0.068	−0.003	−0.035	−0.132	−0.254	−0.104
Balkan	−0.035	−0.100	−0.005	−0.049	−0.183	−0.359	−0.152
Cabco	0.597	−0.112	−0.005	−0.065	−0.251	0.133	0.264
Caeast	0.623	−0.115	−0.005	−0.066	−0.243	0.162	0.283
Camid	4.155	−0.784	−0.036	−0.454	−1.733	0.950	1.857
Canor	3.386	−0.685	−0.032	−0.393	−1.507	0.609	1.478
Caont	0.531	−0.090	−0.004	−0.051	−0.191	0.166	0.247
Usalas	0.177	0.617	0.034	0.284	1.823	2.867	−0.765
Uslake	0.058	0.147	0.008	0.088	0.360	0.656	−0.295
Usnoea	0.052	0.148	0.008	0.084	0.335	0.623	−0.283
Usplai	0.071	0.180	0.010	0.106	0.460	0.820	−0.339
Usrock	0.086	0.214	0.012	0.126	0.593	1.018	−0.382
Ussoea	0.058	0.147	0.008	0.098	0.360	0.668	−0.315
Ussowe	0.119	0.254	0.014	0.174	0.688	1.236	−0.525
Uswest	0.054	0.140	0.008	0.082	0.426	0.704	−0.285
Mexico	0.878	−0.174	−0.008	−0.112	−0.373	0.166	0.404
Amecen	−0.050	−0.101	−0.004	0.465	−0.211	0.075	0.210
Amecen2	−0.739	−1.683	−0.077	5.996	−3.415	−0.204	2.588
Andean	−0.182	−0.383	−0.018	1.390	−0.822	−0.087	0.630
Brazn	−0.070	−0.149	−0.007	0.535	−0.325	−0.044	0.239
Brazne	−0.037	−0.081	−0.004	0.254	−0.178	−0.060	0.114
Brazse	−0.065	−0.139	−0.007	0.418	−0.310	−0.126	0.195
Brazse	−0.038	−0.082	−0.004	0.254	−0.183	−0.068	0.116
Brazco	−0.044	−0.094	−0.005	0.302	−0.207	−0.064	0.136
Argenti	−0.048	−0.102	−0.005	0.323	−0.230	−0.079	0.142
Paragua	−0.049	−0.109	−0.005	0.341	−0.232	−0.072	0.146
Uruguay	−0.049	−0.105	−0.005	0.340	−0.235	−0.072	0.146
Chile	−0.477	−0.994	−0.046	3.517	−2.218	−0.391	1.563
Egypt	−0.066	−0.175	−0.009	−0.098	−0.351	−0.672	−0.276
Medeas	−0.025	−0.065	−0.003	−0.035	−0.131	−0.250	−0.108
Arabia							
Iran							
Afghan	−0.025	−0.060	−0.003	−0.034	−0.146	−0.259	−0.097
Pakista	−0.029	−0.071	−0.004	−0.042	−0.174	−0.308	−0.112
Indcen	−0.030	−0.071	−0.004	−0.043	−0.001	−0.145	0.076
Indne1	−0.045	−0.107	−0.005	−0.065	−0.002	−0.219	0.116
Indne2	−0.039	−0.092	−0.005	−0.056	0.007	−0.181	0.101
Indnor	−0.026	−0.062	−0.003	−0.037	0.013	−0.112	0.067
Indsou	−0.027	−0.064	−0.003	−0.039	0.000	−0.131	0.068

Region	NAFTA	EU	EFTA	South Am	Asia/Pacific	All_5	All_5_uni
Indwes	−0.035	−0.084	−0.004	−0.050	0.007	−0.162	0.090
Asiasou	−0.027	−0.063	−0.003	−0.037	0.011	−0.115	0.067
Srilank	−0.024	−0.056	−0.003	−0.035	0.024	−0.092	0.059
Asean1	−0.039	−0.089	−0.004	−0.055	0.008	−0.177	0.101
Thailan	−0.033	−0.074	−0.004	−0.048	0.009	−0.146	0.085
Singapo	−0.022	−0.048	−0.002	−0.031	0.025	−0.077	0.062
Philipp	−0.029	−0.065	−0.003	−0.041	0.013	−0.122	0.075
Malaysi	−0.076	−0.169	−0.009	−0.112	0.030	−0.328	0.193
Indones	−0.042	−0.092	−0.005	−0.062	0.006	−0.190	0.105
Chicn	−0.022	−0.048	−0.002	−0.030	0.002	−0.097	0.060
Chics	−0.024	−0.053	−0.003	−0.033	−0.004	−0.115	0.064
Chiin	−0.028	−0.062	−0.003	−0.039	−0.007	−0.136	0.075
Chiis	−0.044	−0.097	−0.005	−0.061	−0.014	−0.215	0.116
Chimo							
Chine	−0.030	−0.066	−0.003	−0.041	0.026	−0.111	0.085
Chiwe	−0.303	−0.686	−0.036	−0.419	0.178	−1.236	0.816
Chicm	−0.021	−0.046	−0.002	−0.029	−0.001	−0.097	0.057
Mongol	−0.615	−1.778	−0.086	−0.865	1.556	−1.724	1.616
Korea	−0.023	−0.052	−0.003	−0.032	0.037	−0.072	0.069
Japan	−0.024	−0.052	−0.003	−0.032	0.038	−0.070	0.070
Honkong	−0.022	−0.050	−0.003	−0.031	0.025	−0.078	0.061
Austral	−0.094	−0.196	−0.010	−0.130	0.229	−0.195	0.265
Newzeal	−0.036	−0.074	−0.004	−0.051	0.084	−0.078	0.098
Afrnor	−0.176	−0.488	−0.023	−0.256	−0.882	−1.759	−0.779
Afrwest	−0.073	−0.174	−0.009	−0.109	−0.369	−0.707	−0.329
Afreast	−0.036	−0.087	−0.004	−0.053	−0.196	−0.363	−0.150
Afrcen	−0.107	−0.259	−0.013	−0.158	−0.555	−1.052	−0.463
Afrsadc	−0.097	−0.227	−0.011	−0.147	−0.520	−0.966	−0.411
Afrsacu	0.000	−0.153	−0.007	−0.096	−0.340	−0.637	−0.281

Appendix Table C.12: Global Liberalisation: Reduction of All Trade Costs by 30%. Results for Key Variables from Numerical Simulation. Changes in Percentage from the Base Scenario

Note: Regions with zero manufacturing in the base scenarios have blank cells for manufacturing.

Region	Wage	Welfare	Manufacturing firms
Runwest1	0.617	2.671	0.169
Runwest2	0.000	2.574	
Rucentr	0.438	2.589	0.119
Rusouth	0.580	2.652	0.214
Ruvolga	0.538	2.575	1.853
Ruural	0.000	2.577	
Rusibwe	0.771	2.626	1.363
Rusibno	0.000	2.571	
Rusibea	0.000	2.557	
Rufesou	0.000	2.580	
Rufenor	0.000	2.668	
Rusakha	0.000	2.622	
Belarus	0.713	2.895	0.222
Kaznor	1.872	3.309	0.884
Kazsou	1.836	3.347	0.572
Kazwes	0.000	2.982	
Armen	0.606	2.718	0.196
Kyrgyz	1.700	3.382	0.703
Georgia	0.366	2.455	0.097
Azerb	0.000	2.889	
Tajik	2.389	3.824	0.620
Uzbek	1.676	3.666	1.316
Ukraine	0.640	2.726	0.329
Moldova	0.694	2.841	0.167
Benelux	0.000	1.903	0.000
France	−0.119	1.809	−0.028
Germany	−0.250	1.751	−0.059
Italy	0.097	2.075	0.023
Greece	0.373	2.391	0.089
Unitedk	−0.077	1.824	−0.020
Ireland	0.262	2.009	0.062
Denmark	0.099	1.890	0.029
Spaport	0.331	2.155	0.079
Sweden	0.161	1.926	0.045
Finland	0.267	2.112	0.082

Region	Wage	Welfare	Manufacturing firms
Eucentr	0.119	2.128	0.030
Baltic	0.211	2.201	0.067
Poland	0.180	2.138	0.053
Bulgrom	0.323	2.362	0.098
Norway	0.322	2.004	0.328
Iceland	0.640	2.280	0.147
Switzer	0.095	1.921	0.022
Turkey	0.269	2.450	0.069
Balkan	0.636	2.618	0.219
Cabco	1.100	2.353	0.391
Caeast	0.798	2.209	0.279
Camid	0.981	2.174	2.421
Canor	1.097	2.205	2.419
Caont	0.639	2.144	0.169
Usalas	0.975	2.296	0.888
Uslake	0.156	1.980	0.039
Usnoea	0.016	1.904	0.004
Usplai	0.376	2.090	0.115
Usrock	0.625	2.204	0.228
Ussoea	0.095	1.948	0.025
Ussowe	0.408	2.106	0.190
Uswest	0.458	2.127	0.119
Mexico	0.545	2.626	0.310
Amecen	1.166	2.975	0.378
Amecen2	1.314	3.111	7.587
Andean	1.295	3.039	1.808
Brazn	1.292	3.037	0.725
Brazne	1.140	3.014	0.370
Brazse	0.836	2.860	0.482
Brazse	1.103	3.000	0.370
Brazco	1.187	3.027	0.444
Argenti	1.477	3.179	0.606
Paragua	1.820	3.447	0.743
Uruguay	1.691	3.264	0.701
Chile	1.355	2.632	5.046
Egypt	0.226	2.790	0.156
Medeas	0.311	2.446	0.077
Arabia	0.000	2.492	
Iran	0.000	3.451	
Afghan	1.554	3.538	0.405
Pakista	0.018	2.675	0.006
Indcen	−0.882	2.322	−0.309
Indne1	−0.721	2.430	−0.380
Indne2	−0.439	2.535	−0.196

Region	Wage	Welfare	Manufacturing firms
Indnor	−0.480	2.507	−0.140
Indsou	−0.605	2.430	−0.190
Indwes	−0.751	2.400	−0.303
Asiasou	0.140	2.883	0.041
Srilank	0.791	2.972	0.201
Asean1	−0.133	2.671	−0.058
Thailan	−0.040	2.324	−0.015
Singapo	0.131	1.969	0.030
Philipp	0.137	2.508	0.042
Malaysi	0.178	2.241	0.149
Indones	−0.069	2.536	−0.032
Chicn	−0.916	1.770	−0.222
Chics	−0.754	1.856	−0.206
Chiin	−1.035	1.741	−0.333
Chiis	−1.009	1.815	−0.511
Chimo	0.000	2.127	
Chine	−0.278	2.104	−0.088
Chiwe	−0.302	2.183	−1.008
Chicm	−0.877	1.782	−0.208
Mongol	1.259	3.013	7.549
Korea	−0.002	2.022	0.000
Japan	0.181	1.886	0.042
Honkong	0.411	1.914	0.094
Austral	1.676	2.697	1.380
Newzeal	1.941	2.930	0.608
Afrnor	0.380	2.912	0.639
Afrwest	0.947	3.213	0.652
Afreast	1.226	3.502	0.452
Afrcen	1.694	3.679	1.713
Afrsadc	1.504	3.449	1.428
Afrsacu	1.612	3.050	0.994

Appendix Table C.13: Trade Cost Reduction in Europe Integration Scenarios (Chap. 8)

Note: Cells that are relevant vary across scenarios—for example, for each bi-regional FTA scenario there are two relevant cells, and for "World Integration" all cells with non-zero changes are included, except the cell for intra-West Europe trade costs.

Initial level of trade costs (average in % for all relevant bilateral flows).

	East Europe	West Europe	North Am	South Am	M. East	Asia/ Pacific	Africa
East Europe	46.23	41.90	51.86	75.62	60.10	57.99	78.30
West Europe	56.62	24.86	44.70	66.44	53.55	57.89	68.07
North Am	66.78	45.72	25.99	62.69	69.98	62.62	79.38
South Am	71.15	50.19	46.19	41.54	71.70	68.30	77.38
Mideast	54.63	36.94	50.84	69.74	47.90	55.38	70.66
Asia/Pacific	59.51	46.58	51.21	71.92	61.52	43.93	77.45
Africa	63.97	43.28	52.84	66.24	63.00	62.15	60.51

Level of trade costs in trade liberalisation scenarios (average in % for all relevant bilateral flows).

	East Europe	West Europe	North Am	South Am	M. East	Asia/ Pacific	Africa
East Europe	46.23	27.50	51.86	75.62	60.10	57.99	78.30
West Europe	35.83	18.21	30.83	42.14	34.38	37.79	42.57
North Am	66.78	31.27	25.99	62.69	69.98	62.62	79.38
South Am	71.15	35.02	46.19	41.54	71.70	68.30	77.38
M. East	54.63	25.79	50.84	69.74	47.90	55.38	70.66
Asia/Pacific	59.51	32.60	51.21	71.92	61.52	43.93	77.45
Africa	63.97	30.21	52.84	66.24	63.00	62.15	60.51

Percentage change in trade costs from the base scenario.

	East Europe	West Europe	North Am	South Am	M. East	Asia/ Pacific	Africa
East Europe	0	−34.36	0	0	0	0	0
West Europe	−36.72	−26.75	−31.04	−36.57	−35.81	−34.72	−37.46
North Am	0	−31.61	0	0	0	0	0
South Am	0	−30.22	0	0	0	0	0
M. East	0	−30.19	0	0	0	0	0
Asia/Pacific	0	−30.00	0	0	0	0	0
Africa	0	−30.20	0	0	0	0	0

Appendix Table C.14: Integration Scenarios Between Western Europe and Other World Regions. Impact on Nominal Wage. Changes in Percentage from the Base Scenario. Results from Numerical Simulation

Region	Intra-West Eur.	East Europe	North Am	South Am	M. East	Asia/ Pacific	Africa	World	World/ non-reciprocal
Runwest1	−0.20	1.71	−0.53	−0.28	−0.37	−1.33	−0.33	−1.16	0.43
Runwest2	0.00	0.00	0.00	0.00	0.00	0.00	0.00	0.00	0.00
Rucentr	−0.19	1.60	−0.51	−0.27	−0.38	−1.31	−0.32	−1.21	0.43
Rusouth	−0.19	1.61	−0.49	−0.27	−0.42	−1.31	−0.33	−1.23	0.45
Ruvolga	−0.18	1.54	−0.49	−0.27	−0.39	−1.31	−0.32	−1.25	0.47
Ruural	0.00	0.00	0.00	0.00	0.00	0.00	0.00	0.00	0.00
Rusibwe	−0.16	1.46	−0.47	−0.26	−0.38	−1.35	−0.31	−1.30	0.51
Rusibno	0.00	0.00	0.00	0.00	0.00	0.00	0.00	0.00	0.00
Rusibea	0.00	0.00	0.00	0.00	0.00	0.00	0.00	0.00	0.00
Rufesou	0.00	0.00	0.00	0.00	0.00	0.00	0.00	0.00	0.00
Rufenor	0.00	0.00	0.00	0.00	0.00	0.00	0.00	0.00	0.00
Rusakha	0.00	0.00	0.00	0.00	0.00	0.00	0.00	0.00	0.00
Belarus	−0.22	1.82	−0.55	−0.29	−0.38	−1.38	−0.34	−1.16	0.35
Kaznor	−0.17	1.96	−0.47	−0.27	−0.40	−1.37	−0.32	−0.91	0.83
Kazsou	−0.16	1.90	−0.46	−0.27	−0.41	−1.39	−0.32	−0.98	0.82
Kazwes	0.00	0.00	0.00	0.00	0.00	0.00	0.00	0.00	0.00
Armen	−0.20	1.11	−0.52	−0.28	−0.44	−1.38	−0.34	−1.80	−0.11
Kyrgyz	−0.17	1.66	−0.47	−0.27	−0.42	−1.41	−0.32	−1.24	0.55
Georgia	−0.21	1.01	−0.52	−0.28	−0.44	−1.38	−0.34	−1.89	−0.19
Azerb	0.00	0.00	0.00	0.00	0.00	0.00	0.00	0.00	0.00
Tajik	−0.17	1.98	−0.47	−0.27	−0.44	−1.40	−0.33	−0.96	0.79
Uzbek	−0.17	1.67	−0.47	−0.27	−0.42	−1.38	−0.33	−1.21	0.60
Ukraine	−0.23	1.30	−0.56	−0.29	−0.38	−1.39	−0.34	−1.64	−0.10
Moldova	−0.23	1.26	−0.56	−0.29	−0.39	−1.41	−0.34	−1.72	−0.20
Benelux	0.87	0.81	1.06	0.92	1.52	4.12	1.02	8.83	−1.75
France	0.77	0.79	1.03	0.91	1.50	4.02	1.02	8.67	−1.79
Germany	0.70	0.81	0.99	0.88	1.52	4.03	0.99	8.64	−1.83
Italy	0.88	0.82	1.07	0.94	1.59	4.24	1.09	9.09	−1.67
Greece	1.05	0.86	1.12	0.95	1.69	4.53	1.13	9.55	−1.42
Unitedk	0.77	0.79	1.05	0.92	1.50	4.06	1.02	8.73	−1.80
Ireland	0.96	0.81	1.14	0.96	1.51	4.21	1.04	9.01	−1.58
Denmark	0.93	0.84	1.07	0.91	1.54	4.22	1.01	8.95	−1.62

Region	Intra-West Eur.	East Europe	North Am	South Am	M. East	Asia/ Pacific	Africa	World	World/ non-reciprocal
Spaport	0.95	0.81	1.16	1.01	1.56	4.27	1.13	9.24	−1.62
Sweden	0.93	0.86	1.08	0.91	1.54	4.31	1.00	9.04	−1.53
Finland	0.98	0.89	1.11	0.91	1.57	4.44	1.01	9.25	−1.45
Eucentr	0.99	0.85	1.08	0.92	1.60	4.28	1.06	9.12	−1.66
Baltic	0.98	0.89	1.09	0.91	1.58	4.40	1.02	9.21	−1.49
Poland	0.97	0.89	1.10	0.92	1.62	4.39	1.04	9.26	−1.61
Bulgrom	1.06	0.89	1.12	0.77	1.69	4.53	1.10	9.40	−1.47
Norway	1.05	0.85	1.13	0.94	1.49	4.37	1.10	9.20	−1.53
Iceland	1.14	0.82	1.29	1.01	1.44	3.58	1.10	8.63	−1.27
Switzer	0.96	0.79	1.05	0.93	1.47	3.78	1.14	8.58	−1.63
Turkey	−0.22	−0.26	−0.53	−0.28	0.95	−1.37	−0.34	−1.82	−0.23
Balkan	−0.24	−0.26	−0.58	−0.30	1.45	−1.43	−0.36	−1.51	−0.05
Cabco	−0.16	−0.22	1.05	−0.32	−0.32	−1.26	−0.31	−1.29	0.48
Caeast	−0.17	−0.22	1.08	−0.33	−0.32	−1.24	−0.33	−1.26	0.43
Camid	−0.16	−0.22	1.05	−0.32	−0.32	−1.25	−0.31	−1.28	0.46
Canor	−0.17	−0.23	1.12	−0.31	−0.33	−1.29	−0.32	−1.27	0.45
Caont	−0.17	−0.22	1.00	−0.33	−0.31	−1.21	−0.32	−1.29	0.44
Usalas	−0.16	−0.23	1.04	−0.31	−0.33	−1.29	−0.31	−1.33	0.43
Uslake	−0.16	−0.21	0.86	−0.32	−0.30	−1.18	−0.31	−1.36	0.40
Usnoea	−0.16	−0.21	0.87	−0.32	−0.30	−1.18	−0.31	−1.35	0.39
Usplai	−0.16	−0.21	0.89	−0.32	−0.31	−1.19	−0.31	−1.35	0.41
Usrock	−0.16	−0.21	0.92	−0.32	−0.31	−1.21	−0.31	−1.34	0.43
Ussoea	−0.16	−0.21	0.84	−0.33	−0.30	−1.16	−0.31	−1.36	0.41
Ussowe	−0.15	−0.21	0.87	−0.33	−0.30	−1.18	−0.31	−1.36	0.43
Uswest	−0.15	−0.21	0.88	−0.31	−0.31	−1.21	−0.30	−1.36	0.44
Mexico	−0.16	−0.22	0.54	−0.37	−0.30	−1.18	−0.30	−1.70	0.12
Amecen	−0.17	−0.22	−0.63	1.00	−0.31	−1.22	−0.33	−1.64	0.14
Amecen2	−0.19	−0.24	−0.58	1.04	−0.34	−1.27	−0.36	−1.69	0.05
Andean	−0.17	−0.21	−0.55	1.06	−0.31	−1.20	−0.33	−1.49	0.35
Brazn	−0.16	−0.23	−0.53	1.28	−0.33	−1.19	−0.34	−1.31	0.54
Brazne	−0.16	−0.23	−0.51	1.24	−0.34	−1.19	−0.36	−1.34	0.54
Brazse	−0.15	−0.22	−0.49	1.08	−0.33	−1.16	−0.34	−1.41	0.54
Brazse	−0.15	−0.22	−0.50	1.15	−0.33	−1.17	−0.35	−1.38	0.55
Brazco	−0.16	−0.23	−0.51	1.22	−0.33	−1.18	−0.35	−1.35	0.55
Argenti	−0.15	−0.23	−0.50	1.24	−0.33	−1.19	−0.35	−1.32	0.58
Paragua	−0.17	−0.21	−0.54	1.04	−0.33	−1.24	−0.36	−1.57	0.27
Uruguay	−0.16	−0.23	−0.51	1.31	−0.34	−1.21	−0.36	−1.30	0.57
Chile	−0.16	−0.21	−0.54	0.88	−0.32	−1.24	−0.34	−1.69	0.19
Egypt	−0.20	−0.26	−0.50	−0.30	0.89	−1.31	−0.37	−1.82	−0.15
Medeas	−0.21	−0.26	−0.53	−0.30	0.87	−1.35	−0.36	−1.89	−0.22
Arabia	0.00	0.00	0.00	0.00	0.00	0.00	0.00	0.00	0.00
Iran	0.00	0.00	0.00	0.00	0.00	0.00	0.00	0.00	0.00

Region	Intra-West Eur.	East Europe	North Am	South Am	M. East	Asia/ Pacific	Africa	World	World/ non-reciprocal
Afghan	−0.17	−0.27	−0.46	−0.26	1.36	−1.44	−0.32	−1.41	0.42
Pakista	−0.17	−0.26	−0.45	−0.27	0.75	−1.43	−0.31	−1.91	0.02
Indcen	−0.15	−0.22	−0.41	−0.25	−0.38	−0.68	−0.29	−2.05	0.04
Indne1	−0.15	−0.22	−0.41	−0.25	−0.36	−0.67	−0.29	−2.03	0.06
Indne2	−0.15	−0.22	−0.42	−0.25	−0.36	−0.62	−0.29	−1.99	0.06
Indnor	−0.16	−0.23	−0.43	−0.26	−0.40	−0.56	−0.30	−2.01	0.01
Indsou	−0.15	−0.21	−0.41	−0.26	−0.37	−0.64	−0.30	−2.02	0.06
Indwes	−0.15	−0.22	−0.42	−0.25	−0.39	−0.63	−0.29	−2.04	0.02
Asiasou	−0.15	−0.25	−0.43	−0.25	−0.37	−0.42	−0.30	−1.85	0.13
Srilank	−0.16	−0.23	−0.44	−0.29	−0.41	−0.10	−0.33	−1.64	0.29
Asean1	−0.14	−0.23	−0.42	−0.25	−0.34	−0.42	−0.29	−1.80	0.21
Thailan	−0.14	−0.23	−0.41	−0.26	−0.35	−0.19	−0.30	−1.59	0.42
Singapo	−0.14	−0.21	−0.43	−0.27	−0.36	−0.17	−0.30	−1.59	0.39
Philipp	−0.15	−0.23	−0.43	−0.27	−0.33	−0.45	−0.29	−1.83	0.16
Malaysi	−0.14	−0.23	−0.41	−0.27	−0.36	−0.15	−0.30	−1.58	0.42
Indones	−0.13	−0.22	−0.40	−0.27	−0.35	−0.20	−0.30	−1.59	0.42
Chicn	−0.13	−0.23	−0.40	−0.24	−0.32	−0.31	−0.27	−1.62	0.40
Chics	−0.13	−0.23	−0.40	−0.24	−0.33	−0.32	−0.28	−1.63	0.41
Chiin	−0.13	−0.23	−0.39	−0.23	−0.32	−0.36	−0.27	−1.65	0.40
Chiis	−0.13	−0.23	−0.39	−0.23	−0.33	−0.35	−0.27	−1.65	0.40
Chimo	0.00	0.00	0.00	0.00	0.00	0.00	0.00	0.00	0.00
Chine	−0.14	−0.24	−0.42	−0.25	−0.33	−0.18	−0.28	−1.55	0.42
Chiwe	−0.14	−0.25	−0.42	−0.24	−0.36	−0.16	−0.29	−1.57	0.40
Chicm	−0.13	−0.23	−0.40	−0.24	−0.32	−0.33	−0.27	−1.63	0.41
Mongol	−0.24	−0.26	−0.59	−0.30	−0.39	0.32	−0.36	−1.46	−0.03
Korea	−0.16	−0.23	−0.46	−0.27	−0.33	−0.44	−0.29	−1.86	0.07
Japan	−0.15	−0.23	−0.45	−0.26	−0.33	−0.05	−0.30	−1.48	0.42
Honkong	−0.15	−0.23	−0.44	−0.26	−0.35	−0.10	−0.30	−1.54	0.41
austral	−0.14	−0.22	−0.48	−0.31	−0.35	0.19	−0.33	−1.34	0.56
Newzeal	−0.14	−0.22	−0.48	−0.32	−0.34	0.17	−0.33	−1.37	0.56
Afrnor	−0.23	−0.25	−0.58	−0.33	−0.36	−1.35	1.00	−1.83	−0.31
Afrwest	−0.18	−0.24	−0.51	−0.34	−0.37	−1.26	1.30	−1.40	0.40
Afreast	−0.17	−0.24	−0.48	−0.30	−0.41	−1.33	1.24	−1.48	0.36
Afrcen	−0.18	−0.25	−0.51	−0.32	−0.38	−1.33	1.37	−1.41	0.34
Afrsadc	−0.17	−0.24	−0.48	−0.32	−0.37	−1.32	1.27	−1.44	0.40
Afrsacu	−0.17	−0.24	−0.50	−0.32	−0.38	−1.32	1.12	−1.59	0.22

Appendix Table C.15: Integration Scenarios Between Western Europe and Other World Regions. Impact on Welfare (Real Income Per Capita). Changes in Percentage from the Base Scenario. Results from Numerical Simulation

Region	Intra–West Eur.	East Europe	North Am	South Am	M. East	Asia/ Pac.	Africa	World	World/non–reciprocal
Runwest1	–0.05	1.10	–0.12	–0.07	–0.10	–0.32	–0.08	0.31	0.11
Runwest2	–0.01	0.71	–0.01	0.00	–0.01	–0.02	0.00	0.56	0.01
Rucentr	–0.05	1.05	–0.12	–0.06	–0.10	–0.31	–0.07	0.29	0.11
Rusouth	–0.04	1.01	–0.10	–0.06	–0.09	–0.27	–0.07	0.32	0.10
Ruvolga	–0.01	0.76	–0.03	–0.01	–0.03	–0.07	–0.02	0.50	0.03
Rural	0.00	0.67	0.00	0.00	–0.01	–0.01	0.00	0.55	0.01
Rusibwe	–0.01	0.75	–0.03	–0.02	–0.03	–0.11	–0.02	0.44	0.04
Rusibno	0.00	0.63	0.00	0.00	0.00	0.00	0.00	0.54	0.00
Rusibea	0.00	0.61	0.00	0.01	0.00	0.00	0.01	0.53	0.00
Rufesou	0.00	0.59	0.01	0.01	0.00	0.01	0.01	0.53	0.00
Rufenor	0.00	0.63	0.00	0.00	0.00	0.00	0.01	0.54	0.00
Rusakha	0.00	0.63	0.00	0.00	0.00	0.00	0.00	0.54	0.00
Belarus	–0.06	1.22	–0.13	–0.07	–0.10	–0.33	–0.08	0.39	0.10
Kaznor	–0.03	1.20	–0.09	–0.05	–0.08	–0.25	–0.06	0.54	0.15
Kazsou	–0.04	1.22	–0.10	–0.05	–0.09	–0.30	–0.07	0.48	0.18
Kazwes	–0.01	0.90	–0.01	0.00	–0.01	–0.02	0.00	0.72	0.02
Armen	–0.05	0.80	–0.12	–0.06	–0.11	–0.31	–0.08	0.06	0.00
Kyrgyz	–0.04	1.01	–0.09	–0.05	–0.08	–0.27	–0.06	0.35	0.11
Georgia	–0.05	0.55	–0.13	–0.07	–0.12	–0.34	–0.08	–0.20	–0.02
Azerb	–0.01	0.87	–0.01	0.00	–0.01	–0.02	–0.01	0.69	0.02
Tajik	–0.04	1.33	–0.11	–0.06	–0.10	–0.32	–0.07	0.51	0.18

Region	Intra–West Eur.	East Europe	North Am	South Am	M. East	Asia/ Pac.	Africa	World	World/non–reciprocal
Uzbek	−0.03	1.41	−0.07	−0.04	−0.06	−0.19	−0.04	0.82	0.09
Ukraine	−0.05	0.89	−0.11	−0.06	−0.09	−0.28	−0.07	0.21	0.01
Moldova	−0.07	0.83	−0.15	−0.08	−0.12	−0.38	−0.09	−0.05	−0.01
Benelux	0.52	0.26	0.67	0.34	0.39	1.83	0.34	3.67	1.42
France	0.41	0.25	0.62	0.33	0.37	1.72	0.33	3.48	1.25
Germany	0.41	0.26	0.62	0.32	0.38	1.77	0.33	3.54	1.31
Italy	0.48	0.26	0.64	0.34	0.41	1.83	0.36	3.67	1.35
Greece	0.63	0.29	0.71	0.37	0.46	2.07	0.40	4.06	1.62
Unitedk	0.45	0.25	0.65	0.33	0.37	1.76	0.33	3.54	1.36
Ireland	0.50	0.26	0.67	0.35	0.39	1.81	0.34	3.65	1.34
Denmark	0.48	0.26	0.63	0.32	0.37	1.75	0.32	3.49	1.36
Spaport	0.53	0.26	0.70	0.37	0.41	1.88	0.37	3.81	1.45
Sweden	0.50	0.27	0.64	0.32	0.38	1.83	0.32	3.60	1.41
Finland	0.56	0.28	0.68	0.33	0.39	1.92	0.33	3.75	1.57
Eucentr	0.57	0.28	0.68	0.34	0.41	1.91	0.36	3.79	1.50
Baltic	0.55	0.28	0.66	0.33	0.39	1.88	0.33	3.68	1.54
Poland	0.52	0.27	0.64	0.32	0.39	1.84	0.33	3.63	1.43
Bulgrom	0.60	0.28	0.68	0.31	0.43	1.97	0.36	3.83	1.60
Norway	0.50	0.18	0.52	0.23	0.24	1.39	0.24	2.73	1.55
Iceland	0.63	0.27	0.74	0.38	0.41	1.74	0.38	3.72	1.48
Switzer	0.53	0.24	0.55	0.32	0.39	1.59	0.35	3.31	1.09
Turkey	−0.06	−0.07	−0.13	−0.07	0.68	−0.35	−0.09	−0.07	−0.02
Balkan	−0.07	−0.07	−0.14	−0.08	0.77	−0.36	−0.09	−0.02	0.03
Cabco	−0.03	−0.04	0.59	−0.06	−0.07	−0.24	−0.06	0.09	0.10
Caeast	−0.04	−0.05	0.60	−0.07	−0.07	−0.25	−0.06	0.07	0.09
Camid	−0.01	−0.01	0.45	−0.02	−0.02	−0.07	−0.02	0.26	0.03
Canor	−0.01	−0.02	0.47	−0.02	−0.03	−0.08	−0.02	0.26	0.04
Caont	−0.04	−0.05	0.59	−0.07	−0.07	−0.26	−0.07	0.04	0.10

Region	Intra–West Eur.	East Europe	North Am	South Am	M. East	Asia/ Pac.	Africa	World	World/non–reciprocal
Usalas	–0.02	–0.03	0.54	–0.03	–0.04	–0.15	–0.03	0.21	0.06
Uslake	–0.04	–0.04	0.56	–0.07	–0.07	–0.24	–0.06	0.05	0.09
Usnoea	–0.04	–0.05	0.56	–0.07	–0.07	–0.25	–0.06	0.04	0.09
Usplai	–0.03	–0.04	0.57	–0.06	–0.06	–0.23	–0.06	0.07	0.09
Usrock	–0.03	–0.04	0.57	–0.06	–0.06	–0.22	–0.05	0.10	0.08
Ussoea	–0.03	–0.04	0.55	–0.07	–0.07	–0.23	–0.06	0.05	0.09
Ussowe	–0.03	–0.03	0.53	–0.05	–0.05	–0.18	–0.05	0.12	0.07
Uswest	–0.03	–0.04	0.57	–0.06	–0.07	–0.24	–0.06	0.06	0.09
Mexico	–0.03	–0.03	0.62	–0.06	–0.05	–0.17	–0.04	0.20	0.02
Amecen	–0.04	–0.05	–0.15	0.78	–0.07	–0.24	–0.06	0.13	0.03
Amecen2	–0.01	–0.01	–0.04	0.87	–0.02	–0.05	–0.02	0.62	0.02
Andean	–0.02	–0.02	–0.07	0.81	–0.03	–0.10	–0.03	0.46	0.04
Brazn	–0.03	–0.04	–0.10	1.02	–0.06	–0.18	–0.05	0.47	0.09
Brazne	–0.03	–0.05	–0.11	1.07	–0.07	–0.24	–0.07	0.41	0.11
Brazse	–0.02	–0.03	–0.08	0.95	–0.05	–0.17	–0.05	0.44	0.08
Brazse	–0.03	–0.04	–0.10	1.02	–0.07	–0.22	–0.07	0.39	0.11
Brazco	–0.03	–0.04	–0.10	1.04	–0.07	–0.22	–0.07	0.42	0.11
Argenti	–0.03	–0.04	–0.10	1.07	–0.06	–0.21	–0.06	0.47	0.11
Paragua	–0.03	–0.04	–0.11	0.99	–0.07	–0.23	–0.07	0.37	0.06
Uruguay	–0.03	–0.04	–0.10	1.00	–0.07	–0.22	–0.07	0.39	0.11
Chile	–0.01	–0.01	–0.04	0.44	–0.02	–0.05	–0.01	0.26	0.02
Egypt	–0.04	–0.05	–0.09	–0.06	0.68	–0.25	–0.07	0.12	0.02
Medeas	–0.06	–0.07	–0.13	–0.07	0.69	–0.34	–0.09	–0.05	–0.02
Arabia	–0.01	–0.01	–0.01	0.00	0.56	–0.02	–0.01	0.45	0.02
Iran	–0.01	–0.01	–0.01	0.00	1.63	–0.02	0.00	1.36	0.02

Region	Intra–West Eur.	East Europe	North Am	South Am	M. East	Asia/ Pac.	Africa	World	World/non–reciprocal
Afghan	−0.04	−0.06	−0.10	−0.06	1.03	−0.33	−0.07	0.30	0.10
Pakista	−0.03	−0.05	−0.09	−0.05	0.85	−0.29	−0.06	0.22	0.01
Indcen	−0.03	−0.04	−0.07	−0.04	−0.07	0.49	−0.05	0.20	0.01
Indne1	−0.02	−0.03	−0.06	−0.03	−0.05	0.51	−0.04	0.27	0.01
Indne2	−0.03	−0.03	−0.07	−0.04	−0.06	0.52	−0.04	0.25	0.01
Indnor	−0.03	−0.05	−0.09	−0.05	−0.08	0.54	−0.06	0.19	0.01
Indsou	−0.03	−0.04	−0.08	−0.05	−0.07	0.50	−0.05	0.19	0.02
Indwes	−0.03	−0.04	−0.07	−0.04	−0.07	0.53	−0.05	0.23	0.01
Asiasou	−0.03	−0.05	−0.08	−0.05	−0.07	0.59	−0.06	0.26	0.03
Srilank	−0.04	−0.05	−0.10	−0.06	−0.09	0.54	−0.07	0.16	0.07
Asean1	−0.03	−0.04	−0.07	−0.04	−0.06	0.45	−0.05	0.18	0.04
Thailan	−0.02	−0.04	−0.06	−0.04	−0.06	0.47	−0.05	0.21	0.07
Singapo	−0.03	−0.05	−0.09	−0.06	−0.08	0.23	−0.06	−0.09	0.09
Philipp	−0.03	−0.04	−0.08	−0.05	−0.06	0.36	−0.05	0.07	0.03
Malaysi	−0.02	−0.02	−0.04	−0.03	−0.04	0.38	−0.03	0.20	0.05
Indones	−0.02	−0.03	−0.06	−0.04	−0.05	0.42	−0.04	0.17	0.07
Chicn	−0.03	−0.04	−0.07	−0.04	−0.06	0.36	−0.05	0.09	0.08
Chics	−0.02	−0.04	−0.07	−0.04	−0.06	0.36	−0.05	0.10	0.08
Chiin	−0.02	−0.04	−0.06	−0.03	−0.05	0.35	−0.04	0.11	0.07
Chiis	−0.02	−0.03	−0.05	−0.03	−0.04	0.37	−0.03	0.18	0.05
Chimo	0.00	0.01	0.01	0.01	0.01	0.46	0.01	0.47	−0.01
Chine	−0.03	−0.04	−0.08	−0.04	−0.06	0.43	−0.05	0.15	0.08
Chiwe	0.00	−0.01	−0.01	0.00	−0.01	0.48	0.00	0.41	0.01
Chicm	−0.02	−0.04	−0.07	−0.04	−0.06	0.35	−0.05	0.08	0.08
Mongol	−0.02	−0.02	−0.04	−0.02	−0.04	0.72	−0.02	0.54	0.03

Region	Intra–West Eur.	East Europe	North Am	South Am	M. East	Asia/ Pac.	Africa	World	World/non–reciprocal
Korea	–0.03	–0.05	–0.10	–0.05	–0.07	0.26	–0.06	–0.06	0.02
Japan	–0.03	–0.05	–0.09	–0.05	–0.07	0.32	–0.06	0.01	0.09
Honkong	–0.03	–0.05	–0.09	–0.05	–0.08	0.23	–0.06	–0.08	0.09
Austral	–0.02	–0.02	–0.06	–0.04	–0.04	0.46	–0.04	0.25	0.07
Newzeal	–0.03	–0.04	–0.10	–0.06	–0.07	0.45	–0.06	0.12	0.11
Afrnor	–0.04	–0.04	–0.08	–0.05	–0.07	–0.19	0.87	0.36	0.02
Afrwest	–0.03	–0.04	–0.08	–0.05	–0.07	–0.20	1.14	0.56	0.07
Afreast	–0.04	–0.05	–0.10	–0.06	–0.09	–0.27	1.29	0.57	0.08
Afrcen	–0.03	–0.03	–0.07	–0.04	–0.06	–0.17	1.36	0.81	0.05
Afrsadc	–0.02	–0.03	–0.06	–0.04	–0.05	–0.17	0.99	0.51	0.06
Afrsacu	–0.03	–0.04	–0.08	–0.05	–0.07	–0.22	0.79	0.25	0.05

Appendix Table C.16: Integration scenarios between Western Europe and other world regions. Impact on the number of manufacturing firms. Changes in percentage from the base scenario. Results from numerical simulation

Note: Blank rows have zero manufacturing in both scenarios.

Region	Intra-West Eur.	East Europe	North Am	South Am	M. East	Asia/Pac.	Africa	World	World/non-reciprocal
Runwest1	−0.06	0.47	−0.15	−0.08	−0.10	−0.37	−0.09	−0.32	0.12
Runwest2									
Rucentr	−0.05	0.44	−0.14	−0.07	−0.10	−0.36	−0.09	−0.33	0.12
Rusouth	−0.07	0.59	−0.18	−0.10	−0.16	−0.49	−0.12	−0.46	0.17
Ruvolga	−0.63	5.26	−1.70	−0.93	−1.35	−4.58	−1.10	−4.35	1.60
Ruural									
Rusibwe	−0.29	2.57	−0.83	−0.47	−0.67	−2.42	−0.55	−2.33	0.90
Rusibno									
Rusibea									
Rufesou									
Rufenor									
Rusakha									
Belarus	−0.07	0.56	−0.17	−0.09	−0.12	−0.43	−0.11	−0.37	0.11
Kaznor	−0.08	0.93	−0.23	−0.13	−0.19	−0.66	−0.15	−0.44	0.39
Kazsou	−0.05	0.59	−0.14	−0.08	−0.13	−0.44	−0.10	−0.31	0.26
Kazwes									
armen	−0.07	0.36	−0.17	−0.09	−0.14	−0.45	−0.11	−0.59	−0.04

Region	Intra-West Eur.	East Europe	North Am	South Am	M. East	Asia/Pac.	Africa	World	World/non-reciprocal
Kyrgyz	−0.07	0.69	−0.20	−0.11	−0.17	−0.59	−0.14	−0.52	0.23
Georgia	−0.05	0.27	−0.14	−0.07	−0.12	−0.37	−0.09	−0.50	−0.05
Azerb									
Tajik	−0.04	0.52	−0.12	−0.07	−0.11	−0.37	−0.09	−0.25	0.21
Uzbek	−0.14	1.31	−0.37	−0.21	−0.34	−1.11	−0.26	−0.97	0.47
Ukraine	−0.12	0.67	−0.29	−0.15	−0.20	−0.73	−0.17	−0.85	−0.05
Moldova	−0.06	0.30	−0.14	−0.07	−0.09	−0.34	−0.08	−0.42	−0.05
Benelux	0.21	0.20	0.26	0.22	0.37	0.99	0.25	2.09	−0.43
France	0.18	0.19	0.24	0.21	0.35	0.93	0.24	1.98	−0.42
Germany	0.16	0.19	0.23	0.21	0.36	0.94	0.23	1.97	−0.44
Italy	0.21	0.20	0.25	0.22	0.38	0.99	0.26	2.09	−0.40
Greece	0.25	0.20	0.27	0.23	0.40	1.06	0.27	2.19	−0.34
Unitedk	0.20	0.21	0.28	0.24	0.39	1.05	0.27	2.22	−0.48
Ireland	0.22	0.19	0.27	0.23	0.35	0.98	0.24	2.05	−0.38
Denmark	0.27	0.25	0.31	0.27	0.45	1.22	0.30	2.54	−0.48
Spaport	0.23	0.19	0.28	0.24	0.37	1.00	0.27	2.13	−0.39
Sweden	0.26	0.24	0.30	0.25	0.43	1.18	0.28	2.43	−0.43
Finland	0.30	0.27	0.34	0.28	0.48	1.33	0.31	2.71	−0.45
Eucentr	0.25	0.21	0.27	0.23	0.40	1.07	0.27	2.23	−0.42
Baltic	0.31	0.28	0.34	0.29	0.50	1.37	0.32	2.80	−0.48
Poland	0.29	0.26	0.32	0.27	0.47	1.27	0.31	2.62	−0.48
Bulgrom	0.32	0.27	0.34	0.23	0.51	1.34	0.33	2.73	−0.45
Norway	1.06	0.86	1.15	0.95	1.50	4.33	1.12	8.84	−1.57
Iceland	0.26	0.19	0.30	0.23	0.33	0.81	0.25	1.92	−0.29
Switzer	0.22	0.18	0.24	0.21	0.34	0.86	0.26	1.93	−0.38

Region	Intra-West Eur.	East Europe	North Am	South Am	M. East	Asia/Pac.	Africa	World	World/non-reciprocal
Turkey	−0.06	−0.07	−0.14	−0.07	0.24	−0.35	−0.09	−0.47	−0.06
Balkan	−0.08	−0.09	−0.20	−0.10	0.50	−0.50	−0.12	−0.52	−0.02
Cabco	−0.06	−0.08	0.37	−0.11	−0.12	−0.45	−0.11	−0.46	0.17
Caeast	−0.06	−0.08	0.38	−0.12	−0.11	−0.44	−0.11	−0.45	0.15
Camid	−0.41	−0.56	2.60	−0.79	−0.80	−3.14	−0.78	−3.21	1.15
Canor	−0.38	−0.51	2.47	−0.70	−0.74	−2.88	−0.71	−2.85	1.01
Caont	−0.04	−0.06	0.26	−0.09	−0.08	−0.32	−0.08	−0.34	0.12
Usalas	−0.15	−0.21	0.94	−0.28	−0.30	−1.19	−0.29	−1.23	0.39
Uslake	−0.04	−0.05	0.22	−0.08	−0.08	−0.30	−0.08	−0.34	0.10
Usnoea	−0.04	−0.05	0.21	−0.08	−0.07	−0.28	−0.08	−0.33	0.09
Usplai	−0.05	−0.06	0.27	−0.10	−0.09	−0.37	−0.09	−0.41	0.13
Usrock	−0.06	−0.08	0.34	−0.12	−0.11	−0.45	−0.11	−0.50	0.16
Ussoea	−0.04	−0.05	0.22	−0.09	−0.08	−0.31	−0.08	−0.36	0.11
Ussowe	−0.07	−0.10	0.40	−0.16	−0.14	−0.55	−0.14	−0.64	0.20
Uswest	−0.04	−0.06	0.23	−0.08	−0.08	−0.32	−0.08	−0.36	0.11
Mexico	−0.09	−0.13	0.30	−0.21	−0.17	−0.68	−0.17	−0.98	0.07
Amecen	−0.06	−0.07	−0.21	0.33	−0.10	−0.40	−0.11	−0.54	0.04
Amecen2	−1.11	−1.40	−3.40	6.00	−1.96	−7.48	−2.11	−9.97	0.28
Andean	−0.23	−0.30	−0.78	1.48	−0.44	−1.70	−0.47	−2.12	0.48
Brazn	−0.09	−0.13	−0.30	0.72	−0.19	−0.68	−0.19	−0.75	0.31
Brazne	−0.05	−0.07	−0.17	0.40	−0.11	−0.39	−0.12	−0.44	0.17
Brazse	−0.09	−0.13	−0.28	0.62	−0.19	−0.67	−0.20	−0.83	0.31
Brazse	−0.05	−0.08	−0.17	0.38	−0.11	−0.40	−0.12	−0.47	0.19
Brazco	−0.06	−0.09	−0.19	0.45	−0.13	−0.45	−0.13	−0.51	0.20
Argenti	−0.06	−0.09	−0.21	0.51	−0.14	−0.50	−0.15	−0.55	0.24

Region	Intra-West Eur.	East Europe	North Am	South Am	M. East	Asia/Pac.	Africa	World	World/non-reciprocal
Paragua	−0.07	−0.09	−0.22	0.43	−0.14	−0.51	−0.15	−0.65	0.11
Uruguay	−0.07	−0.10	−0.21	0.55	−0.14	−0.51	−0.15	−0.55	0.24
Chile	−0.61	−0.78	−2.05	3.28	−1.20	−4.72	−1.27	−6.44	0.71
Egypt	−0.14	−0.18	−0.35	−0.21	0.62	−0.92	−0.26	−1.28	−0.10
Medeas	−0.05	−0.06	−0.13	−0.07	0.21	−0.34	−0.09	−0.47	−0.05
Arabia									
Iran									
Afghan	−0.04	−0.07	−0.12	−0.07	0.36	−0.38	−0.08	−0.37	0.11
Pakista	−0.05	−0.08	−0.14	−0.09	0.24	−0.46	−0.10	−0.62	0.01
Indcen	−0.05	−0.08	−0.14	−0.09	−0.13	−0.24	−0.10	−0.72	0.01
Indne1	−0.08	−0.11	−0.22	−0.13	−0.19	−0.35	−0.15	−1.08	0.03
Indne2	−0.07	−0.10	−0.19	−0.11	−0.16	−0.28	−0.13	−0.90	0.03
Indnor	−0.05	−0.07	−0.13	−0.07	−0.12	−0.16	−0.09	−0.59	0.00
Indsou	−0.05	−0.07	−0.13	−0.08	−0.12	−0.20	−0.09	−0.64	0.02
Indwes	−0.06	−0.09	−0.17	−0.10	−0.16	−0.25	−0.12	−0.83	0.01
Asiasou	−0.05	−0.07	−0.13	−0.07	−0.11	−0.12	−0.09	−0.55	0.04
Srilank	−0.04	−0.06	−0.11	−0.07	−0.11	−0.03	−0.08	−0.42	0.07
Asean1	−0.06	−0.10	−0.18	−0.11	−0.15	−0.18	−0.13	−0.79	0.09
Thailan	−0.05	−0.09	−0.15	−0.10	−0.13	−0.07	−0.11	−0.59	0.15
Singapo	−0.03	−0.05	−0.10	−0.06	−0.08	−0.04	−0.07	−0.37	0.09
Philipp	−0.05	−0.07	−0.13	−0.08	−0.10	−0.14	−0.09	−0.57	0.05
Malaysi	−0.12	−0.19	−0.35	−0.23	−0.31	−0.13	−0.25	−1.34	0.35
Indones	−0.06	−0.10	−0.19	−0.13	−0.16	−0.09	−0.14	−0.75	0.20
Chicn	−0.03	−0.06	−0.10	−0.06	−0.08	−0.07	−0.07	−0.39	0.10
Chics	−0.04	−0.06	−0.11	−0.06	−0.09	−0.09	−0.08	−0.45	0.11

Region	Intra-West Eur.	East Europe	North Am	South Am	M. East	Asia/Pac.	Africa	World	World/non-reciprocal
Chiin	−0.04	−0.07	−0.13	−0.07	−0.10	−0.11	−0.09	−0.53	0.13
Chiis	−0.07	−0.11	−0.20	−0.12	−0.17	−0.18	−0.14	−0.84	0.20
Chimo									
Chine	−0.04	−0.08	−0.13	−0.08	−0.10	−0.06	−0.09	−0.49	0.13
Chiwe	−0.48	−0.84	−1.40	−0.81	−1.21	−0.53	−0.96	−5.29	1.31
Chicm	−0.03	−0.05	−0.09	−0.06	−0.08	−0.08	−0.06	−0.39	0.10
Mongol	−1.48	−1.58	−3.56	−1.84	−2.34	1.92	−2.20	−8.93	−0.21
Korea	−0.04	−0.05	−0.11	−0.06	−0.08	−0.10	−0.07	−0.43	0.02
Japan	−0.03	−0.05	−0.10	−0.06	−0.08	−0.01	−0.07	−0.34	0.10
Honkong	−0.03	−0.05	−0.10	−0.06	−0.08	−0.02	−0.07	−0.36	0.09
Austral	−0.12	−0.18	−0.40	−0.26	−0.29	0.15	−0.27	−1.13	0.47
Newzeal	−0.05	−0.07	−0.15	−0.10	−0.11	0.05	−0.10	−0.44	0.18
Afrnor	−0.39	−0.43	−0.97	−0.55	−0.62	−2.30	1.68	−3.13	−0.53
Afrwest	−0.12	−0.17	−0.35	−0.23	−0.25	−0.88	0.89	−0.98	0.27
Afreast	−0.06	−0.09	−0.18	−0.11	−0.15	−0.50	0.46	−0.55	0.13
Afrcen	−0.19	−0.25	−0.52	−0.33	−0.39	−1.37	1.39	−1.46	0.35
Afrsadc	−0.16	−0.23	−0.46	−0.31	−0.36	−1.27	1.21	−1.39	0.39
Afrsacu	−0.11	−0.15	−0.31	−0.20	−0.23	−0.83	0.69	−1.00	0.14

Appendix Table C.17: The Economic Impact of Intra-regional Integration. Changes in Percentage from the Base Scenario. Results for 110 Countries and Regions, Aggregated for World Regions. Shaded Cells: Regions Involved in Trade Integration

Nominal wage								
Impact on:	Integration scenario; trade integration within:							
	WEUR	EEUR	NAM	SAM	MEA	AFR	ASIA	World
EEUR	−0.124	0.502	−0.123	−0.053	−0.067	−0.083	−1.206	0.486
WEUR	0.853	−0.031	−0.199	−0.085	−0.096	−0.137	−1.754	0.023
MEAST	−0.086	−0.014	−0.081	−0.036	0.909	−0.058	−0.840	0.104
North Am	−0.159	−0.028	0.941	−0.097	−0.086	−0.125	−1.720	0.304
South Am	−0.161	−0.029	−0.243	1.163	−0.088	−0.134	−1.721	1.175
Asia/Pacific	−0.139	−0.029	−0.172	−0.077	−0.088	−0.116	1.943	−0.501
Africa	−0.183	−0.031	−0.199	−0.093	−0.102	1.866	−1.842	1.124
World	0.000	0.000	0.000	0.000	0.000	0.000	0.000	0.000
Per capita utility/real income								
Impact on:	Integration scenario; trade integration within:							
	WEUR	EEUR	NAM	SAM	MEA	AFR	ASIA	World
EEUR	−0.031	0.199	−0.022	−0.006	−0.016	−0.011	−0.213	2.751
WEUR	0.479	−0.007	−0.042	−0.014	−0.024	−0.024	−0.318	1.952
MEAST	−0.028	−0.003	−0.015	−0.004	0.408	−0.009	−0.176	2.717
North Am	−0.033	−0.004	0.494	−0.017	−0.015	−0.017	−0.273	2.099
South Am	−0.026	−0.003	−0.042	0.400	−0.012	−0.015	−0.193	2.987
Asia/Pacific	−0.024	−0.004	−0.027	−0.009	−0.015	−0.014	1.433	2.120
Africa	−0.033	−0.004	−0.027	−0.010	−0.016	0.624	−0.215	3.271
World	0.045	0.005	0.054	0.017	0.015	0.024	0.501	2.297
Number of manufacturing firms								
Impact on:	Integration scenario; trade integration within:							
	WEUR	EEUR	NAM	SAM	MEA	AFR	ASIA	World
EEUR	−0.100	0.405	−0.100	−0.043	−0.055	−0.068	−1.000	0.399
WEUR	0.221	−0.008	−0.051	−0.022	−0.025	−0.035	−0.456	0.009
MEAST	−0.069	−0.012	−0.065	−0.030	0.717	−0.047	−0.680	0.082
North Am	−0.052	−0.009	0.311	−0.032	−0.028	−0.041	−0.563	0.115
South Am	−0.105	−0.018	−0.158	0.769	−0.057	−0.087	−1.129	0.768
Asia/Pacific	−0.050	−0.010	−0.061	−0.028	−0.031	−0.042	0.683	−0.169
Africa	−0.134	−0.022	−0.144	−0.067	−0.072	1.307	−1.329	0.776
World	−0.014	0.003	−0.005	0.015	−0.002	0.023	−0.043	0.040

Price level								
Impact on:	Integration scenario; trade integration within:							
	WEUR	EEUR	NAM	SAM	MEA	AFR	ASIA	World
EEUR	−0.103	0.363	−0.110	−0.051	−0.056	−0.078	−1.087	−2.160
WEUR	0.371	−0.024	−0.156	−0.070	−0.072	−0.112	−1.427	−1.899
MEAST	−0.082	−0.016	−0.090	−0.044	0.778	−0.067	−0.954	−2.556
North Am	−0.123	−0.023	0.372	−0.078	−0.069	−0.104	−1.401	−1.811
South Am	−0.123	−0.023	−0.183	0.693	−0.069	−0.108	−1.391	−1.847
Asia/Pacific	−0.112	−0.024	−0.138	−0.066	−0.070	−0.098	0.222	−2.693
Africa	−0.132	−0.024	−0.153	−0.074	−0.077	1.082	−1.473	−2.186
World	−0.079	−0.006	−0.106	−0.016	0.010	0.071	−0.513	−2.417

Note: For World integration, a flat reduction of 30% is applied to all trade costs. For intra-regional trade integration, trade costs are reduced using the same method as in paragraph 8.3, giving the average trade cost reductions shown below. The shorthand acronyms refer to the same world regions as defined in Chap. 2.

WEUR (Western Europe)	−26.75
EEUR (Eastern Europe)	−28.68
NAM (North America)	−25.19
SAM (South America)	−29.59
MEA (Middle East)	−38.28
AFR (Africa)	−39.94
ASIA (Asia/Pacific)	−32.31

Appendix Table C.18: Intra-regional Trade Integration in World Regions: Impact on Real Income Per Capita

Results from numerical simulations. Shaded areas: Regions involved in trade integration. Head row denotes integration scenarios.

Region	Integration scenario:							
	WEUR	EEUR	NAM	SAM	MEA	AFR	ASIA	World
Runwest1	−0.05	0.22	−0.04	−0.01	−0.02	−0.02	−0.35	2.67
Runwest2	−0.01	0.09	0.00	0.00	0.00	0.01	0.03	2.57
Rucentr	−0.05	0.19	−0.04	−0.01	−0.02	−0.02	−0.35	2.59
Rusouth	−0.04	0.21	−0.03	−0.01	−0.03	−0.02	−0.33	2.65
Ruvolga	−0.01	0.11	−0.01	0.00	−0.01	0.00	−0.06	2.57
Ruural	0.00	0.09	0.00	0.00	0.00	0.01	0.01	2.58
Rusibwe	−0.01	0.14	−0.01	0.00	−0.01	0.00	−0.15	2.63
Rusibno	0.00	0.09	0.00	0.00	0.00	0.01	−0.01	2.57
Rusibea	0.00	0.09	0.00	0.00	0.00	0.01	−0.02	2.56
Rufesou	0.00	0.09	0.00	0.00	0.00	0.01	−0.03	2.58
Rufenor	0.00	0.09	0.00	0.00	0.00	0.01	−0.01	2.67
Rusakha	0.00	0.09	0.00	0.00	0.00	0.01	−0.01	2.62
Belarus	−0.06	0.33	−0.04	−0.01	−0.02	−0.02	−0.33	2.89
Kaznor	−0.03	0.36	−0.03	−0.01	−0.02	−0.02	−0.34	3.31
Kazsou	−0.04	0.39	−0.04	−0.01	−0.02	−0.02	−0.43	3.35
Kazwes	−0.01	0.17	0.00	0.00	0.00	0.01	0.02	2.98
Armen	−0.05	0.30	−0.04	−0.01	−0.03	−0.02	−0.36	2.72
Kyrgyz	−0.04	0.37	−0.03	−0.01	−0.02	−0.02	−0.39	3.38
Georgia	−0.05	0.27	−0.04	−0.01	−0.03	−0.02	−0.38	2.46
Azerb	−0.01	0.16	0.00	0.00	0.00	0.01	0.03	2.89
Tajik	−0.04	0.47	−0.04	−0.01	−0.03	−0.02	−0.45	3.82
Uzbek	−0.03	0.35	−0.02	−0.01	−0.02	−0.01	−0.26	3.67
Ukraine	−0.05	0.26	−0.03	−0.01	−0.02	−0.02	−0.25	2.73
Moldova	−0.07	0.38	−0.04	−0.01	−0.03	−0.02	−0.36	2.84
Benelux	0.52	−0.01	−0.04	−0.01	−0.02	−0.02	−0.32	1.90
France	0.41	−0.01	−0.04	−0.01	−0.02	−0.02	−0.32	1.81
Germany	0.41	−0.01	−0.04	−0.01	−0.02	−0.02	−0.32	1.75
Italy	0.48	−0.01	−0.04	−0.01	−0.03	−0.03	−0.33	2.08
Greece	0.63	−0.01	−0.04	−0.01	−0.03	−0.03	−0.36	2.39
Unitedk	0.45	−0.01	−0.04	−0.01	−0.02	−0.02	−0.30	1.82
Ireland	0.50	−0.01	−0.05	−0.02	−0.02	−0.03	−0.33	2.01
Denmark	0.48	−0.01	−0.04	−0.01	−0.02	−0.02	−0.31	1.89
Spaport	0.53	−0.01	−0.05	−0.02	−0.02	−0.03	−0.32	2.15
Sweden	0.50	−0.01	−0.04	−0.01	−0.02	−0.02	−0.33	1.93
Finland	0.56	−0.01	−0.04	−0.01	−0.02	−0.02	−0.33	2.11

Region	Integration scenario:							
	WEUR	EEUR	NAM	SAM	MEA	AFR	ASIA	World
Eucentr	0.57	−0.01	−0.04	−0.01	−0.03	−0.02	−0.33	2.13
Baltic	0.55	−0.01	−0.04	−0.01	−0.02	−0.02	−0.32	2.20
Poland	0.52	−0.01	−0.04	−0.01	−0.02	−0.02	−0.32	2.14
Bulgrom	0.60	−0.01	−0.04	−0.01	−0.03	−0.02	−0.32	2.36
Norway	0.50	0.00	−0.02	0.00	−0.01	−0.01	−0.14	2.00
Iceland	0.63	−0.01	−0.06	−0.02	−0.02	−0.02	−0.37	2.28
Switzer	0.53	−0.01	−0.04	−0.01	−0.02	−0.03	−0.34	1.92
Turkey	−0.06	−0.01	−0.04	−0.01	0.55	−0.02	−0.36	2.45
Balkan	−0.07	−0.01	−0.04	−0.01	0.63	−0.02	−0.30	2.62
Cabco	−0.03	0.00	0.66	−0.02	−0.02	−0.02	−0.31	2.35
Caeast	−0.04	0.00	0.62	−0.02	−0.02	−0.02	−0.28	2.21
Camid	−0.01	0.00	0.46	0.00	0.00	0.00	−0.05	2.17
Canor	−0.01	0.00	0.48	0.00	0.00	0.00	−0.07	2.21
Caont	−0.04	−0.01	0.62	−0.02	−0.02	−0.02	−0.31	2.14
Usalas	−0.02	0.00	0.50	−0.01	−0.01	−0.01	−0.18	2.30
Uslake	−0.04	0.00	0.44	−0.02	−0.02	−0.02	−0.29	1.98
Usnoea	−0.04	0.00	0.40	−0.02	−0.02	−0.02	−0.29	1.90
Usplai	−0.03	0.00	0.49	−0.02	−0.02	−0.02	−0.28	2.09
Usrock	−0.03	0.00	0.52	−0.02	−0.01	−0.02	−0.28	2.20
Ussoea	−0.03	0.00	0.42	−0.02	−0.02	−0.02	−0.28	1.95
Ussowe	−0.03	0.00	0.46	−0.01	−0.01	−0.01	−0.22	2.11
Uswest	−0.03	0.00	0.48	−0.02	−0.02	−0.02	−0.33	2.13
Mexico	−0.03	0.00	0.81	−0.02	−0.01	−0.01	−0.20	2.63
Amecen	−0.04	0.00	−0.08	0.60	−0.02	−0.02	−0.29	2.97
Amecen2	−0.01	0.00	−0.01	0.44	0.00	0.00	0.01	3.11
Andean	−0.02	0.00	−0.03	0.42	−0.01	−0.01	−0.09	3.04
Brazn	−0.03	0.00	−0.05	0.41	−0.01	−0.02	−0.21	3.04
Brazne	−0.03	0.00	−0.05	0.39	−0.02	−0.02	−0.29	3.01
Brazse	−0.02	0.00	−0.04	0.29	−0.01	−0.02	−0.20	2.86
Brazse	−0.03	0.00	−0.05	0.38	−0.02	−0.02	−0.28	3.00
Brazco	−0.03	0.00	−0.05	0.40	−0.02	−0.02	−0.27	3.03
Argenti	−0.03	0.00	−0.05	0.47	−0.02	−0.02	−0.27	3.18
Paragua	−0.03	0.00	−0.05	0.57	−0.02	−0.02	−0.27	3.45
Uruguay	−0.03	0.00	−0.05	0.51	−0.02	−0.02	−0.27	3.26
Chile	−0.01	0.00	−0.02	0.24	0.00	0.00	−0.02	2.63
Egypt	−0.04	0.00	−0.02	−0.01	0.43	−0.02	−0.20	2.79
Medeas	−0.06	−0.01	−0.04	−0.01	0.64	−0.03	−0.37	2.45
Arabia	−0.01	0.00	0.00	0.00	0.15	0.00	0.02	2.49
Iran	−0.01	0.00	0.00	0.00	0.51	0.00	0.02	3.45
Afghan	−0.04	−0.01	−0.04	−0.01	0.84	−0.02	−0.47	3.54
Pakista	−0.03	−0.01	−0.03	−0.01	0.52	−0.02	−0.45	2.67
Indcen	−0.03	0.00	−0.03	−0.01	−0.02	−0.02	1.74	2.32
Indne1	−0.02	0.00	−0.02	−0.01	−0.01	−0.01	1.84	2.43
Indne2	−0.03	0.00	−0.02	−0.01	−0.02	−0.01	2.02	2.54
Indnor	−0.03	−0.01	−0.03	−0.01	−0.02	−0.02	1.96	2.51

Region	Integration scenario:							
	WEUR	EEUR	NAM	SAM	MEA	AFR	ASIA	World
indsou	−0.03	0.00	−0.03	−0.01	−0.02	−0.02	1.84	2.43
indwes	−0.03	0.00	−0.02	−0.01	−0.02	−0.01	1.78	2.40
asiasou	−0.03	−0.01	−0.03	−0.01	−0.02	−0.02	2.41	2.88
srilank	−0.04	−0.01	−0.04	−0.01	−0.02	−0.02	2.59	2.97
asean1	−0.03	0.00	−0.03	−0.01	−0.02	−0.01	2.09	2.67
Thailan	−0.02	0.00	−0.03	−0.01	−0.02	−0.02	1.40	2.32
Singapo	−0.03	−0.01	−0.04	−0.01	−0.02	−0.02	1.27	1.97
Philipp	−0.03	0.00	−0.03	−0.01	−0.02	−0.02	1.57	2.51
Malaysi	−0.02	0.00	−0.02	0.00	−0.01	−0.01	1.28	2.24
Indones	−0.02	0.00	−0.02	−0.01	−0.01	−0.01	1.41	2.54
chicn	−0.03	−0.01	−0.03	−0.01	−0.02	−0.02	1.08	1.77
chics	−0.02	0.00	−0.03	−0.01	−0.02	−0.02	1.14	1.86
chiin	−0.02	0.00	−0.03	−0.01	−0.01	−0.01	1.02	1.74
chiis	−0.02	0.00	−0.02	−0.01	−0.01	−0.01	1.01	1.81
chimo	0.00	0.00	0.01	0.01	0.00	0.01	0.87	2.13
chine	−0.03	−0.01	−0.03	−0.01	−0.02	−0.01	1.28	2.10
chiwe	0.00	0.00	0.00	0.00	0.00	0.00	1.03	2.18
chicm	−0.02	0.00	−0.03	−0.01	−0.02	−0.02	1.09	1.78
mongol	−0.02	0.00	0.00	0.00	−0.01	0.00	1.66	3.01
korea	−0.03	−0.01	−0.04	−0.01	−0.02	−0.02	1.90	2.02
japan	−0.03	−0.01	−0.04	−0.01	−0.02	−0.02	1.60	1.89
honkong	−0.03	−0.01	−0.04	−0.01	−0.02	−0.02	1.71	1.91
austral	−0.02	0.00	−0.03	−0.01	−0.01	−0.01	1.80	2.70
newzeal	−0.03	0.00	−0.05	−0.02	−0.02	−0.02	1.84	2.93
afrnor	−0.04	0.00	−0.02	0.00	−0.01	0.44	−0.06	2.91
afrwest	−0.03	0.00	−0.03	−0.01	−0.02	0.64	−0.20	3.21
afreast	−0.04	−0.01	−0.03	−0.01	−0.02	0.80	−0.34	3.50
afrcen	−0.03	0.00	−0.02	−0.01	−0.01	0.75	−0.17	3.68
afrsadc	−0.02	0.00	−0.02	−0.01	−0.01	0.55	−0.19	3.45
afrsacu	−0.03	0.00	−0.03	−0.01	−0.02	0.52	−0.26	3.05

Appendix D: Teaching Material: A Simple Model of Regional Trade Integration

Building on Krugman (1980), we construct a simple model of regional integration.

There are three countries with subscripts $i, j = 1, 2, 3$. We assume than countries 1 and 2 can integrate whereas country 3 remains outside. There is two-way trade in manufacturing between all three, with trade costs shown in Fig. D.1.

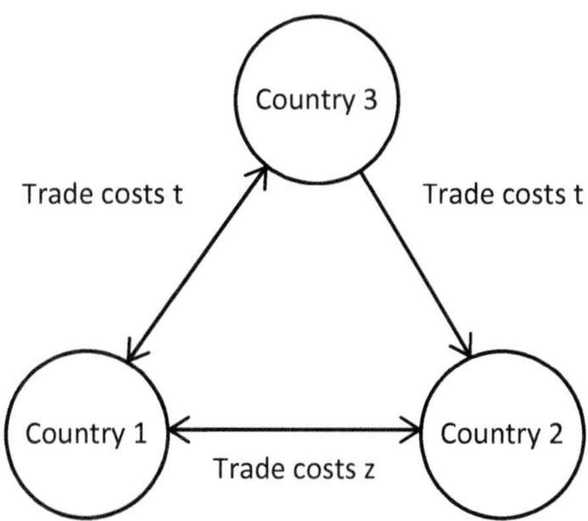

Fig. D.1 Trade costs in manufacturing between three equal countries

A. Melchior, *Free Trade Agreements and Globalisation*,
https://doi.org/10.1007/978-3-319-92834-0

Countries are of equal size and have labour endowments L. These can be used for production in a “numeraire sector” A, where one unit of labour is used to produce one unit of A with constant returns to scale. Goods from this sector are traded internationally at zero cost.

The other sector is a standard “Dixit-Stiglitz” sector where differentiated manufactured goods are produced with economies of scale and under monopolistic competition. We use small x for an individual variety and large X for the aggregate of manufactured goods. Manufactures are traded internationally with trade costs t in both directions between country 3 and the two others and z between countries 1 and 2. These are expressed so that t and z are both larger than one; for example, 10% trade costs between countries 1 and 2 means $z = 1.1$. Trade costs are of the “iceberg type” where some of the goods traded “melt away” in transport. If a quantity q is shipped from country 1 to country 2, only q/z arrives. Trade costs in the home market are zero. In the model, there is two-way trade in manufacturing, and a trade surplus (deficit) in manufacturing must be matched with a trade deficit (surplus) in sector A.

There is a two-level demand system: The choice between A and X is subject to a Cobb-Douglas utility function:

$$U_i = C_{Ai}^{1-\alpha} X_i^{\alpha}$$

where α is the consumption share for manufactured goods and C_{Ai} is the consumption of A goods in country i. The choice between varieties of X is undertaken according to a CES (constant elasticity of substitution) sub-utility function with $\sigma > 1$ as the elasticity of substitution. If Y_j is the income of country i, the demand for an individual variety of X from country i in market j is:

$$x_{ij} = \alpha Y_j p_{ij}^{-\sigma} P_j^{\sigma-1}$$

Here p_{ij} is the price for a manufactured variety shipped from country i to country j, and P_j is the price index for manufactured goods in country j. Readers not familiar with this approach may consult Fujita et al. (1999, Chap. 4) for more details.

We assume that all three countries are diversified in the sense that they have production in both sectors. Free trade in product A assures that the wage is the same in all three countries and equal to one, since A is the numeraire. Given this, we assume that manufacturing firms in all three countries have the same cost function

$$C = f + cx$$

where x is the total quantity produced by the firm, c is marginal cost, and f is a fixed cost. The manufacturing firms maximise profits $\pi = px - C$ under monopolistic competition. This gives the pricing condition

$$p = \sigma^{*} c / (\sigma - 1).$$

So the price is a mark-up on marginal cost, which is inversely related to the substitution elasticity.

Assuming free entry and exit until all firms have zero profits, we set profits equal to zero, substitute for p, and obtain the firm size (measured in quantity):

$$x = (\sigma - 1) f$$

which is the same in all countries. Turning to the three markets, the firm-level allocation of sales are as follows:

$$\begin{aligned} x_{11} + x_{12} + x_{13} &= x \\ x_{21} + x_{22} + x_{23} &= x \\ x_{31} + x_{32} + x_{33} &= x \end{aligned}$$

where x, firm scale, is given above. Now we may use the demand equations to express all x variables in the first column as functions of x_{11}, all in the second column as functions of x_{22}, and all in the third column as functions of x_{33}. Now we must remember that with iceberg trade costs, the shipped and received quantities are not the same, and so the consumed quantity is, for example, x_{21}/t and the "real price" is $p_{21}=pz$, where p is the factory price and this is the same for firms in all countries.

Using this, we must have

$$x_{21} / \left(z^* x_{11}\right) = \left(\alpha Y_1 p_{21}{}^{-\sigma} P_1^{\sigma-1}\right) / \left(\alpha Y_1 p_{11}{}^{-\sigma} P_1^{\sigma-1}\right)$$
$$= \left(\alpha Y_1 \left(pz\right)^{-\sigma} P_1^{\sigma-1}\right) / \left(\alpha Y_1 p^{-\sigma} P_1^{\sigma-1}\right) = z^{-\sigma}$$

which gives,

$$x_{21} = x_{11} z^{1-\sigma}$$

x_{12} must be the same, and x_{13}, x_{23}, x_{31}, and x_{32} are obtained in similar way. Countries 1 and 2 must be identical (same size and same trading costs), and so $x_{11} = x_{22}$. Then it reduces to two equations with two unknowns, and we may solve for x_{11} and x_{33} (also substituting the solution for firm size x) and derive all the other x variables.

The number of manufacturing firms is endogenous and we denote it by n_i, $i = 1, 2$, and 3. Using this, we set up the equations for market clearing for X goods in each country. The consumption share for X is α and the income in all countries must be L, and so we have

$$n_1 p x_{11} + n_2 p\, x_{21} + n_3 p\, x_{31} = aL$$
$$n_1 p x_{12} + n_2 p\, x_{22} + n_3 p\, x_{32} = aL$$
$$n_1 p x_{13} + n_2 p\, x_{23} + n_3 p\, x_{33} = aL$$

Here we use the producer prices and quantities since the product of quantity*price is the same on the producer and consumer side. Here p is known from the pricing condition, the x's are derived from the equations above, and we know that $n_1 = n_2$, since countries 1 and 2 are identical (country 3 has the same size, but faces different trading costs). Using this, the first two equations become identical, and we may solve for n_1 and n_3. Having obtained the solutions for the number of firms, we may analyse how these expressions respond to changes in z. If $z = t$, the three countries are obviously in the same situation. If $t > z$, you will find that $n_1 = n_2 > n_3$.

The solution is left to the reader. The integration between countries 1 and 2 (lowering z) leads to "production shifting" of manufacturing from country 3 to the two integrating countries. The integrating countries also obtain higher welfare, whereas welfare in country 3 declines.

Welfare effects can be studied using the price indexes:

$$P_{x1} = \left[n_1 p^{1-\sigma} + n_2 (pz)^{1-\sigma} + n_3 (pt)^{1-\sigma} \right]^{\frac{1}{1-\sigma}}$$

Since $n_1 = n_2$, the expression for country 2 will be similar. For country 3 we must have:

$$P_{x3} = \left[n_1 (pt)^{1-\sigma} + n_2 (pt)^{1-\sigma} + n_3 p^{1-\sigma} \right]^{\frac{1}{1-\sigma}}$$

Using the solutions for the number of firms, welfare effects may be derived.

In Appendix B, it was noted that integration may give rise to trade effects or wage effects. The model presented here gives trade effects only, since wages are equalised across countries: The improved market access shows up in changed trade flows and production shifting (Baldwin and Venables 1995). The model solution is valid only as long as all three countries are diversified. If differences in market access are large enough, or if there are also country size differences, some countries may lose all its manufacturing production, and the model cannot be solved in the way shown above.

In order to get wage effects instead of trade effects, we can drop the numeraire sector, and so there is only one sector, the manufacturing sector. Then there will only be intra-industry trade, and since trade must be balanced, there are no trade specialisation effects. Integration between countries 1 and 2 will then show up in different wages; the integrating countries will have higher wages and a higher welfare level. With wage effects, it is more difficult to solve the model explicitly, and so we have to use numerical simulation even in this simple setting. In the model presented in Chap. 6 and Appendix B of this book, there are trade effects as well as wage effects.

References

Baldwin, R. E. & Venables, A. J. (1995). Regional Economic Integration. In Grossmann, G. M. & Rogoff, K. (Eds.), *Handbook of International Economics Volume 3* (Chapter 31, pp. 1597–1644). Amsterdam: North-Holland.

Fujita, M., Krugman, P., & Venables, A. J. (1999). *The Spatial Economy. Cities, Regions and International Trade*. Cambridge MA/London: The MIT Press.

Krugman, P. (1980). Scale Economies, Product Differentiation, and the Pattern of Trade. *American Economic Review*, *70*(5), 950–959.

Index[1]

[1] Note: Page numbers followed by 'n' refer to notes.

A. Melchior, *Free Trade Agreements and Globalisation*,
https://doi.org/10.1007/978-3-319-92834-0

CPI Antony Rowe
Chippenham, UK
2020-12-22 12:51